Me

Pes~~~~~~~~ ~~~~

Cookbook

4 Books In 1: 280 Recipes For
Preparing Healthy Food Fish And
Seafood

Emma Yang

Adele Tyler

MEDITERRANEAN COOKBOOK

70 Recipes For Fresh And Healthy
Dishes From Greece Italy Spain
And France

Emma Yang

The trademarks that are used are without any consent, and the publication of the trademark is without permission or backing by the trademark owner. All trademarks and brands within this book are for clarifying purposes only and are the owned by the owners themselves, not affiliated with this document.

Contents

Introduction

Fresh grains, meats, vegetables, and olives are used in Mediterranean foods. Many people all over the world can follow Mediterranean dishes because of the numerous nutritional benefits they provide. The Mediterranean diet is heart-healthy because it emphasizes new, low-fat foods with no lipid. This means you should try this recipe whether you're trying to lose weight or don't like to eat unhealthy foods. While this diet includes some animal protein, the amounts are small, and it is low in fat, which is beneficial to your health. Mediterranean food is popular all over the world due to its delectable flavors and health benefits. This diet has the advantage of allowing you to consume clean, nutritious foods.

Mediterranean food is a term that refers to food patterns that are followed by a diverse range of individuals. It is not the result of a single ethnic group or community. Cooking reflects a wide range of cultural influences. The Mediterranean Sea was home to the world's first civilizations. The good soil and mild climate boosted food land. Their position at the crossroads of Europe, Asia, and Africa attracted merchants who traded cultural products such as seasoning and other foodstuffs. Another aspect that influenced Mediterranean delicacies was colonization. As a result of various societies' attempts to establish empires, the diverse cultures of the Mediterranean came under increasing contact.

The rugged terrain of the Mediterranean does not sustain larger herding livestock like cattle, so goats, pigs, and poultry provide the bulk of the meat. Normally, it is roasted. Milk from goats and sheep can also be used in a number of recipes. Seafood is readily available due to the city's proximity to the Mediterranean Sea.

Mediterranean food is distinguished by fresh herbs such as garlic, marjoram, tarragon, thyme, oregano, shallots, parsley, basil, and cloves. "Mediterranean Cookbook" is rich in tasty and delicious recipes from Mediterranean cuisine. It has four chapters. The first chapter is about traditional Italian cuisine. While Chapters two, three, and four are about Spanish, French, and Greek recipes. Start reading this book and enjoy Mediterranean food with more health benefits.

Chapter 1: Traditional Italian Dishes

1.1 Italian Eggplant Lasagna Recipe

Cooking Time: 1 hour 30 minutes

Serving Size: 4

Ingredients:

- ¼ cup fresh parsley
- 4 cup mozzarella
- ½ cup Parmesan
- 1 large egg
- 2 medium eggplants
- 1 25-oz. jar marinara
- 16 oz. whole milk ricotta
- Kosher salt
- 2 teaspoon oregano
- black pepper
- 3 cloves garlic
- 1 yellow onion
- 1 tablespoon olive oil

Method:

1. Preheat the oven to 400 degrees Fahrenheit.
2. Add the oil to a large frying pan.
3. After 1 minute, add the garlic, peppers, and marjoram to the plate.

4. Heat until vegetables are translucent, seasoning with salt and black pepper. Cook until the marinara has cooked through.

5. Combine gnocchi, Parmesan, cheese, and tarragon in a medium mixing bowl. Season to taste.

6. Apply a thin layer of marinara in a soup pot, then a double layer of eggplant "pasta," a layer of ricotta mixture, and a pesto layer; repeat levels.

7. Finish with marinara, chorizo, and Parmesan cheese on the last layer of eggplant.

8. Wrap in foil and cook for thirty minutes, then serve garnished with rosemary.

1.2 Mediterranean Italian Garlic Shrimp Pasta Recipe

Cooking Time: 10 minutes

Serving Size: 4

Ingredients:

- 3 ripe vine tomatoes
- Parmesan cheese
- 1 lemon zested and juiced
- Large handful of fresh parsley
- ¾ lb. thin spaghetti
- ½ teaspoon red pepper flakes
- 1 cup dry white wine
- Kosher salt
- 5 garlic cloves

- 1 teaspoon dry oregano
- Extra virgin olive oil
- Black pepper
- ½ red onion
- 1 lb. large shrimp

Method:

1. Add the noodles as per the package instructions in lightly salted water.

2. Heat the seafood while the pasta is baking.

3. One tablespoon additional olive oil, heated in a wide large frying pan until glinting but not burning.

4. Cook the seafood for two or three minutes on each hand.

5. Onions, ginger, marjoram, and red pepper flakes should be sautéed.

6. Scrape up any bits of garlic and onions from the bottom of the pan with the wine. Then squeeze in the lemon zest and juice.

7. Toss in the tomato and minced parsley for about up to 60 seconds.

8. Toss the pasta in the skillet to coat it.

9. Add the chopped shrimp last.

10. Finish with a sprinkling of grated cheese and garlic powder.

1.3 Easy Italian Chicken Cacciatore Recipe

Cooking Time: 40 minutes

Serving Size: 6

Ingredients:

- ¾ cup chicken broth
- Fresh basil
- 14.5 oz. diced tomato
- ½ cup red wine
- 4 chicken breasts
- 4 cloves garlic
- 2 teaspoons rosemary
- Salt, to taste
- 1 white onion
- 1 red bell pepper
- 3 tablespoons oil
- 1 lb. Portobello mushroom
- Pepper, to taste

Method:

1. Dress both sides of the chicken thighs with salt and black pepper.

2. Four chicken parts should be seared in a skillet until lightly browned.

3. Mix in the mushrooms for about ten minutes.

4. Put the mushrooms on a tray and toss them aside.

5. In the same pan, heat and cook one tablespoon of olive oil.

6. Sprinkle with salt the vegetables and bell peppers.

7. Two minutes, stirring regularly till the vegetables and peppers have hardened.

8. Stir in the garlic and herbs until the garlic has become fragrant.

9. Mix in the onions, red wine, and stock until the liquid has lightly browned.

10. Return the mushrooms and poultry to the sauces and reduce to low heat.

1.4 Ribollita (Tuscan White Bean Soup)

Cooking Time: 1 hour

Serving Size: 3

Ingredients:

- ¼ cup Parmesan cheese
- Sea salt and black pepper
- 4 thick stale ciabatta bread
- 4 cups vegetable broth
- 3 large lacinato kale leaves
- Balsamic vinegar
- 2 tablespoons white wine
- 3 medium Roma tomatoes
- ½ teaspoon red pepper flakes
- 1 tablespoon rosemary
- 2 garlic cloves

- 1½ cups cannellini beans
- 1 small onion
- 3 carrots
- 2 tablespoons olive oil

Method:

1. In a wide saucepan over medium heat, heat the oil.

2. Cook with the onion and a tablespoon of salt and pepper.

3. Combine the vegetables, thyme, and garlic in a mixing bowl.

4. Cook for an additional four minutes.

5. Add the onions, red pepper flakes, and a sprinkle of salt to taste.

6. Cook for about fifteen minutes, just until the tomatoes are soft and ripe, stirring occasionally. Cook for a few minutes after adding the wine.

7. After that, add the peas and the vegetable broth.

8. Cook for 30 minutes to an hour or until the vegetables are tender.

9. Combine the kale, cut into cubes bread, and rain of balsamic vinegar in a mixing bowl.

10. Cook for a few more moments or until the kale has wilted.

11. Season with salt and pepper to taste, and serve immediately in large bowls.

12. Fresh Parmesan pieces should be shaved on top.

1.5 Simple Italian Minestrone Soup

Cooking Time: 1 hour 5 minutes

Serving Size: 6

Ingredients:

- 2 teaspoons lemon juice
- Parmesan cheese
- 1 can beans
- 2 cups baby spinach
- 4 tablespoons olive oil
- Freshly ground black pepper
- 1 cup whole grain orecchiette
- 2 bay leaves
- Pinch of red pepper flakes
- 2 cups water
- 1 teaspoon fine sea salt
- 1 medium yellow onion
- 1 large can of diced tomatoes
- 4 cups vegetable broth
- 2 medium carrots
- ½ teaspoon oregano
- ½ teaspoon thyme
- 2 medium ribs celery
- 2 cups seasonal vegetables

- 4 cloves garlic
- ¼ cup tomato paste

Method:

1. In a wide Dutch oven or sauté pan, heat three tablespoons of vegetable oil over moderate flame.

2. Add the remaining onion, carrot, carrots, tomato sauce, and a pinch of salt until the oil is glinting. Pan, mixing often.

3. Combine the seasonal veggies, garlic, marjoram, and thyme in a large mixing bowl.

4. In a large mixing bowl, add the pureed tomatoes, their liquids, broth, and water.

5. Combine the salt, garlic cloves, and red pepper flakes in a mixing bowl.

6. Take the water to a boil over a moderate flame, then loosely cover the pot with the cover.

7. Combine the pasta, peas, and greens in a large mixing bowl.

8. Remove the basil leaves after removing the pot from the flame.

9. Combine the lime juice and the leftover tablespoon of olive oil in a mixing bowl.

10. Serve the soup in bowls with grated Parmesan cheese on top.

1.6 Easy Italian Biscotti Recipe with Pistachios

Cooking Time: 58 minutes

Serving Size: 36 cookies

Ingredients:

- 1 cup coarsen pistachios
- Sanding sugar
- 1 teaspoon vanilla extract
- 1 cup sweetened cranberries
- 2 cups all-purpose flour
- ¼ teaspoon salt
- 4 large eggs
- ½ teaspoon baking powder
- 1 cup sugar

Method:

1. Preheat the oven to 350 degrees Fahrenheit.
2. In a mixing bowl, add flour, sugar, brown sugar, and salt.
3. Add the three eggs and vanilla extract and beat on slow speed for 30 seconds, or until just mixed.
4. Combine the cranberries and pistachios in a mixing bowl.
5. Divide the dough in half and put it on a well-floured surface.
6. Brush the leftover egg over the dough in a small tub.
7. Use sanding powder, coat the surface.

8. Bake the logs for thirty minutes or until they are secure to the touch.

9. Preheat the oven to 325 degrees Fahrenheit.

10.　　　Transfer the logs to a baking sheet and quickly remove each into 18 pieces with a serrated knife.

11.　　　Bake for about 10 minutes, or until the edges of the cookies begin to crisp.

12.　　　Enable cookies to cool absolutely on wire racks.

1.7 Italian Oven Roasted Vegetables

Cooking Time: 30 minutes

Serving Size: 6

Ingredients:

- Parmesan cheese
- Crushed red pepper
- 1 teaspoon dried thyme
- Salt and pepper
- 8 oz. baby Bella mushrooms
- Extra virgin olive oil
- ½ tablespoon dried oregano
- 12 oz. baby potatoes
- 2 zucchini or summer squash
- 12 large garlic cloves
- 12 oz. Campari tomatoes

Method:

1. Preheat the oven to 375 degrees Fahrenheit.
2. In a big mixing bowl, combine the mushrooms, vegetables, and garlic.
3. Drizzle a generous amount of olive oil on top.
4. Insert the sesame oil, tarragon, salt, and pepper to taste. Toss all together.
5. Take just the potatoes and lay them out on a baking pan that has been lightly greased.
6. Roast for ten minutes in a preheated oven.

7. Remove the pan from the heat and add half veggies and mushrooms.

8. Return to the oven for a final 20 minutes of roasting or until the vegetables are fork-tender.

9. Mix thoroughly with smashed cayenne pepper and chopped fresh Parmesan cheese.

1.8 Easy Italian Pasta Alla Norma

Cooking Time: 50 minutes

Serving Size: 4

Ingredients:

- ½ teaspoon oregano
- ¾ cup Parmesan cheese
- ½ cup fresh basil
- 1 teaspoon red pepper flakes
- ¼ teaspoon fine salt
- 8 ounces rigatoni
- 2 medium eggplants
- ¼ cup extra-virgin olive oil
- 1 batch Marinara Sauce

Method:

1. Cook the sauce according to the package directions.

2. Preheat the oven to 425 degrees Fahrenheit in the meantime.

3. Remove the end pieces from the eggplants and slice them into 12-inch thick rounds.

4. Arrange the eggplant on the baking dishes that have been lined with parchment paper.

5. Roast for 40 - 45 minutes, or until yellow and tender.

6. Add the noodles until al dente, as per package instructions, in a large pot of simmering water.

7. In a small cup, gently fold the fried eggplant into the liquid.

8. Add 1 teaspoon extra virgin olive oil, fresh herbs, and red pepper flakes.

9. Slowly pour the pasta into the sauce, along with a few tablespoons of the retained pasta braising liquid.

10.   Remove about two-thirds of the cheese and set aside for garnish.

1.9 Tuna Italian Pasta Recipe, Mediterranean-Style

Cooking Time: 10 minutes

Serving Size: 5

Ingredients:

- 1 jalapeno pepper
- Grated Parmesan cheese
- Black pepper
- 8 pitted Kalamata olives
- Handful fresh parsley
- 1 teaspoon oregano
- ¾ lb. spaghetti
- Zest of 1 lemon
- Juice of ½ lemon
- Kosher salt
- 6 garlic cloves
- 2 5- oz. cans albacore tuna
- 1 ½ cups frozen peas
- 1 red bell pepper
- Extra virgin olive oil

Method:

1. Add one tablespoon kosher salt, 3 quarts of liquid to boil.

2. Heat the pasta al dente in hot water as per product instructions.

3. Heat 2 tablespoon extra-virgin canola oil, heated over medium-high until shimmering in a big, deep grill grate.

4. Cook, constantly flipping, for approximately five minutes with the red bell peppers.

5. Cook, regularly flipping, for thirty seconds or until seasoning is aromatic.

6. Toss the pasta with the peas in the bowl to blend.

7. Combine the tuna, lime zest, lime juice, tarragon, marjoram, black pepper, Kalamata olives, Poblano pepper if using, and a generous amount of Parmesan cheese in a large mixing bowl.

8. To serve, divide the tuna pasta among serving bowls.

1.10 Italian Chicken Stew Recipe, Mediterranean-Style

Cooking Time: 45 minutes

Serving Size: 6

Ingredients:

- 1 tablespoon white wine vinegar
- 1 cup fresh parsley
- 1 28 can tomatoes
- 2 cups chicken broth
- 1 teaspoon dry oregano
- 2 sprigs of fresh thyme
- 1½ lb. chicken thighs
- 1 teaspoon paprika
- 1 teaspoon coriander
- Kosher salt and black pepper
- 1 zucchini small
- 1 potato small
- Extra virgin olive oil
- 2 carrots
- 1 red bell pepper
- 3 garlic cloves
- 1 yellow onion

Method:

1. Clean the meat and sprinkle it with coarse salt and black pepper on both ends.

2. 2 tablespoons olive oil in a Dutch oven or Sauté pan over moderate flame until shimmering.

3. Cook the chicken until it is golden brown on both sides.

4. Transfer the onions, cloves, vegetables, bell peppers, sweet potato, and cabbage to the same Dutch oven.

5. Insert the tomatoes and use a rolling pin to break them up.

6. Combine the meat broth and tarragon springs in a large mixing bowl.

7. Boost the heat to high and bring the mixture to a boil.

8. Enable the chicken stew to simmer for thirty minutes over moderate flame.

9. Switch off the heat. Let the thyme sprigs out.

10. Serve with red wine vinegar and new parsley.

1.11 Italian Lemon Chicken Piccata Recipe

Cooking Time: 50 minutes

Serving Size: 4

Ingredients:

- 3 tablespoons butter
- 2 tablespoons Italian parsley
- ¼ cup fresh lemon juice
- 2 tablespoons capers
- 3 large chicken breast

- 1 cup chicken broth

- ½ lemon

- Salt and pepper to taste

- 2 tablespoons vegetable oil

- 1 clove garlic

- ½ cup all-purpose flour

Method:

1. Preheat the oven to 200 degrees Fahrenheit.

2. To steam, a covering platter, place it on the stove.

3. Dredge the grilled chicken parts in flour after seasoning them with salt and pepper.

4. Remove any extra flour by shaking it off.

5. In a pan, heat the olive oil and cook the chicken breasts until lightly brown on both sides, around 3 minutes per hand.

6. In a pan, heat and mix the chopped garlic until moist, about 20 seconds.

7. Transfer the chicken stock to the pot.

8. Bring the water to a boil after adding the lime juice. Cook for another five minutes after adding the lemon juice and capers.

9. Turn off the heat and set it aside from the tarragon.

10. Serve the meat medallions on serving plates with sauce spooned over each section.

1.12 Mediterranean Italian Pasta

Cooking Time: 20 minutes

Serving Size: 6

Ingredients:

- ¼ cup Parmesan cheese
- ¼ cup Italian parsley
- ¼-½ teaspoon red pepper flakes
- ¼ cup lemon juice
- 3 tablespoons olive oil
- ½ teaspoon black pepper
- 1 can artichoke hearts
- 1 can of black olives
- 1 tablespoon kosher salt
- 4 cloves garlic
- 2 cups grape tomatoes
- 6 ounces whole-wheat pasta

Method:

1. Bring one tablespoon salt to boiling in a big pot of water.

2. Add the noodles until it is al dente (firm to the bite).

3. Garlic should be minced; cherry tomatoes should be halved; artichokes should be drained and finely chopped; olives should be drained and sliced in half.

4. In a medium saucepan, heat the olive oil over moderate flame.

5. Combine the tomatoes, cloves, residual salt, pepper, and ground chili flakes in a large mixing bowl.

6. Cook, stirring regularly until the seasoning is fragrant and the tomatoes have broken down.

7. Toss the spaghetti in the skillet to coat it.

8. Combine the artichokes and olives in a bowl.

9. Pour the lime juice over the pasta and toss to combine.

10. Toss for another 2 minutes, or until heated through.

11. Remove from the heat and top with Parmesan cheese and tarragon.

1.13 Italian-Style Sheet Pan Chicken with Vegetables

Cooking Time: 40 minutes

Serving Size: 4

Ingredients:

- ¼ cup balsamic vinegar
- Fresh basil rolled
- 4 slices mozzarella cheese
- 2 tomatoes sliced
- Kosher salt to taste
- Black pepper to taste
- 4 chicken breasts
- ¾ cup marinade

- 3 cups broccoli florets
- 2 tablespoons olive oil
- 4 red potatoes

For the Marinade

- 1 teaspoon sugar
- 1 teaspoon red pepper flakes
- ½ tablespoon kosher salt
- 1 teaspoon black pepper
- 1 cup olive oil
- 1 tablespoon thyme
- 1 tablespoon basil
- 5 cloves garlic minced
- 1 tablespoon oregano
- 1 cup red wine vinegar

Method:

1. Combine all of the marinade ingredients in a mixing bowl and whisk until smooth.
2. Place the chicken in a plastic container with ¾ cup of the marinade and put the lid.
3. Set aside the remainder of the marinade.
4. Remove any excess air from the bag, close it tightly, and marinate for at least a few minutes.
5. Preheat the oven to 475 degrees Fahrenheit.
6. Toss the leftover marinade with the diced potatoes.
7. Arrange the potatoes in a single layer down one side of the plate.
8. Bake for 20 minutes in the oven.

9. Remove the pan from the oven after the chicken and vegetables have cooked for about twenty minutes and add the vegetables.

10. Over the vegetables, sprinkle about 2 tablespoons olive oil and season with salt and pepper.

11. Return the pan to the oven for fifteen minutes after coating the chicken with fresh mozzarella and tomato.

1.14 Italian Eggplant Pizza Recipe with Spinach and Mushrooms

Cooking Time: 20 minutes

Serving Size: 6

Ingredients:

- 1 cup marinara sauce
- 10 oz. fresh mozzarella
- 6 ounces white mushrooms
- 2 cups baby spinach
- 1 eggplant
- Extra virgin olive oil
- Kosher salt

Method:

1. Preheat oven to 425 degrees Fahrenheit.
2. On both ends, sprinkle the eggplant with sea salt.
3. Rub an overly big baking sheet with olive oil.
4. Organize the eggplant slices in a thin layer on a baking sheet.

5. Cook for 20 to 30 minutes on the wire shelf of your preheated oven.

6. In the meantime, heat 1 tablespoon of additional vegetable oil in a pan.

7. Cook the mushroom for about five minutes over moderate flame.

8. Mix in the spinach for a few seconds to wilt it.

9. Return the baking sheet to the stove and set the oven to fry up.

10. Take the eggplant out of the oven and set it aside.

11. Overlay the eggplant slices with the mushrooms and spinach combination.

1.15 Mediterranean Italian Pasta Salad

Cooking Time: 15 minutes

Serving Size: 8

Ingredients:
Mediterranean Pasta Salad

- 4 ounces feta cheese
- Red onion
- 1-pint cherry tomatoes
- 2/3 cup Kalamata olives
- 1 English cucumber
- 12 ounces dry pasta

Lemon-Herb Vinaigrette

- ¼ teaspoon salt
- Pinch of red pepper flakes
- 2 small garlic cloves
- ¼ teaspoon black pepper
- ¼ cup olive oil
- 2 teaspoons dried oregano
- 1 teaspoon honey
- 1 tablespoon lemon juice
- 3 tablespoons red wine vinegar

Method:

1. Cook the noodles al dente as per package directions in a big soup pot of simmering water.

2. Drain pasta and rinse for 20-30 seconds underneath cold water until it is no longer wet.

3. In a large bowl, position the pasta.

4. Toss together the tomatoes, cucumber, feta cheese, Kalamata olives, and red onion in a stand mixer, then sprinkle the vinaigrette over all evenly.

5. Toss till the dressing is uniformly distributed between the components.

6. Serve right away, with extra feta and black pepper on top if needed.

7. Add all ingredients to a mixing bowl and whisk until smooth.

1.16 Italian Baked Chicken Breast Recipe

Cooking Time: 30 minutes

Serving Size: 4

Ingredients:

- ¾ cup bread crumbs
- 4 chicken breast halves
- ½ cup Parmesan cheese
- ¾ teaspoon garlic powder
- ¾ cup mayonnaise

Method:

1. Preheat the oven to 425 degrees Fahrenheit.
2. Combine the mayo, Grated parmesan, and fresh basil in a mixing bowl.
3. Bread crumbs should be dropped in a different dish.
4. To cover the meat, dip it in the mayonnaise combination and then into the bread crumbs.
5. Arrange the poultry on a baking sheet that has been sprayed.
6. In a roasting tin, bake for 20 minutes or until meat juices run transparent and the surface is lightly browned.

1.17 Italian Mediterranean Baked Zucchini with Parmesan and Thyme

Cooking Time: 30 minutes

Serving Size: 4

Ingredients:

- 2 tablespoons olive oil
- 2 tablespoon parsley leaves
- ¼ teaspoon garlic powder
- Kosher salt and black pepper
- 4 zucchini
- ½ teaspoon oregano
- ½ teaspoon basil
- ½ teaspoon thyme
- ½ cup Parmesan

Method:

1. Preheat the oven to 350 degrees Fahrenheit.
2. Set aside a broiler pan that has been sprayed with nonstick cooking spray and placed on a baking sheet.
3. Mix Parmesan, tarragon, marjoram, basil, garlic salt, seasoning, and pepper in a small cup, to fit.
4. Place the zucchini on the baking sheet that has been prepared.
5. Drizzle olive oil over the top and top with the Parmesan combination.
6. Preheat oven to 350°F and bake until vegetables are tender, about thirty minutes.

7. Then reheat for 2-3 minutes, or until lightly browned and crispy.

8. Mix thoroughly with parsley on top, if desired.

1.18 Simple Pancetta Italian Pasta with Peas and Parmesan

Cooking Time: 23 minutes

Serving Size: 4

Ingredients:

- Salt and black pepper
- ½ lemon
- 2 cloves garlic
- ¼ cup Parmesan
- 16 ounces fettuccine
- ½ onion
- 1 (10-ounce) bag frozen peas
- 8 ounces pancetta

Method:

1. Over moderate flame, bring a big pot of salted water on the stove.

2. Cook until the pasta is al dente.

3. Drain the pasta, reserving 1 cup of the cooking liquid.

4. In a wide pan over medium heat, cook pancetta once golden brown, around 6 minutes. Place on a plate lined with paper towels.

5. Sauté onions in the very same pan until melted, around five minutes. Sauté the peas and cloves for three minutes.

6. Combine the Parmesan, pasta, and pancetta in a mixing bowl.

7. Use some of the stored pasta water to moisten the noodles.

8. Toss to mix, sprinkle with salt if desired, and top with lime juice drizzled on top.

1.19 Italian White Bean and Kale Soup with Chicken

Cooking Time: 30 minutes

Serving Size: 6

Ingredients:

- Sea salt + black pepper
- 3 cups kale
- 1 15-oz can white beans
- 2 cups chicken
- 1 strip bacon
- 4 cloves garlic
- 8 cups broth
- 1 cup white onion
- 1 tablespoon avocado oil

Method:

1. Over moderate flame, heat a large pan or casserole dish.

2. Once the pan is warmed, add the bacon or oil.

3. Allow for two minutes of cooking time, stirring occasionally.

4. Cook, stirring periodically, for 4-5 minutes, or until onions becomes transparent and citrusy.

5. Then add garlic and cook for another 2-3 minutes.

6. Carry to a boil the broth, completely soaked white beans, and meat.

7. To blend the flavors, cook for ten minutes.

8. After that, sprinkle with salt and pepper.

9. Insert the kale over the last few minutes before serving. Serve instantly.

1.20 Italian Crispy Fried Calamari Recipe

Cooking Time: 50 minutes

Serving Size: 4

Ingredients:

- 2 tablespoons parmesan
- Black pepper
- Salt
- 1 tablespoon unsalted butter
- 2 tablespoons garlic olive oil
- 250 grams orzo pasta
- 625 milliliters boiling water
- 150 grams petits pois
- 150 grams pancetta

Method:

1. In a heavy-bottomed pan, heat the oil.

2. Heat, occasionally stirring, till the pancetta is crispy and freckled, then add the beans and mix for a minute or so, till the frozen look has disappeared.

3. Put in hot water after tossing the pasta in the pancetta and beans.

4. Add the salt, then reduce the heat to low and allow to simmer for ten minutes, checking on it a few times and stirring it or two to keep it from settling.

5. The water must be consumed by the pasta, which should be fluffy and starchy.

6. In a large mixing bowl, combine the butter and Parmesan, season with salt and pepper, and serve with rice into warm ready bowls.

Chapter 2: Traditional Spanish Dishes

2.1 Fried Chorizo with Chick Peas and Tomatoes

Cooking Time: 20 minutes

Serving Size: 4

Ingredients:

- Salt and pepper
- 3 tablespoons parsley
- 2 pints cherry tomatoes
- 1 teaspoon smoked paprika
- 9 ounces chorizo
- 2 15-oz. cans chickpeas
- 1 onion
- 1 tablespoon olive oil

Method:

1. In a saucepan over medium heat, steam the oil.
2. Sauté onion for three minutes, or until soft.
3. Toss in the chorizo.
4. Sauté for 30 seconds to 1 minute, or until thoroughly hot.
5. Combine chickpeas, grape tomatoes, and paprika in a mixing bowl.
6. Cook for 8 minutes, or until tomatoes are softened and liquids are boiling.
7. Salt and pepper to taste. Serve with a tarragon garnish.

2.2 Boquerones Al Limon

Cooking Time: 30 minutes

Serving Size: 2

Ingredients:

- Chickpea flour
- Salt
- 1 clove of garlic
- 1 bunch of parsley
- 1 lemon
- 350 grams anchovies

Method:

1. The anchovies should be cleaned and dried.
2. Place the garlic, tarragon, and pepper in a mortar and use the pestle to grind them into a powder.
3. Combine the paste with the extract of one lemon.
4. Place the fillets in a crystal tray and spill the marinade over them.
5. Cover the plate with plastic wrap and refrigerate for up to two hours to soak.
6. Take off the extra chickpea flour after passing them through.
7. In a large pan, heat some butter over medium heat.
8. Fry 4-5 at the moment for 1 minute, or till they transform a lovely golden color.
9. To absorb excess oil, place the fried fish on a plate lined with towels.
10. Serve with lime wedges and aioli sauce.

2.3 Pan con Tomate

Cooking Time: 7 minutes

Serving Size: 8

Ingredients:

- 2 medium cloves garlic
- Flaky sea salt
- 1 loaf ciabatta
- Extra-virgin olive oil
- Kosher salt
- 2 large tomatoes

Method:

1. Tomatoes should be cut in half vertically. In a big mixing bowl, grate a box grinder.

2. Preheat the broiler to high and position the rack four inches below it.

3. Spoonful olive oil over the cut side of the bread on a work surface.

4. Use kosher salt, season to taste.

5. Position the bread cutting side up on a rack set in a pan or immediately on the griddle rack and broil for two or three minutes, or until crispy and beginning to char form around edge.

6. Take the bread from the microwave and scrub it with the garlic cloves that have been cut.

7. Spread the tomato mixture on top of the pizza.

8. Dress with flaky sesame oil and rain of extra-virgin canola oil.

2.4 Mediterranean Garlic Soup with Egg and Croutons

Cooking Time: 35 minutes

Serving Size: 2

Ingredients:

- ¼ cup extra virgin olive oil
- Salt and pepper
- 1 teaspoon sweet paprika
- 1-liter chicken broth
- 2 eggs
- 6 garlic cloves
- 2 slices of stale bread

Method:

1. Garlic should be peeled and cut into strips.

2. Heat the olive oil in a saucepan over medium heat.

3. Add garlic and cook for 2-3 minutes, or until it starts to brown.

4. Add the loaf to the pan and fry it with the garlic, allowing it to soak up the oil.

5. Reduce to low heat and stir in the parmesan.

6. Put in the liquid and give it a good swirl.

7. Take the soup to a rolling simmer, reduce to low heat, and continue cooking for about thirty minutes.

8. To taste, season with salt and pepper, using at least ½ teaspoon pepper.

9. In a large mixing bowl, whisk together the eggs and add them to the soup.

2.5 Salmorejo (Spanish Cold Tomato Soup)

Cooking Time: 25 minutes

Serving Size: 4

Ingredients:

- 2 hardboiled eggs
- Diced serrano ham
- A splash of sherry vinegar
- A pinch of salt
- 8 medium tomatoes
- 1 cup olive oil again
- 1 clove of garlic
- 1 medium baguette

Method:

1. Carry a big pot of salted water to a boil on the burner.
2. In the base of each tomato, make a small symbol.
3. Remove the cores from the tomatoes and mix everything else.
4. Use a high-powered blender, combine all ingredients.
5. Remove the "guts" from your baguette and toss them in with the blended vegetables.
6. Mix in the drop of vinegar, pepper, and garlic until the soup has even consistency.
7. Mix in 1 hardboiled egg until completely combined.

8. Offer in big containers with toppings of diced poblano pepper and diced ham. Serve chilled.

2.6 Mediterranean Baked Tapas

Cooking Time: 15 minutes

Serving Size: 4

Ingredients:

- 3 tablespoon olive oil
- 110g sundried tomatoes
- 8 cloves garlic
- 110g chorizo sausages

Method:

1. Set the oven to 150 degrees Celsius.

2. Heat a whole clove, chorizo treats, and quasi tomato in a tiny cast-iron skillet with just a little canola oil for 2-three minutes on the hot plate.

3. Place the whole combination in the oven and continue to cook for 10-12 minutes.

4. Turn off the heat and set aside to cool moderately before brushing with the residual oil and serve with toasted bread.

2.7 Spicy Spanish Meatballs

Cooking Time: 35 minutes

Serving Size: 4

Ingredients:

Spanish Meatballs

- 2 ½ teaspoon smoked paprika
- ¼ cup olive oil
- 2 clove garlic
- 1 egg yolk
- 2 tablespoon milk
- 500 grams beef
- ½ cup breadcrumbs

Smoked Paprika Tomato Sauce

- ½ teaspoon smoked paprika
- 500 grams tomatoes
- 3 cloves garlic
- 1 bay leaf
- 1 onion
- 1 tablespoon olive oil

Method:

1. Soak the breadcrumbs in dairy for five minutes before pressing out any remaining water.
2. Add salt and pepper to taste.
3. Make 12 balls out of the flour mix and place them on a table to work with.

4. In a large skillet, heat the oil over medium heat.

5. Heat the meatballs for four minutes, rotating once or until golden brown.

6. Heat for about four minutes with the spray of excess oil, onions, ginger, and bay leaf.

7. Wait for another minute till the paprika is aromatic.

8. Transfer the meatballs to the bowl after stirring in the tomatoes.

9. Transfer to a serving bowl and serve right away.

2.8 Spanish One-Pan Chicken with Chorizo and Bell Peppers

Cooking Time: 1 hour

Serving Size: 5

Ingredients:
For Chicken

- 3 tablespoon tomato paste
- 3 cups chicken broth
- 2 garlic cloves
- 1 large ripe tomato
- 1 green bell pepper
- 1 red onion
- 1 ½ cup rice
- Olive oil
- 6 oz. Chorizo sausage
- 4 chicken drumsticks
- 4 chicken thighs

For Spice Rub

- 1 teaspoon black pepper
- ½ teaspoon cayenne pepper
- 1 teaspoon garlic powder
- 1 teaspoon salt
- 1 tablespoon smoked paprika

Method:

1. Wash the rice in water for a few minutes.
2. Enable the rice to soak for fifteen minutes after covering it with water.
3. Combine the ingredients, salt, and pepper in a small cup.
4. Season the chicken with salt and pepper.
5. Season the chicken with the spice rub after patting it dry.
6. Both sides of the chicken should be browned.
7. Add 1 tablespoon of additional olive oil, heat until glistening but not burning over medium-high heat.
8. Cook the chorizo and veggies together.
9. Prepare the chicken.
10. Combine the sliced tomatoes, tomato sauce, and chicken stock in a large mixing bowl.
11. Cook the rice in the same pot as the chicken.
12. Allow the chicken and rice to rest in the pan for a few minutes.
13. Remove the pan from the heat but keep it covered and unhindered for another ten minutes. Serve immediately.

2.9 Sizzling Spanish Garlic Prawns

Cooking Time: 13 minutes

Serving Size: 6

Ingredients:

- 6 garlic cloves
- 6 tablespoons dry sherry
- 1 teaspoon chili flakes
- 4 tablespoons olive oil
- 3 tablespoons parsley
- 900g raw king prawns

Method:

1. Preheat the oven to 220 degrees Celsius.
2. Simply cut the prawns lengthwise but not through it and cut the vein to flap the shrimp.
3. Use 6 small oven tray dishes or one big one to separate the shrimp, garlic, chili or pimento, brandy, and balsamic vinegar.
4. Cook for 12 to 15 minutes until it is red and piping hot, based on the pan or pots' size.
5. Serve with toasted bread and citrus wedges, garnished with parsley.

2.10 Super Tasty Spanish Roast Chicken

Cooking Time: 1 hour 40 minutes

Serving Size: 8

Ingredients:

- Olive oil
- 2 cloves garlic
- Freshly ground black pepper
- 300g Iberico chorizo sausage
- 2kg chicken
- Sea salt
- 1.6kg potatoes
- 1 handful parsley
- 4 lemons

Method:

1. Heat your oven to 220°C, and put your vegetables in a large pan of boiling water containing two lemons and simmer for five minutes.

2. Take the leaves from the tarragon stalks and set them aside.

3. Fill the meat with the tarragon stalks and warm lemons.

4. Position the potato in the center of the baking parchment, then the poultry on top and the pancetta on top of that.

5. Whereas the chicken and vegetables are frying, make the gremolata, as the Italians name it.

6. Chop the poultry and serve with the potatoes on eight plates.

2.11 Spanish Mixed Green Salad

Cooking Time: 10 minutes

Serving Size: 4

Ingredients:

- ½ Spanish onion
- 10 -12 green olives
- 2 cups Boston lettuce
- 2 tomatoes
- 1 cup baby spinach
- 2 cups romaine lettuce

Dressing

- 3 tablespoons olive oil
- Sea salt and black pepper
- 1 tablespoon lemon juice

Method:

1. Combine all of the dressing components in a mixing bowl and whisk until thoroughly combined.
2. Toss with salad well before eating.

2.12 Spanish-inspired Tomato Salad

Cooking Time: 40 minutes

Serving Size: 8

Ingredients:

- 16 caper berries
- 6 anchovy fillets
- 3 pounds tomatoes
- 1 cup parsley
- ½ teaspoon sugar
- ¼ teaspoon salt
- 1/3 cup olive oil
- 3 tablespoons sherry vinegar
- 1 teaspoon pepper
- 1 teaspoon paprika
- 1 cup fresh breadcrumbs
- 5 cloves garlic

Method:

1. In a large saucepan, warm 1/3 cup oil over moderate flame.
2. Cook, occasionally stirring, for about 20 seconds, just until the citrus is spicy and piping hot but not crispy.
3. In the same pan, heat and cook 2 tablespoons of oil over moderate flame.
4. Cook, constantly stirring, until the breadcrumbs are crisp and lightly browned, about five minutes.
5. In a mixing bowl, combine the garlic-paprika oil, mustard, spice, cinnamon, and salt.

6. Gently whisk in the onions, tarragon, caper fruit, and minced anchovies.

7. Serve the tomato salad on a large plate with the fried cornmeal on top.

2.13 Spanish-Style Chicken with Mushrooms

Cooking Time: 55 minutes

Serving Size: 4

Ingredients:

- 1½ cups chicken stock
- Fresh parsley to serve
- 4 cloves garlic
- 2 teaspoons Spanish paprika
- 4 chicken thighs
- 1 tablespoon thyme leaves
- 1 yellow onion
- 1 pound button mushrooms
- 2/3 cup dry white wine
- 2 tablespoons olive oil
- Salt and pepper

Method:

1. Dress the chicken breasts with salts and dried basil before cooking.

2. Steam the olive oil in a large cast-iron pan or grill over moderate flame.

3. On both ends, grill the chicken thighs uniformly.

4. Transfer the pan to the heat and add the vegetables, cooking for an additional five minutes.

5. Shift the oven temperature until the wine has decreased.

6. Stir together the carrots, ginger, paprika, and a pinch of salt.

7. Continue to sauté for another minute.

8. Decrease to a moderate heat area.

9. Transfer the chicken thighs to the pan with the chicken broth, then cover with a cap.

10. Serve immediately with clean parsley on top.

2.14 Quick and Easy Paella

Cooking Time: 1 hour 10 minutes

Serving Size: 6

Ingredients:

Saffron Broth

- ½ teaspoon saffron threads
- 2 ¼ cups chicken broth
- 2 teaspoons olive oil
- 1 pound jumbo shrimp

Paella

- 1 teaspoon paprika
- 1 pinch cayenne pepper
- 1 red bell pepper
- Salt to taste
- 1 ⅓ cups Arborio rice
- ½ cup green peas

- 1 tablespoon olive oil
- ½ yellow onion
- 2 cloves garlic
- 8 ounces chorizo sausage

Method:

1. In a pan over medium heat, steam, and mix preserved shrimp shells and two teaspoons canola oil.

2. Saffron should be stirred into the shells, and chicken broth should be added.

3. Preheat the oven to 425 degrees Fahrenheit.

4. In a large oven-safe skillet, heat one tablespoon of olive oil on medium-high heat. In a hot skillet, cook chorizo strips.

5. Continue cooking the garlic into the chorizo combination until moist.

6. Over the rice, place the seafood in a thin layer.

7. Sprinkle with salt, parmesan, and cayenne pepper, and place pepper slices around as well as between shrimp.

8. Cook the rice paste for 20 minutes in a preheated oven.

9. Cook, often stirring, until the rice is soft, the liquid has been absorbed, and the rice has caramelized.

2.15 Champinones Al Ajillo, Spanish Garlic Mushrooms

Cooking Time: 10 minutes

Serving Size: 4

Ingredients:

- ½ teaspoon chili flakes
- 1 tablespoon flat-leaf parsley
- ¼ teaspoon Spanish paprika
- Ground pepper and sea salt
- 10 large button mushrooms
- 1 tablespoon lemon juice
- 2 tablespoons dry sherry
- 3 tablespoons olive oil
- 5 cloves garlic

Method:

1. The mushrooms should be quartered, the parsley should be chopped, and the garlic should be crushed.

2. Add the olive oil and simmer the mushrooms for several moments over moderate flame.

3. Then, with the exception of the parsley, combine the rest of the ingredients.

4. Cook for another five minutes, stirring occasionally.

5. Then take the pan from the heat and whisk in the grated parmesan.

2.16 Classic Spanish Paella

Cooking Time: 45 minutes

Serving Size: 5

Ingredients:

- 2 sprigs of fresh thyme
- ¾ cup frozen peas
- 1 teaspoon sea salt
- Fresh cracked pepper
- 3 tablespoons olive oil
- 1 teaspoon smoked paprika
- ½ teaspoon sweet paprika
- 4 cups vegetable broth
- 1 large tomato
- 1 ½ cups Bomba Rice
- 1 red bell pepper
- 5 cloves garlic
- 1 medium onion
- 1 teaspoon saffron threads

Method:

1. In a small saucepan, insert vegetable broth.
2. In a 12-inch Paella Bowl, heat two tablespoons of oil and add the vegetables and spices.
3. Sauté until the vegetables are tender and golden brown.
4. Sauté for two minutes after adding the garlic.

5. Combine the onions, spicy paprika, and sweet paprika in a mixing bowl.

6. Cook for 1-2 minutes on high heat.

7. In the same pan, add the rice and the leftover 1 tablespoon of oil.

8. Put in the liquid slowly while adding the fresh thyme. Season with salt and pepper.

9. Reduce the heat to a low simmer.

10.   Switch off the heat in the pan. Toss in the peas on top of the rice.

2.17 Mediterranean Chicken & Chorizo Paella

Cooking Time: 50 minutes

Serving Size: 4

Ingredients:

Lemon Yogurt Sauce

- Pinch of cayenne pepper
- Kosher salt
- Zest and juice of 1 lemon
- 2 tablespoons curly parsley
- 1½ cups plain yogurt

For the Chicken

- ½ cup golden raisins
- ½ cup curly parsley sprigs
- 2 cups safflower oil
- ½ cup whole blanched almonds
- 6 chicken thighs

- 2 bay leaves
- 1½ cups basmati rice
- 4 whole cloves
- 2 cinnamon sticks
- 3 cups chicken stock
- 5 cardamom pods
- 6 chicken drumsticks
- 2 tablespoons tomato paste
- 3 strips orange zest
- Kosher salt and pepper
- ½ teaspoon turmeric
- 2 tomatoes
- 2 tablespoons olive oil
- 1 teaspoon cumin
- 1 teaspoon coriander
- 1 large onion
- 2 teaspoons fresh ginger
- ½ cup grated carrot
- 3 cloves garlic

Method:

1. Combine yogurt, lime juice and zest, tarragon, and smoked paprika in a medium mixing cup.
2. Put aside after seasoning with salt.
3. Preheat the oven to 375 degrees Fahrenheit.
4. Season the chicken with salt and pepper before serving.

5. Reduce the heat to medium-low and add the spices.

6. Place them skin-side up golden brown chicken in the boiling liquid and bake for 25 minutes.

7. Take the rice to a boil in a saucepan with the stored liquid ingredients over moderate flame.

8. Stir in the rice, cover, and cook on low heat until the rice is tender about 20 minutes.

2.18 Classic Rice Spanish Vegetables Recipe

Cooking Time: 45 minutes

Serving Size: 8

Ingredients:

- ½ teaspoon salt
- Chopped cilantro
- 2 teaspoons cumin
- 1 teaspoon chili powder
- ¾ cup corn kernels
- ½ cup peas
- 3 tablespoons olive oil
- 1 cup tomatoes
- 2 2/3 cups vegetable broth
- 1 small onion
- 1½ cups white rice
- 1 tablespoon tomato paste
- 1 large carrot
- 3 cloves garlic

- 1 medium green pepper

Method:

1. In a medium saucepan, heat the oil on moderate flame.
2. Add the onion, garlic, and carrots to the hot oil.
3. Cook for an additional minute, just until the vegetables have softened.
4. Cook for thirty seconds, just until the garlic is fragrant. Toss in the rice.
5. Mix in the chopped tomatoes, then insert the tomatoes, stock, corn, peas, cumin, chili powder, and salt to taste.
6. Remove the rice from the heat and set it aside for ten minutes, covered.
7. Toss the rice with a spoon to fluff it up.
8. Taste and sprinkle with more salt if necessary, then top with coriander.

2.19 Saucy Spanish Chicken with Green Olives

Cooking Time: 150 minutes

Serving Size: 8

Ingredients:
- ¼ cup sherry
- 1 tablespoon cornstarch
- 2 teaspoon dried thyme
- 1 teaspoon cumin and paprika
- 8 chicken drumsticks

- 1 small red onion
- 2 large garlic cloves
- 1 cup green olives
- 389ml can tomato sauce

Method:

1. Remove the skin from the chicken and remove any excess fat.

2. Pour the sauce in. Quantify out the artichokes, then cut them up and throw them in.

3. Combine the onion, ginger, thyme, smoked paprika, and tarragon in a mixing bowl.

4. Place the chicken in the paste to coat it, then turn it bone-side out. Push your way into the liquid.

5. Cook for six hours on medium or 2½ to 3 hours on average, or until chicken reaches 165°F.

6. Combine cornstarch and a few tablespoons of water in a mixing bowl and whisk until smooth.

7. Stir frequently in the sauce until it thickens, around five minutes. Chicken should be served over rice.

2.20 Spanish Potato Tortilla

Cooking Time: 50 minutes

Serving Size: 4

Ingredients:

- 8 eggs, beaten
- Handful flat-leaf parsley
- 400g waxy potatoes
- 6 garlic cloves

- 4 tablespoon olive oil
- 25g butter
- 1 large white onion

To Serve

- 4 vine tomatoes
- Drizzle of olive oil
- 1 baguette

Method:

1. Preheat a large nonstick deep fryer to medium.

2. Steadily roast the onion in the butter and oil until it is tender. Slice the tomatoes in the meantime.

3. Add the potatoes to the skillet, wrap, and cook for another 15-20 minutes, occasionally mixing to ensure even cooking.

4. Add 2 garlic cloves crushed and mixed in, followed by pounded eggs.

5. Replace the lid on the pan and bake the tortilla on low heat.

6. When the tortilla is finished, move it to a plate and eat it warm or hot, with grated parmesan on top.

Chapter 3: Traditional French Dishes

3.1 French Chicken Shawarma Fries

Cooking Time: 50 minutes

Serving Size: 6

Ingredients:

- 1- ½ lbs. russet potatoes
- Hot sauce
- 3 cloves garlic
- 1 lb. chicken breasts
- Juice of ½ lemon
- Pinch cayenne pepper
- Salt
- ¼ cup olive oil
- ½ teaspoon allspice
- Pinch cinnamon
- 1 teaspoon paprika
- ½ teaspoon turmeric
- 1 teaspoon cumin

For the Mediterranean Salsa

- Salt and pepper
- Juice of ½ - 1 lemon
- ¼ cup packed parsley
- ¼ teaspoon oregano
- 2 vine-ripened tomatoes

- ¼ small red onion
- 1 clove garlic
- 1 small cucumber

For the Garlic Sauce

- 3 cloves garlic
- Salt
- 2 tablespoons lemon juice
- ½ cup mayonnaise

Method:

1. In a big Ziploc container, mix the lime juice, 2 tablespoons of additional olive oil, herbs, and crushed garlic cloves.

2. Potatoes can be sliced into chips.

3. Preheat the oven to 400 degrees Fahrenheit, then cover a sheet pan with foil and lightly rub with nonstick cooking spray.

4. Cook the meat for 12-15 minutes after spreading it out on a cookie dish.

5. Boost the temperature to 425 degrees Fahrenheit.

6. Sprinkle the leftover two tablespoons extra virgin sunflower oil over the potatoes and sprinkle thoroughly with salt and black pepper.

7. In a blender or food processor, combine all of the Garlic Sauce components and heat until fully smooth.

3.2 Mediterranean French Salmon En Papillote with Potatoes

Cooking Time: 1 hour

Serving Size: 4

Ingredients:

- 1 courgette
- 400g waxy potatoes
- 1 bag of capers
- 1 Romano pepper
- 1 lemon
- 125g cherry tomatoes
- 2 x 110g salmon fillets
- 1 bag of pitted black olives

Method:

1. Preheat the oven to 200 degrees Celsius.
2. Break the corvettes into tiny parts that are easy to eat.
3. Remove the seeds from the Romano pepper.
4. In the center of two parts, place the sliced courgette, Romano peppers, grape tomatoes, and green olives.
5. Cook the fish with a pinch of salt and place it skin-side up over the veggies.
6. Preheat the oven to 250°F and bake the tray for 25-30 minutes, or until the fish is done.
7. Drain and transfer the vegetables to the pot once they've finished cooking.

8. Offer the en papillote Mediterranean fish with the dressing potatoes on the bottom.

3.3 Mediterranean French Lentils with Roasted Eggplant and Tomatoes

Cooking Time: 1 hour 15 minutes

Serving Size: 4

Ingredients:

- ½ cup Greek yogurt
- Fresh ground pepper
- ¾ teaspoon fine sea salt
- 3 tablespoon fresh parsley
- 4 lbs. globe eggplants
- ½ teaspoon dried oregano
- ¼ teaspoon red pepper flakes
- 2½ tablespoon fresh lemon juice
- 3 plump cloves of garlic
- 1 bay leaf
- 2 tablespoon olive oil
- 765g water
- 20 oz. cherry tomatoes
- 175g French lentils

Method:

1. Preheat the oven to 475 degrees Fahrenheit.
2. Prick each eggplant approximately seven times all around with the tines of a knife.
3. Position the tomatoes on the bottom oven and bake until they are lightly seared and burst.

4. Transfer the lentils to a large sauté pan while the eggplants are frying.

5. Pour in the liquid and season with a pinch of salt and a diced tomato.

6. Cut the eggplants wide and pick out the pulp once they've cooled enough to treat.

7. Transfer the olive oil, ginger, lime juice, marjoram, pepper flakes, white pepper, and tarragon to the lentils and vegetables in the cup.

3.4 French Green Beans Mediterranean Style

Cooking Time: 20 minutes

Serving Size: 6

Ingredients:

- 3 tablespoons olive oil
- 2 packages haricots verts
- 2 teaspoons Dijon mustard
- ½ teaspoon sugar
- 1 large shallot
- 2 tablespoons red wine vinegar
- ⅓ cup Kalamata olives

Method:

1. In a big mixing bowl, combine the first five ingredients.

2. Allow for a 10-minute rest period.

3. Insert the olive oil and season with salt and pepper to taste.

4. Green beans should be cooked for approximately 3 minutes in lightly salted water, or until vibrant and buttery; drain.

5. To stop the cooking time, submerge the beans in ice cubes; rinse and dry thoroughly.

6. Toss the beans with the olive mixture.

7. Serve at ambient temperature or cool for up to two hours.

3.5 French Cheese and Tomato Tartlets

Cooking Time: 1 hour 10 minutes

Serving Size: 6

Ingredients:

Tomato Ragu

- 400g tomatoes
- Pinch of salt and pepper
- 1 teaspoon oregano
- 1 teaspoon sugar
- 1 tablespoon olive oil
- 2 cloves garlic
- 1 tablespoon tomato puree
- 1 onion

Tart Cases

- 320g pack pastry

Béchamel Sauce

- 85g mozzarella cheese
- ½ teaspoon black pepper
- 240ml milk
- 75g mature cheddar cheese
- 4 tablespoon plain flour

- 45g unsalted butter

Other Toppings

- 3 tablespoon cheddar cheese
- Small bunch of fresh thyme
- 12 small tomatoes
- 3 tablespoon panko breadcrumbs
- 1 small egg

Method:

1. In a moderate deep fryer or stove pan, add the oil and insert the onions.
2. Cook for five minutes over moderate flame.
3. Cook for another minute after adding the garlic.
4. Combine the tomato sauce, marjoram, sugar, canned tomatoes, salt, and pepper in a large mixing bowl.
5. Make six squares out of the puff pastry.
6. Take the beans from the stove and set them aside.
7. In a small saucepan, melt the butter.
8. Toss in the flour and mix with a fork. Slowly drizzle in the milk.
9. Combine the cheddar, prosciutto, and black pepper in a mixing bowl.
10. Fill the pastry cases with the tomatoes ragu.

3.6 Mediterranean French Barbecued Lamb

Cooking Time: 18 minutes

Serving Size: 6

Ingredients:

For the Lamb

- 1 large lemon, juice of
- 1 small yellow or red onion
- Olive oil
- 2 racks of lamb
- 1 teaspoon black pepper
- 1 tablespoon mint leaves
- 1 teaspoon garlic paste
- ¼ teaspoon sweet paprika
- ½ teaspoon salt
- ½ teaspoon green cardamom
- ½ teaspoon ground nutmeg
- 1 teaspoon allspice

For the Tomato Mint Quinoa

- ½ cup red onion
- ⅓ cup feta cheese
- Salt and pepper
- 1 cup fresh mint leaves
- 3 garlic cloves
- 1 14.5 oz. can petit tomato
- Water

- 2 tablespoon olive oil
- 1 cup dry quinoa

Method:

1. Mix the garlic, seasoning, tablespoon clean, fresh mint, and two tablespoons olive oil in a shallow bowl.

2. Pick the pork chops and brush them with the paprika rub on both ends.

3. In the meantime, prepare the quinoa as per the product directions.

4. 2 tablespoon olive oil, heated in a nonstick medium saucepan.

5. Continue cooking and add diced tomato from a can. Season to taste.

6. Preheat the grill to high heat, then add the pork chops and cook for 2 minutes.

7. Heat for another three minutes on the other hand.

8. Allow ten minutes for the chops to rest while serving.

3.7 French Ratatouille

Cooking Time: 40 minutes

Serving Size: 8

Ingredients:

Veggies

- 2 yellow squashes
- 2 zucchinis
- 6 Roma tomatoes
- 2 eggplants

Sauce

- 28 oz. can of tomatoes
- 2 tablespoons fresh basil
- Salt, to taste
- Pepper, to taste
- 2 tablespoons olive oil
- 1 red bell pepper
- 1 yellow bell pepper
- 4 cloves garlic
- 1 onion

Herb Seasoning

- Pepper, to taste
- 4 tablespoons olive oil
- 2 teaspoons fresh thyme
- Salt, to taste
- 1 teaspoon garlic
- 2 tablespoons fresh parsley
- 2 tablespoons fresh basil

Method:

1. Preheat the oven to 375 degrees Fahrenheit.
2. Cut the eggplant, onions, squash, and sweet potato into thin slices.
3. In a 12-inch stove pan, heat the oil over moderate flame.
4. Sauté the onion, cloves, and bell pepper for about ten minutes, or until soft.

5. Combine the basil, ginger, garlic, tarragon, salt, vinegar, and balsamic vinegar in a small cup.

6. Season the veggies with the herb spice.

7. Bake for thirty minutes with the pan wrapped in foil.

8. Serve as a side dish or main course while still hot.

3.8 Ratatouille French Vegetable Stew

Cooking Time: 45 minutes

Serving Size: 4

Ingredients:

Salad

- 1/3 cup feta
- ¼ cup basil
- ½ cup artichoke hearts
- 1/3 cup Kalamata olives
- 1 cup green lentils
- ½ red bell pepper
- ½ English cucumber
- 3 cups chicken broth

Dressing

- 3 tablespoons olive oil
- Salt and black pepper
- 2 tablespoons balsamic vinegar
- 1 tablespoon lemon juice

Method:

1. Rinse the lentils and exclude any foreign material.

2. Combine with broth or water in a casserole dish.

3. In a mixing bowl, combine the warm lentils.

4. Mix the lime juice and sour cream to make the seasoning.

5. Slowly drizzle in the olive oil and season with salt and pepper to taste.

6. Combine the lentils and vinaigrette in a mixing bowl.

7. Enable to cool to room temperature before adding the remaining ingredients.

3.9 Mediterranean French Chicken Marbella

Cooking Time: 4 hours 15 minutes

Serving Size: 8

Ingredients:

- ½ cup white wine
- 2 tablespoons Italian parsley
- 3 bay leaves
- ¼ cup brown sugar
- 2 chickens
- 8 Spanish green olives
- ¼ cup capers
- ½ head of garlic
- ¼ cup olive oil
- ½ cup prunes
- Coarse salt and pepper
- ¼ cup red wine vinegar

- 2 tablespoons oregano

Method:

1. Conjoin garlic, marjoram, salt, and black pepper to taste, seasoning, canola oil, prunes, artichokes, capers with water, and garlic cloves in a large mixing bowl.

2. Transfer the chicken parts to the marinade and cover absolutely.

3. Place the chicken in a baking pan and pour the marinade, brown sugar, and wine over it.

4. Preheat the oven to 350 degrees Fahrenheit.

5. Bake for 50-100 minutes, basting regularly with cooking liquid.

6. Transfer the chicken, dried apricots, olives, and dill to a baking tray using a slotted spoon.

7. Serve the chicken with a few of the cooking liquid and a generous amount of parsley.

8. In a sauceboat, serve the leftover juices.

3.10 Mediterranean French Fish Soup with Garlicky Rouille

Cooking Time: 2 hours 30 minutes

Serving Size: 8

Ingredients:

- Pinch of dried oregano
- ½ cup Parmesan cheese
- 1 pound tuna

- 1 small baguette
- 1 gold potato
- 1½ pounds monkfish
- 1 pound skinless cod fillet
- 16 garlic cloves
- 12 thyme sprigs
- Freshly ground pepper
- 1 cup dry white wine
- 2 quarts fish stock
- 1½ cups olive oil
- ⅛ teaspoon saffron threads
- 3 tablespoons tomato paste
- Salt
- ½ tablespoon ground cumin
- ½ teaspoon sweet paprika
- ½ tablespoon pepper
- ½ tablespoon fennel seeds
- ¼ teaspoon cayenne pepper
- 1 celery rib
- 1 fennel bulb
- 1 large onion
- 2 large leeks

Method:

1. Heat the potato cubes in a small saucepan of lightly salted water.

2. Mash the potatoes with the stored potato water and the garlic powder until soft.

3. Preheat the oven to 350 degrees Fahrenheit.

4. Heat and cook ½ cup vegetable oil in a large casserole dish until it shimmers.

5. Cook over medium temperature with the leeks, onions, celery, chives bulb, and six doubled garlic cloves.

6. Put the soup to a boil with the fish meal and the thyme package.

7. Organize the baguette pieces on a cookie dish in the meantime.

8. Toast the baguette pieces for about five minutes until its golden brown.

9. Pour the fish soup into shallow bowls and top with a little rouille.

3.11 Mediterranean Loaded French Fry Salad

Cooking Time: 45 minutes

Serving Size: 2

Ingredients:
Yogurt Sauce

- 1 teaspoon kosher salt
- 2 teaspoons lemon juice
- 1 tablespoon fresh dill
- 2 cloves garlic
- ¼ cup fresh parsley
- 1½ cups Greek yogurt

Fries

- 3 medium russet potatoes
- 1 package spice blend
- 2 cups ice
- 2 tablespoons lemon juice
- Coldwater
- 4 cups vegetable oil

Toppings

- ½ cup feta cheese
- 2 tablespoons dill
- 1 plum tomato
- ¼ cup red onion
- ½ cup cucumber
- 1 cup romaine lettuce
- ½ cup chickpeas

Method:

1. Combine the yogurt, parsley, tarragon, cloves, salt, and lime juice in a medium mixing bowl.

2. In a big mixing bowl, combine ice water, ice, and one tablespoon lime juice.

3. Slice the potatoes and cut them into 14-inch thick, 3-inch large pieces.

4. Refrigerate for thirty minutes after adding the leftover tablespoon of lime juice.

5. Heat the potato in the hot oil in groups for 5–10 minutes until it's soft and light yellow.

6. Raise the temperature of the oil to 375°F.

7. Transfer the chips to the hot oil in groups and continue to cook for 5–10 minutes, or until the light is nicely browned.

8. Pour more yogurt sauce on top. Dill should be sprinkled on top.

3.12 Mediterranean French Lentil Salad

Cooking Time: 25 minutes

Serving Size: 6

Ingredients:

- 2 tablespoons parsley
- Lemon juice and zest
- 1/3 cup red onion
- 4 ounces feta cheese
- 2 cups French lentils
- ¾ cup cucumber
- ¾ cup Kalamata olives
- 1 cup lacinato kale
- ¾ cup tomatoes
- ¾ cup red peppers

Dressing

- ½ teaspoon oregano
- Salt and black pepper
- ½ teaspoon Dijon mustard
- ½ teaspoon maple syrup
- 1 tablespoon red wine vinegar
- 2 tablespoons olive oil

Method:

1. Position the lentils in a big saucepan after rinsing them.

2. Cover with around 6 cups of water and a bit of salt to taste.

3. Bring to the boil, reduce to low heat, and cook for twenty minutes or until lentils are soft. If required, remove the excess water.

4. In a big mixing bowl, whisk together the dressing ingredients.

5. Pour in the lentils and the rest of the components.

6. Salad can be eaten right away or kept refrigerated for up to three days.

3.13 French Cauliflower Gratin

Cooking Time: 30 minutes

Serving Size: 4

Ingredients:

- ½ cup Swiss cheese
- Salt and pepper
- 3 tablespoons flour
- 2 ½ cups milk
- 5 tablespoons butter
- 1 large head cauliflower

Method:

1. Cauliflower should be washed and cut into thin strips.

2. Cook the bits for about ten minutes in a big pot of water.

3. Preheat the oven to 350 degrees Fahrenheit.

4. Heat the oil in a saucepan over medium heat to make the béchamel.

5. Mix in the flour with vigor. You will get a dense cream-like substance.

6. Then, when proceeding to combine with the whisk, slowly add the milk.

7. Drop the béchamel over the cabbage, sprinkle with the leftover cream parmesan, and bake for thirty minutes, exposed.

3.14 Mediterranean French Baguette

Cooking Time: 1 hour

Serving Size: 4

Ingredients:

- ½ lb. prosciutto
- Italian dressing
- Sliced mozzarella cheese
- Basil leaves
- Real mayonnaise
- Baby spinach leaves
- Sliced plum tomatoes
- 1 French baguette

Method:

1. Try squeezing arugula, onions, mozzarella, herbs, prosciutto onto a baguette, and layer with real sour cream.

2. The dressing should be drizzled on top.

3.15 Soupe au Pistou

Cooking Time: 2 hours 30 minutes

Serving Size: 6

Ingredients:

For the Soup

- ½ cup soup pasta
- Freshly ground pepper
- 2 medium-size turnips
- ½ pound green beans
- 2 celery stalks
- 1 medium-size zucchini
- 1 ½ cups white beans
- 2 cups green cabbage
- 2 large carrots
- 1 large onion
- 2 leeks
- 1 pound tomatoes
- Salt to taste
- 1 tablespoon olive oil
- 4 large garlic cloves

For the Pistou

- Freshly ground pepper
- ½ cup Parmesan
- ⅓ cup extra virgin olive oil
- ½ cup grated Parmesan

- 2 large garlic cloves

- 2 cups fresh basil leaves

- Salt to taste

Method:

1. In a big, heavy casserole dish or Dutch oven, pour the white beans and add 2 quarts of liquid. Get the water to a boil.

2. In a large skillet, heat the oil, then put the rest sliced onions and a large salt pinch. Insert the leeks and the rest of the garlic.

3. Transfer all of the leftover vegetables, except for the black beans, to the casserole dish and whisk to blend.

4. In a mixer, grind the herb a pinch at a time to a mixture, then throw the garlic back in and blend well.

5. 10 minutes before eating, add the noodles to the boiling soup and cook until al dente.

6. Season with pepper and salt to taste.

7. Warm the soup while stirring in the blanched black beans.

3.16 French Sea Bass with Olives and Cherry Tomatoes

Cooking Time: 25 minutes

Serving Size: 4

Ingredients:

- 4 6-ounce fillets sea bass
- ¼ cup fresh basil
- 1 tablespoon olive oil
- Kosher salt and pepper
- 1 shallot
- 2 cups cherry tomatoes
- ½ cup green olives
- 2 garlic cloves

Method:

1. Preheat the broiler by putting a rack in the upper third of the oven.

2. In a medium mixing bowl, mix the shallot, garlic, onions, olives, and butter, sprinkle with salt, and toss properly.

3. Season the fish with salt and black pepper in a ceramic baking dish.

4. Sprinkle tomato combination over salmon and broil for 10–13 minutes, or until salmon is opaque throughout vegetables have begun to burst.

5. Serve with a sprinkling of basil on top.

3.17 Mediterranean French Spinach Strata

Cooking Time: 40 minutes

Serving Size: 10

Ingredients:

- 5 large eggs
- 4 large egg whites
- 2 tablespoons Dijon mustard
- 1 ½ teaspoons oregano
- ¾ cup Asiago cheese
- 3 cups milk
- 3 cups plum tomato
- 1 (4-ounce) package feta cheese
- 2 loaves French bread baguette
- Cooking spray
- ½ teaspoon salt
- ½ teaspoon black pepper
- 1 cup onion
- 1 tablespoon all-purpose flour
- 2 (7-ounce) bags of baby spinach
- 1 package mushrooms
- 4 garlic cloves

Method:

1. Preheat the oven to 350 degrees Fahrenheit.
2. Position slices of bread on a cookie dish in a thin layer.

3. Preheat oven to 350°F and bake for ten minutes, or until golden brown.

4. Over moderate flame, brush a large sauté pan with olive oil.

5. Add the onion, garlic, and mushrooms and cook over medium heat until the mushrooms are tender. Toss in the spinach container.

6. Top with sliced tomatoes, feta cheese, and a quarter of the Asiago cheese.

7. Place the leftover bread slices on top of the cheese.

8. Then use a fork, combine ¼ minced peppers, ¼ teaspoon salt, milk, and the rest of the ingredients.

9. Pour over the bread and top with the rest of the Asiago cheese. Chill for 8 hours or overnight, covered.

3.18 French Mediterranean-Style Fish Soup

Cooking Time: 40 minutes

Serving Size: 6

Ingredients:

The Fish Broth

- 6 fresh thyme
- A 2-inch strip of orange zest
- 1 fennel bulb
- 1 medium-size onion
- 3 tablespoons olive oil
- 6 garlic cloves
- 8 pounds whole fish

The Soup Base

- ½-inch French baguette
- 2 cups garlic mayonnaise
- 8 medium-size tomatoes
- ¼ cup Pernod
- 3 tablespoons olive oil
- 3 medium-size leeks

Method:

1. Fill a pot halfway with ice water and soak the fish bones and faces for at least 30 minutes.

2. In a 4-quart bath, heat 3 tablespoons of canola oil.

3. Combine the garlic, fennel, onion, spices, and lime zest in a large mixing bowl. Cook, boiling periodically, over medium-high heat.

4. Mix in the veggies with a rolling pin for another ten minutes or until they begin to fall apart.

5. Remove the bones and veggies and toss them out.

6. Heat the leeks softly in the olive oil for about ten minutes or until they soften and become somewhat transparent.

7. Bake the bread slices under the grill just before eating the stew.

3.19 Mediterranean French Bread Pizza

Cooking Time: 50 minutes

Serving Size: 4

Ingredients:

- 2 ounces goat cheese
- 4 fresh basil leaves
- 2 ounces provolone
- 2 ounces feta
- 1 12 inch loaf bread
- ¼ teaspoon black pepper
- 2 ounces mozzarella
- 10 ounces heavy pizza sauce
- 4 ounces of a portabella mushroom
- ½ teaspoon salt
- 1 fire-roasted red pepper
- 8 ounces of baby spinach
- 1-ounce olive oil
- 6 ounces artichoke hearts
- 2 cloves garlic

Method:

1. The loaf of bread should be split in half longways.

2. On both halves of the crust, distribute the pizza sauce.

3. Artichoke cores, mushrooms, and roast bell pepper are sautéed in a hot pan with canola oil, followed by spinach, garlic powder, and pepper.

4. Cover the sauces with the hot mixture that has been split between the French toast's two halves.

5. Bake for four to five minutes at 400°F in a preheated pan or your bread oven.

6. Take the pizza from the microwave and scatter the basil leaves on top.

3.20 Mediterranean Veggie Sauté

Cooking Time: 15 minutes

Serving Size: 4

Ingredients:

- ⅛ teaspoon garlic powder
- ⅛ teaspoon Sicilian sea salt
- 2 teaspoons olive oil
- ¼ teaspoon sugar
- 2 medium zucchini
- 2 teaspoons Greek seasoning
- 2 teaspoons balsamic vinegar
- 1 small red bell pepper
- 1 medium yellow onion

Method:

1. On moderate flame, heat a large Sautee pan sprayed with cooking spray until warm.

2. Cook and mix for 6 minutes until either zucchini, onions, and bell pepper are caramelized on the edges.

3. In a small cup, combine the rest of the ingredients.

4. Switch off the heat in the skillet. Toss in the spice mixture softly to coat.

Chapter 4: Greek Traditional Dishes

4.1 Mediterranean Greek Breakfast Wrap

Cooking Time: 15 minutes

Serving Size: 4

Ingredients:

- 2 tablespoon Kalamata olives
- 3 tablespoon feta cheese
- 4 scrambled eggs
- 4 cherry tomatoes
- 2 tablespoon tzatziki sauce
- 2 tortillas

Method:

1. Place the tortillas on a floured work surface and scatter the tzatziki down the middle of each one.

2. Scrambled eggs, onions, olives, and parmesan cheese are uniformly distributed on top.

3. Fold the tortillas' bottoms out over the stuffing, then pull in the sides and roll them up securely.

4.2 Mediterranean Greek Potato Skillet

Cooking Time: 20 minutes

Serving Size: 4

Ingredients:

- 2 tablespoons flat-leaf parsley
- 4 eggs
- ¾ ounce Kalamata olives
- 3 tablespoons feta cheese
- ¼ teaspoon kosher salt
- 3 cloves garlic
- 2 cups spinach
- ¼ teaspoon ground pepper
- 4 teaspoons olive oil
- 12 grape or cherry tomatoes
- 1 pound package potatoes

Method:

1. Prepare the potato as per the box instructions, stirring the spice package with two tablespoons of olive oil.

2. Over moderate flame, heat a large sauté pan.

3. Stir in the potatoes, then simmer for two minutes.

4. Mix in the tomatoes and simmer until the potatoes begin to yellow and the tomatoes begin to peel, stirring periodically.

5. To one bottom of the plate, move the tomatoes and potatoes and add the remaining two teaspoons of olive oil.

6. Transfer the cloves and spinach to the olive oil.

7. Cook for about two minutes, stirring continuously until the spinach is wilting.

8. Free from the heat. Mix in the pine nuts, coriander, and feta.

9. Cook the eggs, crispy side up, in a small nonstick pan while the potatoes and tomato combination is frying.

10. Divide the mixture of potatoes into four plates.

11. Cover with a fried egg for each meal.

4.3 Mediterranean Greek Eggs Kayana

Cooking Time: 6 minutes

Serving Size: 4

Ingredients:

- Sea salt
- Freshly ground pepper
- 3 tablespoon extra-virgin olive oil
- Dry oregano
- 2 large tomatoes
- 2 cloves garlic
- 6 eggs organic free-range

For Serving

- Chili pepper flakes

- Feta cheese

Method:

1. In a saucepan, stir in the olive oil.

2. Stir in the diced cloves and sauté for two minutes over medium-high heat.

3. Put some tomatoes. With salt and black pepper, mix.

4. Spray 1 tablespoon of oregano over everything.

5. Stir in the tomatoes and fry for 5-6 minutes, stirring regularly.

6. To the pot, add the egg mixture and gently blend it.

7. Stir in the tomatoes and egg combination three times.

8. Cook the eggs according to the texture you like.

9. Serve instantly with a swirl of hot chili flakes, a crumbled feta cheese, or both.

10. If you like, add some chopped herbs, such as mint or basil.

4.4 Mediterranean Greek Garden Appetizer

Cooking Time: 15 minutes

Serving Size: 4

Ingredients:

- 2 tablespoons ripe olives
- Miniature pita pockets
- ¼ teaspoon pepper
- 1-½ cups cucumber
- 1 cup tomatoes

- ½ teaspoon garlic
- ¼ teaspoon oregano
- ½ cup green onions
- 2 cups feta cheese
- ¼ cup plain yogurt
- 1 carton garden cream cheese

Method:

1. Mix the sour cream, feta, yogurt, garlic, oregano, and peppers in a big mixing bowl.

2. Fill a 9-inch pie plate halfway with the mixture.

3. Over the cheese mixture, scatter the cucumber, onions, tomatoes, and artichokes.

4. Pita bread is a good component.

5. Keep leftovers refrigerated.

4.5 Mediterranean Style Feta and Greek Yogurt Pita Appetizer

Cooking Time: 30 minutes

Serving Size: 4

Ingredients:

- Fresh ground pepper
- 1 teaspoon olive oil
- Four tablespoons Greek yogurt
- 2-3 tablespoons mint
- 2 tablespoons crumbled feta
- 2 round medium pita bread

Method:

1. Preheat the oven to 400 degrees F.

2. Stir the feta with the yogurt in a medium bowl until smooth.

3. Mix in the mint and olive oil thoroughly.

4. Around each pita, distribute the yogurt-feta mixture.

5. Bake for about ten minutes, just until the tops of the pita begin to brown.

6. Remove the pitas and cut them into 6 or 8 pieces with a pizza cutter before serving.

4.6 Mediterranean Greek Layer Dip

Cooking Time: 20 minutes

Serving Size: 8

Ingredients:

- 2 tablespoons parsley
- Pita chips, broccoli, bell peppers, carrots
- ½ cup crumbled feta cheese
- ¼ cup Kalamata olives
- 1 tomato
- ½ cup seeded cucumber
- 1 container hummus
- ½ cup plain Greek yogurt

Method:

1. Place the hummus on the base of an 8x8-inch round roasting pan, a deep pie dish, or a specific glass baking dish in a smooth coat.

2. Spoonful the Greek yogurt over the top with a tiny spoonful, then sprinkle lightly to make a fresh coat.

3. Spread the top of onions, cucumbers, feta, and olives.

4. Use clean parsley to scatter.

5. Put it in the fridge until prepared to eat, then mix as needed with crackers, pita chips, and diced vegetables.

4.7 Mediterranean Greek Stuffed Chicken

Cooking Time: 55 minutes

Serving Size: 4

Ingredients:

- ¼ teaspoon salt
- 4 boneless skinless chicken breast
- 4 garlic cloves
- ½ teaspoon ground pepper
- 2 tablespoons lemon juice
- 2 teaspoons lemon zest

Zucchini Mixture

- ¼ cup prepared pesto
- 4 ounces fresh mozzarella cheese
- ¼ teaspoon red pepper flakes
- ¼ teaspoon ground pepper
- 2 garlic cloves
- ¼ teaspoon salt
- ¼ cup sun-dried tomatoes

- 1 teaspoon olive oil
- 4 large zucchini

Method:

1. Blend the first five ingredients in a large pan.

2. Use chicken to insert; shift to cover. Let the 15 minutes stay.

3. In the meantime, trim the ends of the zucchini for the noodles.

4. Cut the zucchini down the middle into thin, small strips using a bread slicer or filet knife.

5. Break the zucchini on both sides until the beans become apparent, like peeling a potato.

6. Dump and save the seeded part for another use.

7. Cook chicken barbecue, wrapped, over medium heat or 4-inch broil.

8. A thermometer reads a thermometer inserted into the chicken from 4-5 minutes of heat on either side or until 165°. Take from the grill; load up.

9. Heat the vegetables and olive oil in a large nonstick bowl.

10. Add the garlic, cinnamon, flakes of pepper, and salt; boil for thirty seconds and mix.

11. Insert zucchini; fry and mix for three minutes or until soft and crispy.

12. Withdraw from the heat. Stir the pesto in.

13. Get the chicken sliced into strips. With zucchini noodles, eat. Cover with mozzarella cheese.

4.8 Mediterranean Greek Stuffed Peppers

Cooking Time: 4-½ hours

Serving Size: 8

Ingredients:

- ½ teaspoon red pepper flakes
- ½ teaspoon pepper
- 2 tablespoons olive oil
- ½ teaspoon salt
- Chopped fresh parsley
- ½ cup Greek olives
- 1 cup cooked barley
- 1 cup crumbled feta cheese
- 1 can crushed tomatoes
- 1 pound ground lamb
- 1-½ teaspoons dried oregano
- 3 garlic cloves, minced
- 2 medium peppers
- 1 small fennel bulb
- 1 package frozen spinach
- 1 small red onion

Method:

1. Heat the oil over moderate heat in a large pan.
2. Insert fennel and onions; continue cooking for ten minutes until soft.
3. Add the garlic and veggies; cook for one minute longer. Mildly cool.

4. Break the peppers and save the tops; extract and discard the seeds.

5. Pour 1 cup of chopped tomatoes into the 6- or 7-quarter rim.

6. Combine the lamb, rye, 1 cup of feta cheese, olives, and spices in a large mixing bowl; add the mixture of fennel.

7. Mix the spoon into the peppers; place in a slow cooker.

8. Pour the remainder of the crushed tomatoes over the peppers; replace the tops with pepper.

9. Cook, wrapped, until peppers are soft, 4 to 5 hours on medium.

10.   Serve with extra feta and minced parsley if needed.

4.9 Avgolemono: Greek Lemon Chicken Soup

Cooking Time: 35 minutes

Serving Size: 6

Ingredients:

- 2 large eggs
- Fresh parsley for garnish
- 2 cooked chicken breast pieces
- ½ cup lemon juice
- Extra-virgin olive oil
- 1 cup rice
- 8 cups chicken broth

- 2 bay leaves
- Salt and pepper
- 1 cup green onions
- 2 garlic cloves
- 1 cup celery
- 1 cup carrots

Method:

1. Add 1 tablespoon olive oil, heated on moderate in a big Dutch oven or large pot.

2. Toss in the carrot, fennel, and fresh basil, and cook for a few minutes before adding the garlic.

3. Boost the heat to medium and add the garlic broth and coriander seeds.

4. Reduce to low heat and cook for 20 minutes, just until the rice is soft.

5. In a medium cup, whisk together all the lime juice and whites to make the egg-lemon mixture.

6. Mix the sauce into the chicken soup until it's completely mixed.

7. Remove the pan from the heat as soon as possible.

8. If desired, garnish with grated parmesan.

9. Serve with your favorite bread while it's still sweet.

4.10 Greek Bowls with Roasted Garbanzo Beans

Cooking Time: 45 minutes

Serving Size: 4

Ingredients:

- 1 cup cherry tomatoes
- 1 lemon
- ½ cup Kalamata olives
- ½ cup feta cheese
- 1 pound fresh baby spinach
- 1 English cucumber
- 2 teaspoon chili powder
- 1 teaspoon ground cumin
- 1 (14.5 ounces) can garbanzo beans
- 1 tablespoon olive oil
- 2 (6-8 ounce) chicken breasts

Marinade

- 2 garlic cloves
- 1 lemon
- ¼ teaspoon pepper
- 2 teaspoons dried oregano
- ½ cup Kalamata olives
- ½ teaspoon salt
- ½ cup white wine or chicken stock

Method:

1. Mix in a big zip lock bag with all the marinade ingredients.

2. Chicken breasts are added. Stock for thirty minutes or up to eight hours in the refrigerator.

3. Preheat the oven to 400°.

4. Drain the garbanzo bean and wash them. Pat with a clean cloth to rinse.

5. Break the zip lock bag and transfer meat, and remove the marinade.

6. Sprinkle with one tablespoon olive oil in a wide baking sheet.

7. Place one half of the dry garbanzo bean and put the meat on the other.

8. Spray the chili powder and cilantro with the garbanzo bean.

9. Add a dash of pepper and salt. Transfer to the garbanzo bean an extra teaspoon of coconut oil and shake.

10. Cook the chicken and bean for about 30 minutes at 400° or until the chicken is cooked completely.

11. During baking, toss beans each time.

12. Before moving them to your boxes, cool fully.

13. Align boxes. In one side of the box, put ¼ of the spinach.

14. On the other, meat. Divide the remaining ingredients similarly.

15. Load the Tzatkiki dressing into a little bowl and store it in the fridge.

Conclusion

Most people enjoy Mediterranean cuisine because it is among the healthiest on the planet. Since Mediterranean dishes are made from fresh ingredients, these recipes' positive effects make them even more delicious. New whole foods such as berries, grains, herbs, vegetables, and nuts are emphasized in the diet. Olive oil is one of the most widely used ingredients in Mediterranean cuisine. Olive trees can be found in abundance in the area. Olives are a key food in many dishes. Veggies are also a must-have. Common vegetables include zucchini, green beans, carrots, tomatoes, nuts and seeds, mushrooms, garlic, okra, eggplants, and a broad range of greens and courgettes. Food is seldom eaten. Mediterranean food is distinguished by fresh herbs such as garlic, marjoram, tarragon, thyme, oregano, shallots, parsley, basil, and cloves. Since the diet is mainly fruits, nuts, and veggies, you are also mindful of what you are consuming. Try Mediterranean recipes and make healthier meals for your family.

The 365 Days a Year Mediterranean Diet

Cookbook

Over 100 Easy Recipes for Preparing Tasty Meals for Weight Loss and Healthy Lifestyle All Year Round

Adele Tyler

The trademarks that are used are without any consent, and the publication of the trademark is without permission or backing by the trademark owner. All trademarks and brands within this book are for clarifying purposes only and are the owned by the owners themselves, not affiliated with this document.

Contents

Introduction

A lot of people wish to find an effective diet that can help them to lose weight and live a healthy lifestyle. Most people think dieting is all about restricting the calories-intake, but what if you find a diet that lets you enjoy your favorite foods as well as give you some amazing health benefits. The Mediterranean diet is not about calorie restriction. That is why it has long term benefits. It is a healthy way of living life as it sustains weight loss. As this diet is dense mono-saturated having healthy fats like nuts, olive oil, and avocados, it indeed keeps you full for a very long time, so it will make it possible for you to feel satisfied with even less food consumption. Unlike other diets, the carbs-intake is not followed here; however, emphasis is on vegetables and fruits intake along with some whole grains that are full of fiber.

It is mostly a plant-based diet. It focuses on the consumption of healthy fat and whole foods. Even for beginners, it is much easier to understand and follow this diet. The Pyramid of Mediterranean diet guides you about the foods that must be consumed in large, moderate, and low amounts. The most amazing fact is that the Mediterranean diet works very well as your daily practice. There are no unnecessary restrictions on some foods. The Mediterranean diet is a lifestyle, not just a diet plan for some weeks. It is based on the consumption of enjoyable foods. This book has covered almost everything with over 100 delicious and healthy recipes for all seasons at your table that you need to know to follow this diet. You will learn how you can start your Mediterranean diet. These recipes are easy to make. A comprehensive step-by-step guide has been provided to cook these recipes. This book offers all the crucial information you need to know to get your diet done right.

As mentioned earlier, the Mediterranean diet includes healthy fats like olive oil and plant-based dishes. It is famous for its benefits related to heart and brain health. It does not just help in weight-loss, but also assists in maintaining weight in the long-term. This diet is easy to follow, and it has numerous health benefits and richness. To know how to lose weight with the help of Mediterranean diet, you should be clear about certain things. You must have an understanding of the healthy foods. You should make yourself aware of the consequences of eating processed foods that come with chemicals which sabotage your weight loss journey. You should start your diet journey by cutting these unhealthy foods and begin to consume healthy foods. Let's look at the food you should put emphasis on during your Mediterranean diet!

Healthy Fats

While getting to start your Mediterranean diet, you need to switch to some healthy fats like olive oil. It is very healthy and rich in some mono-saturated fatty acids that help in maintaining the cholesterol levels. It is used while cooking, or it can be drizzled on the finished dishes for boosting the flavor.

Eggs and Fish

Add eggs and fish at least 2-3 times a week. Keeping eggs in the diet meals is a healthy way to lose weight successfully.

Whole Grains

The refined carbs lack essential nutrients. They negatively impact the blood sugar levels. Adding whole grains in the diet is one of the best decisions. These should be consumed protein and healthy fats. It helps in nutrient absorption and easy digestion.

Seeds and Nuts

Seeds and nuts are a rich source of fiber and protein. They provide healthy fats and antioxidants. You should use re

asonable portions of nuts on daily basis.

Dairy

Adding dairy like cheeses and yogurt in your diet is one of the best decisions in adapting to a Mediterranean diet. It is a rich source of the beneficial bacteria to improve your digestive system.

Spices and Herbs

These are rich in plant compounds and antioxidants that help you in fighting the inflammation.

Now let's look at the food, which you should avoid in the Mediterranean diet.

Refined Grains

White pasta, white bread, and white flour pizza dough are some of the white grains that you altogether avoid. Brown rice should be replaced with the white rice. Stay away from the white flour as it is low in nutritional value and fiber. So, use whole grains, such as pita bread, whole-wheat pasta, and brown rice.

Refined Oils

Soybean oil and canola oil and butter should be replaced with olive oil when possible.

On the Mediterranean diet, use coconut oil and olive oil instead of the palm oil. Olive oil is always encouraged in the Mediterranean diet. Avoid the hydrogenated oils, such as palm oil.

Sugary Foods

Avoid pastries, candies, artificial juices, and sodas. Do not add sugars. Natural sweeteners such as honey help sweeten the tea or coffee. Added sugars must be limited to stick to the Mediterranean diet. To get a sweet fix, eat fruit and natural sweeteners such as cinnamon.

Processed Food

Hot dogs, processed meats, and Deli meats should be avoided. Processed foods have certain chemicals in them that are not recommended as these are harmful to the body in the long-term.

Meat

The meat intake must be limited. The Mediterranean diet avoids meat. It has a vegetarian angle. So, to make your Mediterranean diet a successful journey, limit meat intake, particularly the red meat. Processed meats should also be avoided. Fish and chicken are friendlier in this diet than bacon. Also, abstain from the processed meats cured like sausage, etc.

You should also look at your behavioral habits. See how you handle a new diet pattern. Control the overconsumption of unhealthy foods and the foods that must be taken in moderate amounts. The quantity of what you eat does matter as it enhances weight loss. There might be a little stress, in the beginning, to adapt it. It will help your process to address the weight gain. Engage yourself in productive activities to help you stay active during your process. Making these eating habits the only way of life on a daily basis will give you long-term benefits. The behavioral change will help you to adapt this lifestyle easily.

In chapter one, you will be introduced to the Mediterranean diet, how it works, and the numerous health benefits associated with this diet. The rest of the book has been divided into two parts.

The first part includes the recipes for the winter and autumn season. You will find recipes for all the meals of the day, including breakfast, lunch, and dinner. You will also find healthy soup and snack recipes for your winter and autumn. No meal is completed without desserts. So, enjoy cooking and eating some of the tasty desserts for these seasons of the year. The second part of this cookbook includes recipes for spring and summer. Over 50 recipes have been given in this part to cook any meal of the day and some soups and desserts too. Put on your chef hat, and enjoy these recipes to live a healthy lifestyle and to achieve sustainable weight-loss.

Chapter 1: Getting Started with the Mediterranean Diet

The Mediterranean diet includes eating food that is linked to the traditional cuisine of the countries that border the Mediterranean Sea. A Mediterranean diet is full of fruits, vegetables, whole grains, nut, beans, seeds, and olive oil. It includes the daily consumption of some healthy fats, fruits, and vegetables. It requires the intake of poultry, fish, eggs, and beans on a weekly basis.

The use of dairy products should be moderate, and there should be limited red meat intake. Another crucial element of this diet is to remain physically active. In this chapter, you will learn the basics of the Mediterranean Diet. We will discuss how the Mediterranean Diet helps in leading a healthy lifestyle.

1.1 The Basics of the Mediterranean Diet

The food we eat contributes to our long term health. Eating unhealthy foods cause many health problems, including some severe heart-related diseases. So, the diet you adopt should be chosen carefully. Eating food as per the Mediterranean diet is one of the healthiest diet patterns in the world. It is an eating pattern that focuses on eating the whole foods full of fantastic flavor. It is a diet abundant in whole grains, fruits, vegetables, olive oil, and legumes. It features the protein. The Mediterranean diet is one of the well-known diets worldwide, and it is not that kind of diet that just focuses on losing weight. It is about a healthy lifestyle that is capable of being more sustainable. The Mediterranean diet includes healthy and traditional living habits of the countries bordering the Mediterranean Sea, like Greece, Morocco, France, Italy, Spain, etc.

The diet might vary by the region and country, so that it might have a little variation. However, it mainly consists of a sufficient intake of legumes, vegetables, fruits, beans, nuts, grains, fish, and olive oil. It includes a low intake of the meat and dairy foods.

There are numerous benefits associated with this diet, like a healthy heart. Those who consume healthy fats, fish, and whole grains not only experience the decreased heart risks, depression, and dementia. According to the Mediterranean diet, eating leaves a little space for the processed foods and unhealthy junk that lead to issues like being obese and overweight. Here are given some interesting facts about your Mediterranean diet:

- You do not need to have a calculator for this diet. Instead of struggling with the numbers, all you have to do is to swap the bad fats with the healthy ones. Choose olive oil. Replace meat with fish, and enjoy the fresh fruit instead of sugary and fancy desserts. Eat flavorful beans and veggies. Nuts are one of the best options to include in your diet, but just a handful per day. Choose whole-grain food, but that too in the moderate quantity.

- The Mediterranean diet includes a lot of fresh food. The main focus is the seasonal food that is simple and mouth-watering in many ways. Building a yummy and delicious salad from cucumbers, tomatoes, and spinach will make your day. Add the Greek ingredients, such as feta cheese and black olives in your recipes. You can enjoy colorful and veggie-filled recipes with minimum effort.

- Replacing white grains with whole grains will do a lot for you. It has more minerals and protein. It is a healthier option. Try to use it with olive oil, tahini, or hummus.

- Eat the healthier fats. You can easily find them in nuts, olive oil, and olives. These fats are not saturated like those found in the processed foods. They add flavor. You can fight various diseases, from cancer to diabetes.

- Cilantro, bay leaves, cinnamon, coriander, garlic, rosemary, and pepper add flavor to your meals. Most of them have numerous health benefits, as well. Rosemary and coriander have nutrients and antioxidants that help in disease-fighting.

- Exercise plays a crucial part in any diet plan. Physical activity on daily basis is encouraged during your Mediterranean diet. Try to attain the target from moderate to the vigorous weekly exercise. These exercises include walking, biking, and swimming. The activities that increase the heart rate are recommended. Choose those exercises, which give you enjoyment too.

1.2 The Mediterranean Diet Pyramid

The Mediterranean Pyramid specifically takes into consideration both the quantitative and qualitative elements for eating choices. This Pyramid has evolved. It has adopted a new way of life. The Mediterranean Pyramid follows a specific pattern, in which the base of the Pyramid consists of the foods that are required to sustain this diet. These foods provide the protective substances and the critical nutrients necessary for the overall well-being. These foods must be consumed in greater frequency and portions than those in the middle and upper part of the Pyramid. At the higher level, it consists of the foods required in the moderate amounts. So, you should focus on the kind of foods that are linked to the sustainability.

The Mediterranean Pyramid was initially developed in 1990s as one of the collaborations between Oldways and Harvard School. In 1950s, Ancel Keys, an American physiologist, found out that some people had lower tendencies of the heart diseases.

He attributed this to the traditional diet that those people were following. That diet had low saturated fat. This Pyramid made its way for the popularity of this diet in the USA. It has become a useful tool to lead a healthy lifestyle. Fruits, whole grains, vegetables, beans, olive oil, legumes, spices, seeds, nuts, and herbs are at the base of this Pyramid. As we move up on the Pyramid, seafood and fish are the most prominent elements. Further up, you will find poultry, cheese, yogurt, and eggs that are used in the moderate amounts. The top consists of sweets and meats that should be consumed in the least often and small quantities.

While you can decide on the main protein first, then select a starch and a vegetable to have the best combination. You do not necessarily have to add more meals than normal consumption. You just need to approach your meal's composition and plan differently. Whatever you are eating, just ensure to add moderation in your intakes. It is a fact that the portions should be small in your Mediterranean diet. It is all about a composition that includes the moderate portions of various dishes.

The small portion of meat and cheese is used as the seasonings. Recipes are not drizzled with the sauce but with the yogurt or olive oil to add richness and flavor. Many American dishes consist of chicken or meat, but Mediterranean dishes are different. Meat is just a small part of the diet, as it is served with the plant-based ingredients like vegetables, bean dishes, whole grains, and fresh salads. The benefits of making these changes go beyond the cardiovascular health. Its health effects can be shown in the long term. With high portions of olive oil and vegetables, which consist of mono-unsaturated healthy fats, this diet promotes the healthy levels of blood sugar. Also, it improves the cognitive function, Alzheimer's, and cancer.

1.3 Health Benefits of the Mediterranean Diet

Consuming the Mediterranean diet minimalizes the use of processed foods. It has been related to a reduced level of risk in developing numerous chronic diseases. It also enhances the life expectancy. Several kinds of research have demonstrated many benefits in the prevention of the cardiovascular disease, atrial fibrillation, breast cancer, and type 2 diabetes. Many pieces of evidence indicated a pattern that leads to low lipid, reduction in oxidative stress, platelet aggregation, and inflammation, and modification of growth factors and hormones involved in cancer.

Reduces Heart Diseases

According to research studies, the Mediterranean diet, which focuses on omega-3 ingredients and mono-saturated fats, reduces the risk of the heart disease. It decreases the chances of cardiac death. Use of olive oil maintains the blood pressure levels. It is suitable for reducing hypertension. It also helps in combating the disease-promoting impacts of oxidation. This diet discourages the use of hydrogenated oils and saturated fats, which can cause heart disease.

Weight-loss

If you have been looking for diet plans for losing weight without feeling hungry, the Mediterranean diet can give you long term results. It is one of the best approaches. It is sustainable as it provides the most realistic approach to eat to feel full and energetic. This diet mostly consists of food that is nutrient-dense. It gives enough room for you to choose between low-carb and lower protein food.

Olive oil consumed in this diet has antioxidants, natural vitamins, and some crucial fatty acids. It all improves your overall health. The Mediterranean diet puts focus on the natural foods, so there is a very little room for junk and processed foods that contribute to the health-related issues and also the weight gain.

Most people trying Mediterranean diet have gained positive results in cutting their weight. It is one of the useful options for someone who is looking forward to weight-loss as it provides the most unique and simple way to lose the overall calories without even changing your lifestyle that much. When you try to decrease the calorie intake, losing weight is inevitable dramatically. But it will not benefit you. It will cause many health problems for you, including severe muscle loss. When you go for Mediterranean diet, the body moves towards a sustainable mode that burns calories slowly. So, it is crucial to practice the right approach and choose the one that goes for fat burning and more effective weight loss.

Prevents Cancer

The cornerstone of this diet is the plant-based ingredients, especially vegetables and fruits. They help in preventing cancer. A plant-based diet provides antioxidants that help in protecting your DNA from the damage and cell mutation. It also helps in lowering inflammation and delaying tumor growth. Various studies found that the olive oil is the natural way to prevent cancer. It also decreases the colon and bowel cancers. The plant-based diet balances blood sugar. It also sustains a healthy weight.

Prevents Diabetes

Numerous studies found that this healthy diet functions as the anti-inflammatory pattern, which helps in fighting the diseases related to the chronic inflammation, Type 2 diabetes, and the metabolic syndrome. It is considered very effective in preventing the diabetes as it controls the insulin levels, which is a hormone to control the blood sugar levels and causes weight gain. Intake of a well-balanced diet that consists of fatty acids alongside some healthy carbohydrates and proteins is the best gift you can give to your body. These foods help your body in burning fats more efficiently, which also provides energy. Due to the consumption of these kinds of foods, the insulin resistance level becomes non-existent, so it becomes impossible to have high blood sugar.

Anti-aging

Choosing Mediterranean diet without suffering from malnutrition is the most efficient and consistent anti-aging intervention. It undoubtedly expands lifespan according to the research. The study found that the longevity biomarkers, i.e., body temperature and insulin level, and also the DNA damage decreased significantly in humans by the Mediterranean diet. Other mechanisms also prove the claim made by researchers in explaining the anti-aging effects by adopting Mediterranean diet, including reduced lipid peroxidation, high efficiency of the oxidative repair, increased antioxidant defense system, and reduced mitochondrial generation rate.

Maintains Blood Sugar Level

The Mediterranean diet focuses on the healthy carbs and whole grains. It has a lot of significant benefits. Consumption of whole-grain foods, like buckwheat, quinoa, and wheat berries as opposed to the refined foods, helps you in maintaining the levels of blood sugar that ultimately gives you enough energy for the whole day.

Enhances Cognitive Health

The Mediterranean diet helps in preserving memory. It is one of the most useful steps towards Alzheimer's treatment and dementia. Cognitive disorders occur when our brain does not get sufficient dopamine, which is a crucial chemical that is vital for the mood regulation, thought processing, and body movements. Healthy fats like olive oil and nuts are good at fighting the cognitive decline, which is mostly an age-related issue. They help in countering some harmful impacts of the free radicals, inflammation, and toxins, which are caused by having a poor diet. The Mediterranean diet proves to be beneficial in decreasing the risk of Alzheimer's to a great extent. Foods like yogurt help in having the healthy gut that helps in improving the mood, cognitive functioning, and memory.

Better Endurance Level

Mediterranean diet helps in fat loss and maintains the muscle mass. It improves physical performance and enhances the endurance levels. Research done on mice has shown positive results in these aspects. It also improves the health of our tissues in the long-term. The growth hormone also offers increased levels as a result of Mediterranean diet. Which ultimately helps in improving metabolism and body composition.

Keeps You Agile

The nutrients from the Mediterranean diet reduces your risk muscle-weakness and frailty. It increases longevity. When your risk of heart disease reduces, it also reduces the risk of early death. It also strengthens your bones. Certain compounds found in the olive oil help in preserving the bone density. It helps in increasing the maturation and proliferation of the bone cells. Dietary patterns of the Mediterranean diet help in preventing osteoporosis.

Healthy Sleep Patterns

Our eating habits have a considerable impact on sleepiness and wakefulness. Some Mediterranean diet believers have reported an improved sleeping pattern as a result of changing their eating patterns. It has a considerable impact on your sleep because they regulate the circadian rhythm that determines our sleep patterns. If you have a regulated and balanced circadian rhythm, you will fall asleep quite quickly. You will also feel refreshed when you wake up. There is another theory that states that having the last meal early will help you to digest the food way before going to sleep. Digestion works best when you are upright.

Apart from the focus on the plant-based eating, the philosophy behind Mediterranean diet emphasizes the variety and moderation, living a life that has a perfect harmony with the nature, valuing essential relationships in life, which includes sharing and enjoying meals, and having a perfectly active lifestyle.

The Mediterranean diet is at the crossroads. With traditions and culture of three millennia, the Mediterranean diet lifestyle made its way to the medical world a long time ago. It has progressively recognized and became one of the successful and healthiest patterns that lead to a healthy lifestyle.

Besides metabolic, cardiovascular, cognitive, and many other benefits, this diet improves the quality of your life. Therefore, it is recommended today by many medical professionals worldwide. Efforts are being made in both non-Mediterranean and Mediterranean populations to make everyone benefit from the fantastic network of eating habits and patterns that began in old-time and which became a medical recommendation for a healthy lifestyle.

Chapter 2: Mediterranean Breakfast Recipes

2.1 Roasted Cherry Tomatoes with Garlic and Balsamic

Cooking Time: 30 minutes

Serving Size: 2 servings

Calories: 150 kcal

Ingredients

- 1/2 tsp. dried thyme
- 1 tbsp. minced garlic
- 1 pint of cherry tomatoes
- 2 tbsp. olive oil
- 1/2 tsp. kosher salt
- 1 tbsp. balsamic vinegar
- 1/4 tsp. black pepper

Method

1. Preheat the oven to 425^0 F.
2. Take a baking dish. Put the cherry tomatoes into it.
3. Mix garlic.
4. Put balsamic vinegar and olive oil.
5. Sprinkle with black pepper, kosher salt, and thyme.
6. Roast it for about 20 minutes.

7. Tomatoes should be soft.

8. Put the tomatoes in plate.

9. Drizzle with cooking juices and serve immediately.

2.2 Kale and Roasted Sweet Potato Hash

Cooking Time: 35 minutes

Serving Size: 4 servings

Calories: 217 kcal

Ingredients

- 1 red onion, sliced
- 2 tbsp. canola oil
- 1 pound of diced sweet potatoes
- 1 pinch salt
- 1 tsp. garlic powder
- Black pepper, to taste
- 4 eggs
- 4 cups of chopped kale

Method

1. Preheat the oven to 425^0 F.

2. Take a baking sheet, put it in an oven.

3. Put onion and sweet potatoes with oil, garlic powder, and salt in a bowl, then spread a layer onto the baking sheet, and roast for about 20 minutes.

4. Mix kale with oil, garlic powder, and salt.

5. Take pan out of the oven, mix vegetables, and then put kale on the top.

6. Keep roasting until sweet potatoes are softened and turn brown, and kale is slightly crisp for almost 10 minutes.

7. Bring some water in the pot to boil.

8. Reduce the heat to low for maintaining the gentle simmer.

9. Put each egg in a bowl, then slip them into simmering water. Make sure the yolks are not broken.

10. Poach for almost 4 minutes to get the soft-set, around 5 minutes to get medium-set, and around 8 minutes to get the hard-set.

11. Transfer eggs with a spoon to a kitchen towel.

12. Drain them.

13. Divide vegetable hash in 4 plates, top each with one egg.

14. Sprinkle pepper, and serve.

2.3 Quinoa and Chia Oatmeal Mix

Cooking Time: 10 minutes

Serving Size: 12 servings

Calories: 196 kcal

Ingredients

- 1 cup of rolled wheat or the barley flakes
- ¾ tsp. salt

- 2 cups of rolled oats
- 1 cup of quinoa
- ½ cup of chia seeds
- 1 cup of dried fruit
- 1 tsp. ground cinnamon

Method

1. For making the dry mix, mix wheat or barley flakes, oats, quinoa, seeds, salt, dried fruit, and cinnamon in the airtight container.

2. For making a single serving of the hot cereal, mix 1/3 cup of dry mix with the 1 1/4 cups of milk or water in a saucepan, and bring to boil.

3. Lower the heat, cover it partially, and simmer.

4. Stir occasionally for about 12-15 minutes.

5. Put aside for around 5 minutes.

6. Add sweetener as per your choice.

7. Add nuts and other dried fruit, and serve.

2.4 Apple Cinnamon Chia Pudding

Cooking Time: 15 minutes

Serving Size: 4 servings

Calories: 230 kcal

Ingredients

For Chia pudding:

- 1/2 cup of coconut milk
- 5 tbsp. of chia seeds
- 1/2 cup of almond milk
- 1 tsp. of vanilla extract
- 1 tbsp. of maple syrup
- 1/3 cup of apple sauce, unsweetened

For Sauteed apples:

- 2 medium apples, diced
- 1 tbsp. of coconut oil
- 1/2 tsp. of cinnamon
- 2 tbsp. of maple syrup

Method

1. Mix together all ingredients of chia pudding in a medium bowl.
2. Put it in the refrigerator for overnight.
3. Heat the oil on the medium heat in the pan.
4. Put apples, cinnamon, and maple syrup into it and cook for almost 2 minutes.
5. Lower the heat and cook for another 5 to 6 minutes.
6. Stir often. When apples are softened, remove them from heat.
7. Put apples and chia pudding in bowls, and enjoy.

2.5 Southwestern Waffle

Cooking Time: 10 minutes

Serving Size: 1 serving

Calories: 207 kcal

Ingredient

- 1 tbsp. of fresh salsa
- 1 large egg, cooked
- 1 waffle, whole-grain and frozen
- ¼ avocado, halved and chopped

Method

1. Toast the waffle as per the package directions.
2. Put egg, salsa, and avocado onto it.
3. Serve and enjoy.

2.6 Pumpkin Overnight Oats

Cooking Time: 5 minutes

Serving Size: 1 serving

Calories: 274 kcal

Ingredients

- 1/2 cup of almond milk, unsweetened
- 1/4 cup of plain Greek yogurt
- 1/4 cup of pumpkin puree
- 1/2 tsp. vanilla extract
- 2 tbsp. maple syrup
- 1/2 cup of Oats
- 1/8 tsp. ground ginger
- 1/4 tsp. cinnamon
- 2 tsp. chia seeds
- 1/8 tsp. nutmeg

Method

1. Take a bowl, and mix together almond milk, Greek yogurt, pumpkin puree, maple syrup, and vanilla.
2. Add oats, spices, and chia seeds.
3. Put in a jar, and then put it in the fridge for about 4 hours or preferably overnight.
4. Serve and enjoy.

2.7 Egg Salad Avocado Toast

Cooking Time: 16 minutes

Serving Size: 3 servings

Calories: 213 kcal

Ingredients

- 3 pieces of bread, whole-grain
- 2 eggs
- 1 avocado
- Salt, to season
- 1 tsp. of lemon juice
- 1 tsp. of light mayo
- 1 tsp. of bagel seasoning
- 1/2 tsp. of Dijon mustard

Method

1. Put eggs in a saucepan.
2. Bring them to boil for almost 4 minutes.
3. When eggs are boiled, add lemon juice, avocado, and salt to a bowl.
4. Mash them, then add a small pinch of pepper.
5. Season with pepper and salt.
6. Toast bread.
7. Put eggs in a bowl, and add Dijon, mayo, and salt.
8. Season pepper and with salt.
9. Place avocado on the toast.
10. Add egg salad on the top.
11. Sprinkle with seasoning, and serve.

2.8 Fruit and Yogurt Smoothie

Cooking Time: 5 minutes

Serving Size: 2 servings

Calories: 145 kcal

Ingredients

- ½ cup of yogurt
- 1 banana
- 1 ½ tsp. white sugar
- 1 cup of strawberries
- 1 tsp. milk
- ¼ cup of pineapple juice
- 1 tsp. orange juice

Method

1. Blend the yogurt, banana, sugar, strawberries, pineapple juice, milk, and orange juice.
2. Blend until smooth, and serve.

2.9 Mediterranean Scramble

Cooking Time: 15 minutes

Serving Size: 2 servings

Calories: 249 kcal

Ingredients

- 1 diced yellow pepper
- 1 tbsp. of oil
- 2 sliced spring onions
- 2 tbsp. of black olives, sliced
- 7 cherry tomatoes
- 1 tbsp. of capers
- 1/4 tsp. of dried oregano
- 4 eggs
- Fresh parsley, for serving
- Black pepper, to taste

Method

1. Take a pan and heat oil.
2. Add diced peppers and spring onions.
3. Cook over the medium heat for around 2-3 minutes.
4. Add quartered tomatoes, capers, and olives, then cook for almost 1 minute.
5. Put eggs in the pan, and scramble with a spatula or a spoon.
6. Add oregano and black pepper.
7. Keep stirring. When eggs are cooked, turn off the heat.
8. Top with parsley and serve warm.

Chapter 3: Mediterranean Lunch and Dinner Recipes

3.1 Gratin of Tomatoes and Zucchini

Cooking Time: 45 minutes

Serving Size: 2 servings

Calories: 163 kcal

Ingredients

- ½ tsp. garlic powder
- 2 firm zucchinis
- Olive oil for spray
- 2 firm tomatoes
- ¼ tsp. Black pepper
- ½ tsp. kosher salt
- 1/4 cup of shredded Parmesan
- ½ tsp. dried thyme

Method

1. Preheat the oven to 400^0 F, and apply olive oil spray to a dish.
2. Cut tomatoes and zucchinis crosswise.
3. Place the alternate layers of zucchini and tomatoes on a baking dish.

4. Put salt, garlic powder, dried thyme, and pepper on top of it.

5. Spray vegetables with the olive oil.

6. Add Parmesan.

7. Bake gratin until it is golden-brown, for around 30 minutes.

8. Drain the juice and serve.

3.2 Spanish Moroccan Fish

Cooking Time: 1 hour 20 minutes

Serving Size: 12 servings

Calories: 268.2 kcal

Ingredients

- 1 chopped onion
- 1 tbsp. vegetable oil
- 1 finely chopped garlic clove
- 2 medium bell peppers, red
- 1 can of garbanzo beans
- 1 large thinly sliced carrot
- 4 olives, chopped
- 3 tomatoes, chopped
- ¼ cup of fresh parsley
- 3 tbsp. paprika
- ¼ cup of ground cumin
- 2 tbsp. of chicken bouillon
- Salt, to taste
- 1 tsp. cayenne pepper

- 5 pounds of tilapia fillets

Method

1. Take a pan and heat oil over the medium heat.
2. Add garlic and onion, and cook until onions are softened, for around 5 minutes.
3. Mix garbanzo beans, olives, carrots, bell peppers, tomatoes, and keep cooking for around 5 minutes.
4. Sprinkle cumin, parsley, paprika, cayenne, and chicken bouillon on top of the vegetables.
5. Add salt.
6. Put tilapia on the top, and cover vegetables with enough water.
7. Lower the heat, and cook for around 40 minutes.
8. Serve ad enjoy.

3.3 Slow Cooker Mediterranean Roast Turkey Breast

Cooking Time: 7 hours 50 minutes

Serving Size: 8 servings

Calories: 333.4 kcal

Ingredients

- ½ cup of chicken broth
- 1 turkey breast, boneless
- 2 tbsp. lemon juice
- ½ cup of calamite olives
- 2 cups of chopped onion
- 3 tbsp. flour
- ½ cup thinly sliced tomatoes
- ½ tsp. salt
- 1 tsp. Greek seasoning
- ¼ tsp. of black pepper

Method

1. Place 1/4 cup of chicken broth, turkey breast, lemon juice, kalamata olives, onion, tomatoes, salt, pepper, and Greek seasoning in the slow cooker.

2. Cook while keeping it covered for around 7 hours.

3. Mix the flour and remaining chicken broth in a bowl.

4. Cook while keeping it covered for another 30 minutes.

5. Serve and enjoy.

3.4 Flounder Mediterranean

Cooking Time: 45 minutes

Serving Size: 4 servings

Calories: 281.6 kcal

Ingredients

- 2 tbsp. olive oil
- 5 tomatoes
- ½ chopped onion
- 1 pinch of Italian seasoning
- 2 chopped garlic cloves
- 24 kalamata olives, chopped
- ¼ cup of capers
- ¼ cup of white wine
- 1 tsp. lemon juice
- 6 leaves of fresh basil
- 3 tbsp. of Parmesan cheese, freshly grated
- 6 leaves of chopped fresh basil
- 1 pound of flounder fillets

Method

1. Preheat the oven to 425^9 F.

2. Boil water in the saucepan.

3. Put tomatoes in the water, and then put in the ice water in a bowl.

4. Drain, discard skins and then chop them.

5. Take oil in a skillet, and heat over the medium heat.

6. Cook onion for around 5 minutes.

7. Add tomatoes, Italian seasoning, and garlic—Cook for 5-7 minutes.

8. Add olives, capers, wine, basil, and lemon juice.

9. Lower the heat, add Parmesan cheese.

10. Cook for around 15 minutes.

11. Put flounder in the baking dish.

12. Add sauce on top of the fillets.

13. Top with basil leaves, and bake for 12 minutes in an oven.

14. Serve and enjoy.

3.5 Tomato & Smoked Mozzarella Sandwiches

Cooking Time: 25 minutes

Serving Size: 4 servings

Calories: 385 kcal

Ingredients

- 1 clove garlic
- 1/3 cup of tomatoes
- ¼ tsp. salt
- 1 cup of basil leaves

- 1 tbsp. lemon juice
- 2 tbsp. Olive oil
- ⅛ tsp. red pepper, crushed
- 8 slices of whole-grain bread
- ¼ cup of chopped olives
- 4 ounces of fresh mozzarella, sliced
- 3 sliced tomatoes
- Ground pepper, to taste
- 2 tsp. balsamic vinegar

Method

1. Place tomatoes in the boiling water. Let it rest for around 10 minutes.
2. Cut garlic and add salt.
3. Put it in a bowl; whisk in oil, lemon juice, and the red pepper.
4. Finely chop the tomatoes. Add them with the dressing in the bowl.
5. Add olives.
6. Put tomato mixture onto the bread.
7. Place cheese slices, pepper, and tomato slices onto it.
8. Add vinegar and salt.
9. Top with basil leaves.
10. Put the remaining oil over other bread slices.

11.   Place them on each other to make the sandwiches.

12.   Serve and enjoy.

3.6 Roasted Salmon with Smoky Chickpeas & Greens

Cooking Time: 40 minutes

Serving Size: 4 servings

Calories: 447 kcal

Ingredients

- 1 tbsp. smoked paprika
- 2 tbsp. Olive oil
- ½ tsp. salt
- ⅓ cup of buttermilk
- 1 can of chickpeas
- ¼ cup of mayonnaise
- ½ tsp. ground pepper
- ¼ cup of chopped chives
- ¼ tsp. garlic powder
- ¼ cup of water
- 10 cups of chopped kale
- 1 ¼ pound of wild salmon

Method

1. Put the racks in the oven, and preheat it to 425^0 F.
2. Mix oil, salt, and paprika in a bowl.
3. Pat the chickpeas dry, and toss with paprika mixture.

4. Place on the baking sheet, and bake them on the rack for about 30 minutes.

5. Put buttermilk, herbs, pepper, garlic powder, and mayonnaise in the blender.

6. Heat the oil in a skillet over the medium heat.

7. Mix kale in it, and cook for almost 2 minutes.

8. Put water into it, and cook for around 5 minutes.

9. Turn off the heat.

10. Add just a pinch of the salt.

11. Take the chickpeas out of oven, and put them on the side of the skillet.

12. Put salmon on the opposite side.

13. Season with pepper and salt, and bake for 5-8 minutes.

14. Pour dressing, and garnish with herbs.

15. Serve with chickpeas and the kale.

3.7 Hasselback Caprese Chicken

Cooking Time: 30 minutes

Serving Size: 4 servings

Calories: 401 kcal

Ingredients

- 4 boneless chicken breasts
- 1 tbsp. of olive oil
- 3 thinly sliced tomatoes
- 1/2 cup of basil leaves
- 1 log of mozzarella

- Salt, to taste
- Pepper, to taste

For Balsamic glaze:
- 3 tbsp. of brown sugar
- 1/2 cup of balsamic vinegar

Method

1. Preheat the oven to 400^0 F.

2. Cut each chicken breast.

3. Apply olive oil to the chicken; season with pepper and salt.

4. Slice mozzarella and tomatoes, then put into the cuts of chicken breast.

5. Add basil.

6. Bake for almost 25 minutes in the oven.

7. Bring brown sugar and balsamic vinegar to boil in a pot over the stove, and cook for almost 10 to12 minutes over medium heat. Set it aside.

8. Take the chicken out, and pour balsamic glaze onto it.

9. Garnish it with fresh basil, and serve with a side dish or salad.

3.8 Vegan Roasted Vegetable Quinoa Bowl with Creamy Green Sauce

Cooking Time: 30 minutes

Serving Size: 4 servings

Calories: 340 kcal

Ingredients

- 8 ounces of cremini mushrooms quartered
- 4 cups of broccoli florets
- 2 large sliced shallots
- ½ tsp. salt, divided
- 2 tbsp. Olive oil
- ¼ tsp. ground pepper
- ½ cup of water
- 1 cup of red cabbage, shredded
- ¾ cup of raw cashews
- ¼ cup of parsley leaves
- ½ tsp. soy sauce or tamari
- 1 tbsp. cider vinegar
- 2 cups of cooked quinoa

Method

1. Preheat the oven to 425^0 F.
2. Mix shallots, mushrooms, and broccoli in a bowl.
3. Put 1 tbsp. Oil, 1/4 tsp. pepper and salt in it.
4. Transfer it to a baking sheet; roast until vegetables are browned and tender, for around 20 minutes.

5. Combine water, cashews, parsley, tamari, vinegar, 1/4 tsp. salt, and remaining 1 tbsp. oil in the blender.

6. Divide the cooked quinoa, sauce, roasted vegetables, and cabbage among four bowls, and serve.

3.9 Chickpea Curry with Easy Brown Rice

Cooking Time: 35 minutes

Serving Size: 4-6 servings

Calories: 534 kcal

Ingredients

- 2 tbsp. vegetable oil
- 2 cups of brown rice
- 1 large chopped onion
- 2 tsp. curry powder
- Kosher salt, to taste
- Black pepper, to taste
- 2 cloves chopped garlic
- Two cans of chickpeas
- 1 cup of vegetable stock
- One can of coconut milk
- 1-2 tbsp. sriracha sauce
- Cilantro, for garnishing
- 1-2 tbsp. honey
- Naan bread, to serve

Method

1. Prepare the rice as per package instructions.
2. Take a skillet, and heat oil over the medium heat.
3. Put onions into it.

4. Add pepper and salt; cook until onions are caramelized and dark brown for around 10 minutes.

5. Add garlic and curry powder; cook for almost 30 seconds.

6. Add vegetable stock; stir.

7. Mix chickpeas, honey, sriracha, and coconut milk, and bring it to boil.

8. Lower the heat; simmer for almost 10 minutes. Adjust seasoning if required.

9. Put naan in a microwave to warm it, and serve it with curry on the rice.

10. Garnish with cilantro, and serve.

3.10 Hummus Vegetable Wrap

Cooking Time: 23 minutes

Serving Size: 4 servings

Calories: 320 kcal

Ingredients

- 2 tsp. olive oil
- 2 zucchini, sliced
- 1/8 tsp. salt
- 1 cup of hummus
- Black pepper, to taste
- 1/4 cup of pine nuts
- 4 pieces of wrap bread, whole-wheat
- 1 thinly sliced bell pepper, red
- 1/2 cup red onion, sliced

- 2 ounces of spinach leaves
- 1/4 cup of mint leaves

Method

1. Preheat a grill over the medium heat.
2. Apply oil on zucchini slices; sprinkle with pepper and salt.
3. Grill each side until slightly browned and tender for 4 minutes.
4. Put 1/4 cup of hummus on top of each bread.
5. Add 1 tbsp. pine nuts on the top.
6. Add zucchini, red pepper, spinach, sliced onions, and mint.
7. Roll them up, and cut into half, and serve.

3.11 Braised Potatoes

Cooking Time: 1 hour

Serving Size: 4 servings

Calories: 369 kcal

Ingredients

- 3 tbsp. butter
- 2 pounds of potatoes
- 1 onion, diced
- 2 cups of turkey, vegetable, or chicken stock
- 1 sprig rosemary or thyme, for

garnishing

- 1 tsp. minced garlic
- Salt, to taste
- Pepper, to taste

Method

1. Scrub potatoes, and cut them into chunks.
2. Take a skillet or pot, and heat 3 tbsp. of butter over the medium heat.
3. Add onions, potatoes, garlic, pepper, salt, and rosemary or thyme.
4. Cook until potatoes turn to golden in color, for about 10 minutes.
5. Put stock to cover potatoes, and bring it to boil.
6. Lower the heat, and occasionally stir for around 30 minutes.
7. Add pepper and salt to taste.
8. Garnish with rosemary or thyme, and serve.

3.12 Baked Pasta with Zucchini

Cooking Time: 1 hou

Serving Size: 12 servings

Calories: 220 kcal

Ingredients

- 1 chopped onion
- 3 cups of uncooked cavatappi
- 2 zucchini, sliced
- 6 ounces of spinach leaves
- 1 cup of sliced mushrooms
- 8 ounces of mozzarella cheese
- 24 ounces of pasta sauce
- 1 tsp. of Italian seasoning
- 15 ounces of Ricotta cheese

Method

1. Heat the oven to 375 degrees F.
2. Take a saucepan, and cook pasta as per package instructions. Do not add salt.
3. Cook onions in a nonstick skillet over the medium heat for 3-4 minutes or crisp-tender.
4. Put mushrooms and zucchini, and cook for 3-4 minutes, or until it is tendered, stir frequently.
5. Put half of the spinach, and cook for 2-3 minutes, or until wilted.
6. Do the same with remaining spinach.

7. Turn off the heat.

8. Add pasta it to the vegetable mixture and pasta sauce in the skillet.

9. Add ricotta, 1 cup of mozzarella, and Italian seasoning.

10. Spoon it into the baking dish; top it with the remaining mozzarella, and bake for 20-25 minutes, or until mozzarella is completely melted.

11. Serve and enjoy.

3.13 Mediterranean Quinoa Bowls

Cooking Time: 20 minutes

Serving Size: 8 servings

Calories: 381 kcal

Ingredients

For roasted red pepper sauce:

- 1 garlic clove
- 1 jar of red peppers, roasted
- 1/2 tsp. salt
- 1/2 cup of olive oil
- One lemon
- 1/2 cup of almonds
- 1 cucumber
- 20 ounces feta cheese
- 20 kalamata olives
- 1 red onion
- Fresh basil

Method

1. Take a blender or food processor, and put all ingredients of the sauce into it.
2. Blend until it is smooth. Make sure its texture is thick.
3. Cook quinoa as per package directions, and when it is done, serve and enjoy.

4. Store the leftovers in a container; assemble bowl just before the serving.

5. To get the vegan version, put the white beans instead of feta cheese.

3.14 Mediterranean Dip

Cooking Time: 15 minutes

Serving Size: 4 servings

Calories: 49.4 kcal

Ingredients

- 1 tomato
- 8 ounces hummus
- 1/2 cup of diced cucumber
- 1/8 tsp. salt
- 1/2 cup of Greek yogurt
- 1/4 tsp. paprika
- 2 red peppers, roasted and diced
- 2 artichoke hearts, canned
- 1/4 cup of feta cheese, crumbled
- Kalamata olives for garnishing
- 2 tbsp. of minced parsley

Method

1. Take a serving dish, and spread hummus on its bottom.

2. Put cucumber and tomatoes over the top.

3. Pour yogurt on the vegetables.

4. Add paprika and salt.

5. Place and feta cheese, roasted red peppers, and artichoke heart on top of yogurt.

6. Add parsley, garnish it with olives, and then serve with pita chips, vegetables, or crackers.

Chapter 4: Mediterranean Salad and Snacks Recipes

4.1 Mediterranean Tuna-Spinach Salad

Cooking Time: 10 minutes

Serving Size: 1 serving

Calories: 375 kcal

Ingredients

- 1 diced orange
- 1 ½ tbsp. lemon juice
- 1 can of chunk tuna
- 1 ½ tbsp. water
- 4 chopped Kalamata olives
- 2 tbsp. parsley
- 2 tbsp. feta cheese
- 1 ½ tbsp. tahini
- 2 cups of baby spinach

Method

1. Mix lemon juice, tahini, and water in a medium bowl.
2. Put tuna, feta, parsley, and olives in it, and stir to mix well.
3. Serve tuna salad on top of 2 cups of spinach; place an orange on one side.

4.2 Citrus Salad Dressing

Cooking Time: 10 minutes

Serving Size: 16 servings

Calories: 41 kcal

Ingredients

For Garlic and Lemon Dressing:

- 2 lemon
- 1/2 cup of olive oil
- 2 chopped clove garlic
- 1/8 tsp. black pepper
- 1/8 tsp. salt

For Orange Dressing:

- 2 tsp. honey
- 1/2 lemon
- 1/4 tsp. orange zest
- 1/2 cup of olive oil
- 1/2 orange

Method

1. Use garlic for the lemon version, and zest orange for the orange version.
2. Mix all ingredients in a blender.
3. Put on the salad or use it as the marinade.
4. It can be refrigerated for two weeks.
5. Shake or whisk well before use.

4.3 Wild Rice and Lentil Salad

Cooking Time: 20 minutes

Serving Size: 8 servings

Calories: 461 kcal

Ingredients

- 1 cup of rinsed dried lentils
- 2 1/4 ounces of wild rice
- 2 cups of water
- 2 tbsp. lemon juice
- 1/4 cup of olive oil
- 2 tbsp. of red wine vinegar
- 1/2 tsp. salt
- 1 minced garlic clove
- 2 chopped tomatoes
- 2 cups of baby spinach or fresh arugula
- 6 chopped green onions
- 1/4 cup of feta cheese, crumbled

Method

1. Prepare rice as per the package directions, then drain and rinse with water.

2. Put lentils in the saucepan. Bring water to the boil in it.

3. Lower the heat, and simmer for about 20 to 25 minutes, then drain and rinse with water.

4. Take a small bowl, and whisk oil, vinegar, lemon juice, salt, and garlic until blended.

5. Take another bowl, mix rice, tomatoes, green onions, and lentils.

6. Pour dressing onto it.

7. Before serving, add cheese and arugula.

4.4 Mediterranean Grilled Chicken Salad

Cooking Time: 25 minutes

Serving Size: 4 servings

Calories: 575 kcal

Ingredients

For Marinade:

- 1 tbsp. of dried oregano
- 1/4 cup of olive oil
- 3 chopped green onions
- 1/4 cup of lemon juice
- 1/2 tsp. of salt
- 1/4 tsp. of pepper
- 1 tbsp. of dried basil

For Dressing:

- 1 tsp. of dried oregano
- 1/4 cup of lemon juice
- 1 tsp. of dried basil
- 1/2 tsp. of pepper

- 1/4 cup of olive oil
- 1/2 tsp. of salt

For Salad:
- 1 chopped Romaine lettuce
- 4 boneless chicken breasts
- 1 sliced English cucumber
- 1 chopped bell pepper, green
- 1/2 chopped red onion
- 2 cups of chopped cocktail tomatoes
- 1/2 cup of crumbled feta cheese
- 1/2 cup of Kalamata olives
- 1 sliced avocado

Method

1. Take a bowl, and whisk all marinade ingredients.
2. Place chicken breasts in it; toss them with the marinade, then cover them with the plastic wrap.
3. Refrigerate for half an hour to almost 4 hours.
4. Preheat the grill on 400^0 F.
5. Mix all dressing ingredients in a bowl; set aside.
6. Take a large bowl, and toss cucumber, lettuce, red onion, tomatoes, olives, and bell pepper together.
7. Grill both sides of chicken breasts for 5 minutes each side.
8. Discard any remaining marinade.

9. Cool down the chicken for 5 minutes, then cut into slices.

10. Pour the dressing on top of the salad; toss well.

11. Put crumbled feta in it and mix well.

12. Serve with sliced chicken on top of the avocado slices and salad.

4.5 Mediterranean Winter Salad

Cooking Time: 20 minutes

Serving Size: 2 servings

Calories: 534 kcal

Ingredients

- 2 tsp. of Cranberry dry
- 1 small red onion, thinly sliced
- 5 Bell peppers, colored, cut into discs
- 1 small Zucchini, cut into half-moons
- Cherry Tomatoes - ¼ cup, halved
- 3 Tomatoes, cut into pieces,
- 10 Black olives, sliced
- ¼ cup Feta cheese, crumbled
- 2 tsp. of Pine nuts
- 2 handful of Salad Greens
- ½ tbsp. Balsamic Vinegar
- Black pepper, to taste
- ½ tsp. Oregano, dry
- ½ tsp. Sumac

- Salt, to taste
- ½ tbsp. Olive Oil

Method

1. Wash baby greens; dry thoroughly. Put them in two salad bowls.

2. Heat olive oil in a pan. Lower the heat; add onions into it. Cook while keeping it covered for almost 3 minutes till tendered and brown lightly.

3. Put bell peppers and zucchini slices into it. Toss them; cook for 3 minutes until slightly cooked.

4. Put oregano, pepper, and salt. Toss well.

5. Put cherry tomatoes, tomatoes, and balsamic vinegar. Toss well for a few seconds; turn off the heat.

6. Add Sumac; toss again.

7. Put warm vegetables on top of greens.

8. Add dried cranberries, feta cheese, sliced olives, and pine nuts.

9. Enjoy your salad.

4.6 Herbed Olives

Cooking Time: 10 minutes

Serving Size: 16 servings

Calories: 47 kcal

Ingredients

- 2 tsp. olive oil
- 3 cups olives
- ⅛ tsp. dried oregano
- 1 crushed clove garlic
- ⅛ tsp. dried basil
- Black Pepper, to taste

Method

1. Mix all ingredients in a bowl.
2. Toss well, and serve.

4.7 Garlic Bread

Cooking Time: 8 minutes

Serving Size: 20 servings

Calories: 258 kcal

Ingredients

- 2 tbsp. fresh parsley, minced
- 3-4 minced garlic cloves
- 1/2 cup melted butter
- 1 French loaf bread

Method

1. In a bowl, mix garlic and butter.

2. Over the sides of the bread, add parsley.

3. Put on the baking sheet, and bake at 350 degrees for about 8 minutes.

4. Broil for about 2 minutes until it is golden brown.

5. Serve warm.

4.8 Chocolate Chip Cookies

Cooking Time: 30 minutes

Serving Size: 24 servings

Calories: 187 kcal

- 1 tbsp. vanilla extract
- 1 cup of olive oil
- ¾ cup of granulated sugar
- 1 tsp. Kosher salt
- ¾ cup of brown sugar
- 1 egg
- ½ tsp. baking soda
- 2 cups of flour
- 2 cups of unsweetened chocolate chips

Method

1. Preheat the oven to 350 degrees F.
2. Add olive oil, both sugars, salt, and vanilla in a large bowl. Toss until there is a smooth consistency.
3. Add egg. Blend well to make it smooth.
4. Put baking soda and flour in the bowl; mix until fully incorporated.
5. Add chocolate chips.
6. With your hands, make balls from the batter by taking 2 tbsp.

7. Put shaped to baking sheets.

8. Gently flatten all the balls with your hands.

9. Sprinkle each ball with salt.

10.   Transfer baking sheets to the oven, and cook until golden brown for about 10-12 minutes.

11.   Set aside, let cool for almost 5 minutes.

12.   Serve and enjoy.

4.9 Sous Vide Egg Bites

Cooking Time: 15 minutes

Serving Size: 7 servings

Calories: 82 kcal

Ingredients

- ½ cup of Monterey jack cheese
- 4 eggs
- ½ cup of cottage cheese
- ½ red pepper
- 1 chopped green onion
- ¼ cup of spinach
- 1/4 cup of green chilis
- 1/2 cup of cheddar cheese
- 1/4 cup of cooked broccoli
- 1/4 cup of cooked bacon
- 1 tbsp. fresh basil
- 1/4 cup of cooked sausage
- 1/2 cup of swiss cheese

- 1/4 cup of cooked mushrooms
- 1 tbsp. green onions
- 1/4 cup of diced tomatoes

Method

1. Add water in the Instant Pot; place the trivet inside.
2. Put eggs, cottage, Monterey Jack, and cheddar cheese in a blender; process for almost 30 seconds.
3. Mix all remaining ingredients, combine well.
4. Put egg mixture into the compartments of the silicone mold, and cover tightly with the aluminum foil.
5. Put the lid on Instant Pot, and press the 'STEAM' button; set timer for 10 minutes.
6. Remove silicone mold, and cool down egg bites.
7. Serve and enjoy.

4.10 Cheddar Basil Bites

Cooking Time: 47 minutes

Serving Size: 24 servings

Calories: 58 kcal

Ingredients

- 2 tbsp. of Cream
- 6 tbsp. of butter at room temperature
- 1 cup cheddar cheese
- 1/4 cup of Coconut flour
- 1/4 cup of parmesan cheese
- 2 tbsp. of chopped fresh basil

Method

1. Preheat oven to 325^0 F.
2. Put soft butter in the mixing bowl.
3. Mix heavy cream; combine using the hand mixer.
4. Add Parmesan cheese and cheddar cheese; combine well.
5. Mix coconut flour; combine well.
6. Add basil.
7. On the parchment, place cheese dough forming a ball with hands.
8. Put one more parchment paper on the top. Use a cookie cutter to cut 24 crackers, then remove them gently; place onto baking sheets.
9. Bake for almost 12 minutes.
10. Serve and enjoy!

4.11 Easy Almond Butter Fat Bombs

Cooking Time: 5 minutes

Serving Size: 6 servings

Calories: 189 kcal

Ingredients

- 1/4 Cup of Coconut Oil
- 1/4 Cup of Almond Butter
- 1/4 Cup of Erythritol
- 2 tbsp. of Cacao Powder

Method

1. Combine almond butter and coconut oil in the medium bowl, then microwave for about 30 to 45 seconds.

2. Mix well to make a smooth mixture.

3. Add cacao powder and erythritol.

4. Put in silicone molds, and refrigerate until it is firm.

5. Serve and enjoy!

Chapter 5: Mediterranean Soup Recipes

5.1 Lentil Soup with Olive Oil and Orange

Cooking Time: 1 hour 15 minutes

Serving Size: 4 servings

Calories: 172 kcal

Ingredients

- 1 diced onion
- 2 tbsp. butter
- 3 cups of chicken broth
- ½ cup of red lentils
- 1 chopped stalk celery
- ½ cup of orange juice
- ½ shredded carrot
- ½ tsp. dried thyme
- 1 large bay leaf
- Black pepper, to taste

Method

1. Cook onions until softened in the pot over the medium heat.
2. Add lentils, celery, orange juice, carrot, thyme, bay leaf, pepper, and ½ chicken broth; simmer for 40 minutes.

3. Puree in the food processor, and put it back in the pot.

4. Add remaining broth; heat through.

5. Serve and enjoy!

5.2 Vegetarian Moroccan Harira

Cooking Time: 55 minutes

Serving Size: 4-6 servings

Calories: 335 kcal

- 1 sliced white onion
- 1½ tbsp. of coconut oil
- 5 minced cloves garlic
- 3 stalks finely sliced celery
- 2 diced carrots
- 2 tsp. of ground cumin
- 2 tsp. of smoked paprika
- 1½ tsp. of ground cinnamon
- ½ tsp. of ground nutmeg
- ½ tsp. of fresh ginger
- ¼ tsp. of red chili powder
- ½ tsp. of saffron threads
- 4 large of chopped ripe tomatoes
- 2 tbsp. of tomato paste
- 800 ml of water or vegetable stock
- ½ cup of uncooked green lentils
- 1½ cup of cooked chickpeas
- ½ cup uncooked quinoa
- ½ lemon
- ⅓ cup of finely chopped fresh parsley and coriander

- Sea salt, to taste

- Black pepper, to taste

Method

1. Saute the onion, celery, and carrots with oil in the pot.

2. Add sea salt; cook on the low heat until soft for about 5 to 10 minutes.

3. Add garlic, tomato puree, and spices; turn up heat, then cook until fragrant for about 3 to 5 minutes.

4. Put tomatoes, chickpeas, stock, quinoa, and lentils. Simmer, and then turn down heat.

5. Cook for almost 30 to 45 minutes stir occasionally.

6. Add water as required.

7. Your soup is ready when the vegetables and lentils are thoroughly cooked.

8. Turn off the heat, taste for any adjustment in the seasonings.

9. Stir lemon juice and fresh herbs. Serve hot.

5.3 Creamy Italian White Bean Soup

Cooking Time: 50 minutes

Serving Size: 4 servings

Calories: 244 kcal

Ingredients

- 1 chopped onion
- 1 tbsp. vegetable oil
- 1 chopped stalk celery
- 2 cans of white kidney beans
- 1 minced clove garlic
- 1 can of chicken broth
- ⅛ tsp. dried thyme
- ¼ tsp. black pepper
- 2 cups of water
- 1 tbsp. lemon juice

1 bunch of fresh spinach, thinly sliced

-

Method

1. Heat oil in a saucepan.
2. Cook celery and onion in the oil for 5-8 minutes.
3. Put garlic, cook for almost 30 seconds, and stir continually.
4. Add beans, pepper, chicken broth, 2 cups of water, and thyme. Bring it to boil, then reduce heat, simmer for almost 15 minutes.

5. Remove 2 cups vegetable and beans mixture from the soup; set aside.

6. Blend the remaining soup in the blender until smooth.

7. Once it is done, pour the soup back to the stockpot; stir in beans.

8. Then bring it to boil, stir occasionally.

9. Add spinach; cook for 1 minute, until wilted.

10. Add lemon juice; remove it from the heat.

11. Serve with Parmesan cheese.

5.4 Slow Cooker Vegetarian Minestrone

Cooking Time: 6 hours 35 minutes

Serving Size: 8 servings

Calories: 138 kcal

Ingredients

- 1 can of crushed tomatoes
- 6 cups of vegetable broth
- 1 can of kidney beans
- 2 stalk diced ribs celery
- 1 chopped large onion
- 2 diced large carrots
- 1 zucchini
- 1 cup of green beans
- 3 minced cloves garlic
- 1 ½ tsp. dried oregano

- 1 tbsp. fresh parsley, minced
- 4 cups of fresh spinach, chopped
- 1 tsp. salt
- ¼ tsp. black pepper, freshly ground
- ¾ tsp. dried thyme
- ½ cup of elbow macaroni
- ¼ cup Parmesan cheese, finely grated

Method

1. Mix vegetable broth, kidney beans, tomatoes, onion, carrots, celery, green beans, garlic, zucchini, parsley, salt, black pepper, oregano thyme in a slow cooker, and cook on for 6-8 hours on low heat.

2. Cook the elbow macaroni in boiling water in a pot, stir occasionally, and cook for almost 8 minutes.

3. Add macaroni and spinach into minestrone, and cook for 15 minutes more.

4. Top with the Parmesan cheese, and serve.

5.5 Roasted Butternut Squash Soup

Cooking Time: 1 hour 10 minutes

Serving Size: 4 servings

Calories: 292 kcal

Ingredients

For Squash Soup:

- 1 tbsp. of avocado oil
- 3 1/2 pound butternut squash
- 1 yellow onion
- 1/2 tbsp. of maple syrup
- 1 peeled garlic clove
- 1 tsp. of salt
- 1/4 tsp. of ground ginger
- 1/4 tsp. of ground nutmeg
- 4 cups of vegetable broth
- 2 tbsp. of butter
- Black pepper, to taste

For Garnishing:

- Parsley
- Pepitas
- Black pepper

Method

1. Preheat the oven to 425⁰ Fahrenheit.

2. Carefully slice butternut squash to remove membrane and seeds.

3. Put butternut squash in the baking tray; sprinkle avocado oil, pepper, and salt.

4. Flip butternut squash on the other side; roast for almost 60 minutes.

5. After 30 minutes, put half onion and avocado in the baking tray.

6. After completion of time, take it out of the oven.

7. Transfer butternut squash to the blender.

8. Put onion, garlic, salt, maple syrup, nutmeg, butter, vegetable broth, and ginger in the blender.

9. Add 3 cups vegetable broth; add more as required.

10.   Blend until creamy.

11.   Taste to check the seasoning adjustment; add pepper and salt if required.

12.   Garnish with pepitas, black pepper, and parsley.

5.6 Minestrone Soup

Cooking Time: 1 hour

Serving Size: 6 servings

Calories: 298 kcal

Ingredients

- 4 tbsp. olive oil
- 1 chopped yellow onion
- 2 chopped carrots, peeled
- 2 chopped ribs celery
- ¼ cup of tomato paste
- 4 minced cloves garlic
- 2 cups of chopped vegetables, seasonal
- ½ tsp. dried oregano
- 1 can diced tomatoes,
- ½ tsp. dried thyme
- 4 cups (vegetable broth
- 1 tsp. fine sea salt
- 2 cups of water
- 3 bay leaves
- 1 pinch red pepper
- Black pepper, to taste
- 1 cup of orecchiette
- 1 ½ cups of cooked beans
- 2 tsp. lemon juice

- 2 cups of baby spinach, chopped
- Freshly Parmesan cheese, to garnish

Method

1. Warm 3 tbsp. of olive oil in an oven over the medium heat.

2. When oil starts shimmering, put chopped onion, celery, carrot, tomato paste, and salt, and cook until vegetables are softened for around 7-10 minutes.

3. Put seasonal vegetables, oregano, thyme, and garlic—Cook for around 2 minutes.

4. Add diced tomatoes, water, and broth.

5. Add salt, red pepper flakes, and bay leaves. Season with fresh black pepper.

6. Take the heat to the medium-high; bring mixture to the boil.

7. Partially cover the pot with a lid, and reduce heat to maintain the gentle simmer, and cook for almost 15 minutes.

8. Remove lid; add pasta, greens, and beans.

9. Cook for another 20 minutes.

10. Remove pot from heat when pasta and greens are cooked.

11. Remove bay leaves.

12. Add remaining tbsp. of the olive oil and lemon juice.

13. Add more pepper and salt if required to get the flavors to sing.

14.   Then garnish the bowls with the grated Parmesan, and serve.

5.7 Tuscan White Bean Soup with Sausage and Kale

Cooking Time: 55 minutes

Serving Size: 10 servings

Calories: 198 kcal

Ingredients

- 2 tbsp. olive oil
- 1 pound Italian sausage
- 1 tsp. fresh garlic, minced
- 3 cans of cannellini beans,
- Black pepper, to taste
- 1 can of diced tomatoes
- 4 cups of chicken broth
- 1 bunch of fresh kale, roughly chopped
- Salt, to taste
- Fresh parsley, chopped

Method

1. Take a pot, and heat the oil over the medium heat.
2. Put garlic and sausage in it; cook, and stir regularly for about 5 to 7 minutes.
3. Put all of the beans except 1 cup.

4. Add tomatoes, and set aside remaining beans for later use. Simmer while keeping it covered for around 5 minutes.

5. Put remaining beans in the food processor and blend; put pureed beans in the pot.

6. Add kale and broth. Bring it to boil.

7. Lower the heat, and simmer while keeping it covered for around 30 minutes.

8. Season with pepper and salt, if required.

9. Turn off the heat; garnish with parsley.

10.   Serve with the toasted bread.

5.8 Greek White Bean Soup with Orange Slices and Olive Oil

Cooking Time: 45 minutes

Serving Size: 8 servings

Calories: 265 kcal

Ingredients

- 4 sliced thin carrots
- 5 sliced thin celery sticks
- 1 sliced thin onion
- 2 cups of water
- 1 cup of olive oil
- 1 bay leaf
- ½ tsp. dried oregano
- 3 slices of orange
- 2 tbsp. tomato paste

15 ounces cannellini white beans

Method

1. Sauté carrots, onion, and celery in the olive oil on the medium heat.

2. Put bay leaf and oregano in it.

3. Add the tomato paste and orange slices, and sauté for almost 2 minutes.

4. Put Cannellini beans.

5. Add water.

6. Cook for almost 30 to 40 minutes stir occasionally.

7. Serve and enjoy!

5.9 Bean Counter Chowder

Cooking Time: 30 minutes

Serving Size: 8 servings

Calories: 196 kcal

Ingredients

- 1/2 cup of chopped onion
- 2 minced garlic cloves
- 1 tbsp. canola oil
- 1 chopped tomato
- 1 tbsp. minced parsley
- 1 3/4 cups of water
- 2 cans vegetable or chicken broth
- 1/2 tsp. dried basil, celery flakes, and oregano

- 3 cans of northern beans
- 1/4 tsp. pepper
- 1 cup of elbow macaroni, uncooked

Method

1. In a saucepan, cook onion in the oil for 3 minutes.
2. Put garlic into it, and cook for about 1 minute.
3. Put tomato into it, and simmer for almost 5 minutes.
4. Then add broth, seasonings, and water.
5. Bring it to boil, and cook for almost 5 minutes.
6. Put macaroni and beans; bring it to boil.
7. Cook for another 15 minutes.
8. Sprinkle parsley, and serve.

5.10 Italian Sausage Kale Soup

Cooking Time: 35 minutes

Serving Size: 8 servings

Calories: 217 kcal

Ingredients

- 1 package of sausage links, Italian turkey
- 1 chopped medium onion
- 8 cups fresh kale, chopped
- 2 minced garlic cloves
- 1/4 tsp. red pepper flakes, crushed
- 1/2 cup of chicken stock
- 3 1/4 cups of chicken stock
- 1 can of cannellini beans
- 1/4 tsp. pepper
- 1 cup of diced tomatoes

1/2 cup of tomatoes, sun-dried and chopped

Method

1. Take a stockpot, and cook onion and sausage over the medium heat for about 6 to 8 minutes.
2. Put kale in the pot; cook for 2 minutes.
3. Put garlic and pepper flakes, and cook for 1 minute.
4. Put wine into it, and cook for almost 2 minutes.
5. Add remaining ingredients and sausage mixture. Bring it to boil.
6. Lower the heat, and simmer for 15 to 20 minutes.
7. Serve and enjoy!

5.11 Shrimp and Cod Stew in Tomato-Saffron Broth

Cooking Time: 20 minutes

Serving Size: 4-6servings

Calories: 172 kcal

Ingredients

- 1 orange
- 790 ml can of undrained tomatoes
- 2 bay leaf
- 4 cups of water
- 1/4 tsp. of dried saffron
- 4 minced garlic cloves
- 1/2 tsp. of dried thyme
- 1/2 tsp. of ground fennel
- 1/2 tsp. of salt
- 1/4 tsp. of black pepper
- 1/4 tsp. of celery salt
- 1/3 cup of cold water
- 1/4 cup of fresh parsley, chopped
- 1/3 cup of flour
- 250 g of frozen or fresh shrimp
- 500 g frozen or fresh fish fillets, boneless
- 500g of mussels

Method

1. Put tomatoes in the food processor, and blend slightly.

2. Take a saucepan, add tomatoes, water, peel strip, saffron, and bay leaf.

3. Place over the medium heat.

4. Add garlic, fennel, thyme, salt, black pepper, and celery salt. Bring it to boil.

5. Lower the heat, and simmer for almost 15 minutes; stir occasionally.

6. In a cup, mix flour with the cold water.

7. When tomato mixture is simmered for almost 15 minutes, add it to the water and flour mixture, stir constantly. Cook for almost 10-15 minutes.

8. Add pepper and salt, if needed.

9. Remove any shells or bones, cut seafood, and fish into small chunks.

10. Before serving, remove the orange peel and bay leaf from broth. Add hot stew; simmer for 10 minutes.

11. Add fish, mussels, parsley, and seafood into the simmering stew.

12. Cook for around 8 minutes.

13. Add chopped parsley.

14. Serve with sourdough bread or crisp baguette.

15. Enjoy!

Chapter 6: Mediterranean Desserts Recipes

6.1 Mediterranean feta and quinoa egg muffins

Cooking Time: 45 minutes

Serving Size: 12 servings

Calories: 114 kcal

Ingredients

- 1/2 cup of onion, finely chopped
- 2 cups of finely chopped baby spinach
- 1 cup of sliced tomatoes
- 1 tbsp. of fresh oregano, chopped
- 1/2 cup of chopped kalamata olives
- 2 tsp. sunflower oil
- 1 cup of cooked quinoa
- 8 eggs
- 1 cup of feta cheese, crumbled
- 1/4 tsp. salt

Method

1. Preheat the oven to 350 Fahrenheit.

2. Prepare 12 muffin tins on the baking sheet; set aside.

3. Cut vegetables; heat the skillet to the medium.

4. Put onions and vegetable oil in it; saute for almost 2 minutes.

5. Put tomatoes in it; saute for 1 minute.

6. Put spinach; saute for almost 1 minute, then turn off the heat.

7. Add oregano and olives; set aside.

8. Put eggs in the blender and blend until combined.

9. Add quinoa, veggie mixture, salt, and feta cheese; stir until combined.

10. Transfer mixture to the muffin tins by equally dividing the mixture.

11. Bake in the oven for almost 30 minutes; wait until eggs are set.

12. When muffins turn golden brown, take it out of the oven.

13. Allow them to cool before serving.

6.2 Greek Yoghurt with Honey and Walnuts

Cooking Time: 10 minutes

Serving Size: 7 serving

Calories: 284 kcal

Ingredients

- 3/4 tsp. of vanilla extract
- 2 1/2 cups of Greek yogurt
- 1 cup of walnuts
- Cinnamon powder

- 1/2 cup hone

Method

1. Preheat oven to 180^0 C, and spread walnuts in the layer on the baking sheet.

2. Toast the walnuts for almost 7 to 8 minutes until fragrant and golden.

3. Put toasted walnuts into a bowl, and add honey; blend well.

4. Set them aside for 1to 2 minutes to let them cool down.

5. Mix vanilla extract and Greek yogurt; divide the mixture among 6 to 7 dessert bowls.

6. Add the walnut-honey mixture on the top; sprinkle with a pinch of cinnamon powder.

7. Store in refrigerator or serve immediately. Enjoy!

6.3 Orange Creamsicle Ice Cream

Cooking Time: 40 minutes

Serving Size: 6 servings

Calories: 386 kcal

Ingredients

- 2 orange
- 1 3/4 cup of coconut milk
- 4 tbsp. of Sweetener
- 1 tsp. of vanilla extract

Method

1. Peel the oranges, and put them flat on the tray; freeze until they are hardened.

2. In the blender, mix coconut milk with half orange sections, and blend until the mixture is smooth.

3. Add remaining oranges; continue blending.

4. Put sweetener (as per your choice).

5. Add vanilla extract, and blend.

6. Put into the freezer until solid.

7. Before serving, let them sit for some time. Enjoy!

6.4 Pistachio Pudding

Cooking Time: 10 minutes

Serving Size: 12 servings

Calories: 236 kcal

Ingredients

- 3.4 ounces of pistachio pudding mix
- 16 ounces of whipped topping
- 3 cups of miniature marshmallows
- 1/2 cup of chopped walnuts or pistachios
- 6-7 drops of green food color
- 20 ounces of pineapple tidbits

Method

1. Take a bowl, and combine pudding mix, food coloring, and whipped topping.
2. Add pineapple and marshmallows.
3. Refrigerate while keeping it covered for almost 2 hours.
4. Before serving, add more whipped topping and nuts.
5. Enjoy!

6.5 Moroccan Orange Cake

Cooking Time: 1 hour

Serving Size: 12 servings

Calories: 289 kcal

Ingredients

- 1 1/2 cups of granulated sugar
- 4 eggs
- 1/2 cup of canola oil
- 4 tsp. of baking powder
- 2 cups of all-purpose flour
- 1/2 tsp. salt
- Powdered sugar
- Two oranges
- 1/2 cup of orange juice
- 1 tsp. of vanilla extract

Method

1. Preheat the oven to 350° degrees F. Grease and spray the pan with the baking spray, and set aside.
2. In a bowl, mix sugar and eggs until thick, then gradually add the oil.
3. Mix flour, salt, orange juice, and baking powder. Beat until it is smooth.
4. Add the vanilla and orange zest.
5. Transfer the batter to the pan, and remove any air bubbles.
6. Bake for almost 40 to 50 minutes.

7. Remove the cake from the oven; allow it to cool down for about 10 minutes.

8. Turn the cake out on the cooling rack; let it cool completely.

9. Sprinkle with powdered sugar.

10. Serve and enjoy!

6.6 Peanut Butter Chocolate Cheesecake

Cooking Time: 7 hours 25 minute

Serving Size: 10-12 servings

Calories: 550 kcal

Ingredients

For Crust:

- 4 tbsp. of melted butter
- 3 tbsp. of granulated sugar
- 15 chocolate crackers
- 1/8 tsp. of kosher salt

For Cheesecake:

- 1 cup of packed brown sugar
- 4 packages of softened cream cheese
- 1/2 tsp. of kosher salt
- 4 eggs, at room temperature
- 1 tbsp. of vanilla extract
- 1 cup of peanut butter

- 1/2 cup of sour cream
- Chopped Reese's

For Chocolate Ganache:

- 3/4 cup of heavy cream
- 6 ounces of coarsely chopped semisweet chocolate
- 1/8 tsp. of kosher salt

Method

1. To make the crust, butter a pan, and preheat oven to 350°.

2. Take a blender, and grind chocolate crackers to make fine crumbs.

3. Put salt and sugar into it, and combine well.

4. Transfer it to a bowl, and add butter; use fingers or fork to blend the mixture.

5. Freeze for 10 minutes.

6. Put the pan on the baking sheet; bake the crust for almost 10 minutes.

7. Let it cool down, reduce the temperature of the oven to 325°.

8. Take water in a tea kettle or saucepan, and bring it to boil.

9. To make cheesecake, take a bowl and beat the cream cheese until smooth for about 3-4 minutes.

10. Put salt and sugar in it and beat until fluffy and smooth for 3-4 minutes.

11. Put vanilla in it; beat for almost 30 seconds.

12.   Put eggs, one by one, and beat for almost 1 minute.

13.   Mix peanut butter, sour cream, and heavy cream; beat slowly until smooth for 1 minute.

14.   Put the cheesecake batter in the cooled crust.

15.   Wrap the bottom of the pan with aluminum foil; place in the roasting pan, and pour boiling into it.

16.   Bake the cheesecake until its top start to brown, for 1.30 hour.

17.   Let the cheesecake cool in the water for an hour.

18.   Take the roasting pan out of the oven, and carefully lift pan from water; remove foil.

19.   Let the cheesecake come to the room temperature, then cover it with the plastic wrap; refrigerate for at least 4 hours.

20.   Before serving, carefully remove the sides of the pan, and place the chocolate in a dry and clean bowl.

21.   Take a saucepan over the medium heat, and warm cream.

22.   Pour the warm cream on top of the chocolate; let it sit about 10 minutes.

23.   Add salt; stir until completely smooth.

24.   Pour the ganache over the cheesecake; spread it evenly.

25.   Sprinkle chopped Reese's over it.

26.   Serve and enjoy!

Part 2: Mediterranean Spring Summer Recipes

Chapter 7: Mediterranean Breakfast Recipes

7.1 Mediterranean Broccoli & Cheese Omelet

Cooking Time: 30 minutes

Serving Size: 4 servings

Calories: 229 kcal

Ingredients

- 6 eggs
- 2 1/2 cups of broccoli florets
- 1/4 cup of 2% milk
- 1/4 tsp. pepper
- 1/2 tsp. salt
- 1/3 cup of Romano cheese
- 1 tbsp. olive oil
- 1/3 cup of sliced Greek olives

Method

1. Preheat the broiler.

2. Take a saucepan, put steamer basket on 1 inch of the water.

3. Put broccoli in the basket. And bring the water to boil.

4. Lower heat to simmer, and steam while keeping it covered for about 4 to 6 minutes until it is crisp-tender.

5. Take a bowl, mix eggs, salt, pepper, and milk.

6. Add cooked broccoli, olives, and grated cheese.

7. Take a 10-inch skillet, and heat the oil over the medium heat.

8. Add egg mixture, and cook while keeping it uncovered for about 4 to 6 minutes until eggs are set.

9. Let stand for 5 minutes, then cut into the wedges.

10. Add parsley and shaved cheese and serve.

7.2 Slim Greek Deviled Eggs

Cooking Time: 20 minutes

Serving Size: 1 dozen

Calories: 42 kcal

Ingredients

- 3 tbsp. of mayonnaise, reduced-fat
- 6 boiled eggs
- 2 tbsp. of feta cheese, crumbled
- 1/2 tsp. of lemon zest grated
- 1/8 tsp. salt
- Greek olives
- 1/2 tsp. lemon juice

- 1/8 tsp. pepper

Method

1. Cut all eggs into half.

2. Remove the yolks, and set aside the egg whites and four yolks.

3. Take a bowl, and mash the reserved yolks.

4. Add mayonnaise, oregano, Feta, lemon zest, salt, pepper, and lemon juice.

5. Stuff into the egg whites.

6. Garnish with the olives.

7. Chill, and serve.

7.3 Low-carb baked eggs with avocado and Feta

Cooking Time: 40 minutes

Serving Size: 2 servings

Calories: 391 kcal

Ingredients

1 avocado

- 4 eggs
- Olive oil spray
- Salt, to taste
- Black pepper, to taste
- 2 cups Feta Cheese, crumbled

Method

1. Break the eggs into ramekins; let avocado and eggs set at room temperature for about 15 minutes.

2. Preheat the oven to 200C, and put gratin dishes over the baking sheet; heat them for about 10 minutes.

3. Peel avocado; cut into six slices.

4. Remove the dishes from oven; spray with oil or spray.

5. Put sliced avocados in a dish.

6. Tip two eggs in the dish.

7. Add crumbled Feta; season with black pepper and salt.

8. Bake for 12 to 15 minutes.

9. Serve hot.

7.4 Mediterranean eggs

Cooking Time: 30 minutes

Serving Size: 6 servings

Calories: 154 kcal

Ingredients

- Olive oil
- 1 large chopped yellow onion
- 2 chopped green peppers
- 2 chopped garlic cloves
- 1 tsp. of ground coriander
- 1 tsp. of sweet paprika
- 1/2 tsp. of ground cumin
- 1 Pinch of red pepper flakes
- Salt, to taste
- Black pepper, to taste
- 6 Vine-ripe chopped tomatoes
- 1/4 cup of chopped mint leaves
- 6 eggs
- 1/2 cup of tomato sauce
- 1/4 cup of chopped parsley leaves

Method

1. Heat oil in the pan.

2. Add onions, garlic, green peppers, spices, pepper, and pinch salt, and cook for 5 minutes until vegetables are softened.

3. Add tomato sauce and tomatoes, and cover it; let it simmer for 15 minutes. Cook while keeping it uncovered to allow mixture to thicken and reduce.

4. Adjust seasoning as you like.

5. Use the wooden spoon, make 6 wells in the mixture, and then gently crack eggs in each indention.

6. Lower the heat, and cover skillet; cook on the low heat until egg whites have set.

7. Add mint and fresh parsley.

8. Add additional black pepper, if desired.

9. Serve with the challah bread, warm pita, or crusty bread of your choice.

7.5 Mediterranean egg white sandwich with roasted tomatoes

Cooking Time: 30 minutes

Serving Size: 1 serving

Calories: 458 kcal

Ingredients

- 1/4 cup of egg whites
- 1 tsp. butter
- Salt, to taste
- Black pepper, to taste
- 1–2 slices of muenster cheese
- 1 ciabatta roll, whole grain

- 1 tsp. chopped herbs (basil, parsley, rosemary)
- 1 tbsp. pesto
- 1/2 cup of roasted tomatoes

For Roasted Tomatoes:

- 1 tbsp. olive oil
- 10 ounces of grape tomatoes
- Kosher salt, to taste
- Black pepper, to taste

Method

1. Melt butter in the skillet.
2. Add egg whites.
3. Season with pepper and salt.
4. Add fresh herbs, and cook for almost 3 to 4 minutes, until egg white is done.
5. Take a toaster, and toast the ciabatta bread.
6. Add pesto to both halves when done.
7. Put an egg on half of the sandwich roll, then add cheese.
8. For making roasted tomatoes, slice the tomatoes into half.
9. Preheat the oven to 400^0 F.
10. Put on the baking sheet; drizzle with olive oil.
11. Toss well, and season with pepper and salt.
12. Roast for almost 20 minutes.

13.   Put roasted tomatoes on the sandwich and serve.

14.   Enjoy!

7.6 Smoked Salmon and Poached Eggs on Toast

Cooking Time: 15 minutes

Serving Size: 2 servings

Calories: 439 kcal

Ingredients

- 4 halved muffins
- 15g of butter
- 240g bag of baby spinach
- 4 eggs
- 2 tsp. of vinegar, white wine
- 6 tbsp. of hollandaise sauce
- Finely chopped Chives
- 120g of smoked salmon

Method

1. Preheat oven to 150°C.
2. Bring a pan of the water to boil.
3. Toast the muffins, keep them warm in an oven.
4. Add spinach, and toss in pan.

5. Pour vinegar into boiling water, and reduce the heat to simmer.

6. Crack two eggs in the separate cups.

7. Slide-in eggs in the water one at a time, then cook for almost 3 to 4 minutes.

8. Remove them with the slotted spoon, and repeat the process with remaining eggs.

9. Heat hollandaise in the bowl in the simmering water.

10.   When it is time to serve, put muffins on the plates.

11.   Top each with spinach, poached eggs, and smoked salmon.

12.   Sprinkle hollandaise, chives, and black pepper, and serve.

7.7 Eggs with Summer Tomatoes, Zucchini, and Bell Peppers

Cooking Time: 40 minutes

Serving Size: 2 servings

Calories: 226 kcal

Ingredients

- 1 thinly sliced yellow onion
- 1 tbsp. olive oil
- 1 minced clove garlic
- 2 tomatoes, chopped
- 2 zucchini or summer squash
- 1/2 tsp. of fresh thyme
- 2 eggs

- 1 bell pepper, red
- 1 tsp. of Spanish paprika or piquillo pepper
- Salt, to taste
- Black pepper, to taste

Method

1. Heat oil in the skillet over the medium heat.
2. Put onion in it, and cook for almost 5 minutes.
3. Put garlic in it, and cook for 1 minute.
4. Pour squash in it, and cook for around 10 minutes.
5. Put tomatoes, thyme, and paprika in it; let simmer for around 20 minutes.
6. Roast pepper on a stovetop.
7. When it is cooled, remove seeds and core, then cut into pieces.
8. Add roasted peppers, pepper, and salt.
9. Fry all eggs, then divide vegetables between the two plates.
10. Top the dish with eggs, and serve with the buttered toast.

7.8 Caprese Avocado Toast

Cooking Time: 10 minutes

Serving Size: 1 serving

Calories: 173 kcal

Ingredients

- ½ avocado, mashed
- 1 handful of chopped fresh basil
- 1 bread, toasted
- Salt, to taste
- 2 sliced heirloom tomatoes
- Pepper, to taste
- 1 sliced mozzarella ball

Method

1. Mash avocado.
2. Add pepper and salt, and mix well.
3. Spread mashed avocado across the toast; top with the heirloom tomatoes, chopped basil, and mozzarella.
4. Enjoy!

7.9 Spinach Feta Breakfast Wraps

Cooking Time: 10 minutes

Serving Size: 1 serving

Calories: 550 kcal

Ingredients

- 1/2 cup of roughly chopped fresh spinach
- 2 eggs
- 1 1/2 tbsp. diced butter

- 4 chopped Kalamata olives
- 1/4 cup of crumbled feta cheese
- Salt, to taste
- Black pepper, to taste
- 1 tortilla, whole wheat

Method

1. Heat a pan over the medium heat.
2. Melt 1/2 tbsp. butter in the pan.
3. Scramble all eggs in the bowl.
4. Put butter chunks, pepper, and salt.
5. Add egg mixture to pan.
6. Let eggs cook, then push them with the spatula.
7. When eggs are about to be cooked, add spinach, combine well and cook.
8. Turn off the heat; lay them on top of the tortilla.
9. Add eggs, feta cheese, and Kalamata olives on it.
10. Wrap together.
11. Serve and Enjoy!

7.10 Spinach Artichoke Frittata

Cooking Time: 25 minutes

Serving Size: 4-6 servings

Calories: 316 kcal

Ingredients

- 1/2 cup sour cream, full-fat

- 10 eggs
- 1 tbsp. Dijon mustard
- 1/4 tsp. of black pepper, freshly ground
- 2 minced cloves garlic
- 1 tsp. kosher salt
- 1 cup Parmesan cheese, grated
- 14 ounces of artichoke hearts
- 2 tbsp. olive oil
- 5 ounces of baby spinach

Method

1. Preheat the oven to 400°F.
2. Put eggs, mustard, sour cream, pepper, salt, and Parmesan in the bowl; whisk well, and set aside.
3. Take a skillet, and heat oil over the medium heat.
4. Put artichokes, and cook, until browned, for 6-8 minutes.
5. Put in garlic and spinach, and cook for 2 minutes.
6. Pour egg mixture on top of the vegetables, and sprinkle with remaining Parmesan.
7. Cook for almost 2-3 minutes.
8. Then bake for 12-15 minutes until eggs are set.
9. Let the pan cool down for almost 5 minutes, slice into the wedges.
10. Serve warm.

7.11 Hearty Breakfast Fruit Salad

Cooking Time: 15 minutes

Serving Size: 5 servings

Calories: 282 kcal

Ingredients

For Grains:

- 1/2 tsp. kosher salt
- 3 cups of water
- 1 cup of whole grain
- 3 tbsp. of vegetable oil or olive oil

For Fruits:

- 1/2 pineapple, cut into chunks
- 6 mandarins or tangerines
- 5 large oranges
- 1 bunch of fresh mint
- 1 1/4 cups of pomegranate seeds

For the Dressing:

- 1 lemon, juice, and grated zest
- 1/3 cup of honey
- 2 limes, juice, and grated zest
- 1/4 cup of olive oil
- 1/2 tsp. kosher salt
- 1/4 cup of toasted nut or hazelnut oil

Method

1. Line two baking sheets with the parchment paper, then rinse barley in the strainer with cold water for around 1 minute—shake strainer to remove excess water.

2. Put barley on the baking sheet; use spatula to place and even out the grains to make a layer, and dry completely for 3-5 minutes.

3. Warm water in a microwave and set aside.

4. Heat 2 tbsp. of oil in the saucepan over the high heat.

5. Add the toast and barley, constantly stirring— Cook for about 90 seconds.

6. Add salt and warm water; bring it to boil.

7. Lower the heat, cover, and then cook until it is tender for about 40-45 minutes.

8. Turn down the heat; let it stand while keeping it covered for around 10 minutes.

9. Prepare mint, fruit, and the dressing.

10. Put pineapple chunks in the containers.

11. Cut the oranges, tangerines, and mandarins.

12. Put them in another container, and refrigerate.

13. Put the pomegranate seeds in the refrigerator separately in a separate container.

14. Thinly slice mint leaves, and refrigerate in a separate container.

15. Whisk honey, zests, salt, and juice in a bowl.

16.   Add olive oil and nut oil, whisk constantly. Refrigerate in the jar.

17.   Put the cooked barley in the baking sheet, spread into a layer, and let cool for 10-20 minutes.

18.   Add remaining oil to the barley, and mix well.

19.   Put barley in a container, cover it, and then refrigerate.

20.   For serving, put 2/3 cup barley into a bowl.

21.   Add pineapple, orange segments, and pomegranate seeds.

22.   Add mint and dressing in each bowl.

23.   Mix well and then coat with dressing.

7.12 Mediterranean Breakfast Pita

Cooking Time: 25 minutes

Serving Size: 2 servings

Calories: 267 kcal

Ingredients

- 1/4 cup of chopped onion
- 1/4 cup of chopped red pepper
- 1 cup of egg substitute
- 1/8 tsp. pepper
- 1/8 tsp. salt
- 1 chopped small tomato
- 2 tbsp. feta cheese, crumbled
- 1-1/2 tsp. fresh basil, minced

- 1/2 cup of baby spinach, torn fresh
- 2 pita bread

Method

1. Take a nonstick skillet, and coat it with the cooking spray.
2. Put onion and red pepper over the medium heat for about 3 minutes.
3. Put the egg substitute, pepper, and salt in it.
4. Mix tomato, basil, and spinach; spoon them onto pitas.
5. Add egg mixture on the top; sprinkle with the feta cheese, and serve immediately.

Chapter 8: Mediterranean Lunch and Dinner Recipes

8.1 Mahi-Mahi and Veggie Skillet

Cooking Time: 30 minutes

Serving Size: 4 servings

Calories: 307 kcal

Ingredients

- 3 tbsp. Olive oil
- 4 Mahi-mahi
- ½ pound mushrooms
- 3 red peppers
- 1 sweet onion
- 1/3 cup Lemon juice
- ¾ tsp. Salt
- ½ tsp. Pepper
- 1/3 cup Pine nuts

Method

1. Place the skillet over the medium heat; add 2 tbsp. olive oil.
2. Put fillets in it; cook each side for almost 5 minutes, then take out of the pan.
3. Put remaining oil, onion, peppers, mushrooms, ¼ tsp. salt, and lemon juice in the pan, and cook

while keeping it covered for almost 8 minutes until vegetables are thoroughly tender.

4. Put the fish on vegetables.

5. Sprinkle with pepper and salt, and cook for almost 2 minutes while keeping covered.

6. Add pine nuts and chives before serving.

8.2 Feta Frittata

Cooking Time: 20 minutes

Serving Size: 4 servings

Calories: 300 kcal

Ingredients

- 1/4 cup of heavy cream
- 6 eggs
- 1 tbsp. fresh dill, finely chopped
- 1/4 tsp. black pepper, freshly ground
- 1/2 tsp. kosher salt
- 1 tbsp. olive oil
- 4 ounces of baby spinach
- 1/2 diced yellow onion
- 3 ounces of feta cheese, crumbled

Method

1. Preheat the oven to 400°F.

2. Put eggs, dill, cream, pepper, and salt in a bowl; whisk and set aside.

3. Take oil in a nonstick skillet, and heat it over the medium heat until shimmering.

4. Put the onion in it, and cook for almost 5 minutes.

5. Mix spinach, and toss for 3 minutes.

6. Spread an even layer on the skillet; sprinkle with cheese.

7. Put egg mixture on the cheese and vegetables.

8. Cook undisturbed for almost 2 minutes.

9. Put pan in the oven; bake until eggs are set for 8-10 minutes.

10. Slice frittata into wedges; serve warm.

8.3 Spanish Prawns with Vegetables

Cooking Time: 20 minutes

Serving Size: 4 servings

Calories: 420 kcal

Ingredients

- 600g Frozen raw prawns
- 2 tbsp. Barbecue spice
- ½ cup of butter spread, Garlic
- 500g of mixed vegetables, Frozen
- 3 Chopped tomatoes
- Crusty bread, for serving

Method

1. Mix prawns with spices; cook in 2 batches.

2. Put the skillet over the medium heat.

3. Put butter in it, and spread.

4. Add the prawns into skillet; cook each side for almost 3 minutes.

5. Take them out of the skillet.

6. Add more butter in the pan.

7. Put tomatoes in it; cook for 1 minute, then return the prawns back into the pan.

8. Add 2 tbsp. of water.

9. Add salt; cook for almost 3 minutes.

10. Microwave vegetables until they are tender, and serve vegetables with the prawn and crusty bread.

8.4 Mediterranean Chickpeas

Cooking Time: 25 minutes

Serving Size: 4 servings

Calories: 340 kcal

Ingredients

- ¾ cup wheat couscous
- 1 medium onion, chopped
- 1 tbsp. Olive oil
- 2 cloves garlic, minced
- 1 can Chickpeas

- 1 can stewed tomatoes
- 1 can Water packed chopped artichoke hearts
- ½ cup coarsely chopped olives
- ½ tsp. Dried oregano
- 1 Pinch pepper
- 1 Pinch cayenne
- 1 tbsp. Lemon juice
- 1 cup Water

Method

1. Put the saucepan over the medium heat; add water in it, and bring it to boil.
2. Add the couscous in boiling water, keep it that way for about 2 minutes, and then turn off the heat.
3. Let it stay in the saucepan to absorb water for almost 10 minutes.
4. Put the skillet over the medium heat; add the olive oil.
5. Put onion in it, and cook until it is tender.
6. Put garlic; cook for 1 minute.
7. Add remaining ingredients, let them heat through.
8. Serve with the couscous.

8.5 Penne and Fresh Tomato Sauce with Spinach and Feta

Cooking Time: 30 minutes

Serving Size: 4 servings

Calories: 282 kcal

Ingredients

- 1 tbsp. olive oil
- 12 ounces of uncooked penne, whole-wheat
- 1 diced medium onion
- 1 1/2 cups of pear or cherry tomatoes
- 2 minced garlic cloves
- 1/2 cup of feta cheese, crumbled
- 3/4 cup of fat-free, chicken broth
- 1/4 tsp. salt
- 6 ounces fresh arugula leaves or baby spinach
- 1/4 tsp. pepper

Method

1. Cook pasta as per the package directions; do not add salt.
2. Heat olive oil in the skillet over the medium heat.
3. Put onion in it; cook for almost 4 minutes.
4. Put garlic in it, and cook for 30 seconds.

5. Mix broth and tomatoes; bring it to simmer, then cook for almost 5 minutes, until tomatoes are soften.

6. Using a spoon, lightly crush the tomatoes.

7. Slowly add spinach; cook for almost 2 minutes.

8. Drain the pasta.

9. Take a serving bowl, and toss pasta with the warm spinach-tomato sauce.

10. Add pepper and salt.

11. Garnish with the cheese, and serve.

8.6 Summer Vegetable Gratin

Cooking Time: 1 hour 20 minutes

Serving Size: 4 servings

Calories: 228 kcal

Ingredients

- 1 tbsp. minced garlic
- 1 cup shallots, thinly sliced
- 1/2 cup olive oil
- 1 large sliced eggplant
- 1 tbsp. chopped thyme leaves
- 1 large sliced yellow squash
- Kosher salt, to taste
- Black pepper, to taste
- 1 large sliced zucchini
- 4 vine-ripe sliced tomatoes
- 1 crusty bread, for serving

- 1/4 cup of grated Parmesan
- 1/2 cup of shredded fontina
- 4 leaves of fresh basil

Method

1. Preheat the oven to 400⁰ F.

2. Mix shallots, 2 tbsp. of olive oil, 1 tsp. of thyme and garlic in the baking dish, and bake until caramelized for 15-20 minutes, then let it cool.

3. Divide eggplant, zucchini, and yellow squash between 2 sheets.

4. Add salt to vegetables, and let stand for 30 minutes.

5. Press vegetables with the kitchen towel.

6. Transfer vegetables to sheet trays.

7. Put tomatoes to the sheet trays, and toss all vegetables with the olive oil, thyme, pepper, and salt.

8. Make 1 stack of all vegetables on the baking sheet.

9. Add one tomato slice, 1-2 slices of the zucchini, 1 slice of the eggplant, and 1-2 slices of the yellow squash.

10. Put stack in baking dish on the top of caramelized shallots, then repeat making the stacks.

11. Sprinkle with Parmesan and fontina, and bake until vegetables are thoroughly tender and cheese is completely melted, for 35 minutes, then let it cool for 15 minutes.

12.   Add basil.

13.   Serve with the crusty bread.

8.7 Tomato-Poached Halibu

Cooking Time: 30minutes

Serving Size: 4 servings

Calories: 224 kcal

Ingredients

- 2 finely chopped poblano peppers
- 1 tbsp. olive oil
- 1 finely chopped small onion
- 1 can diced tomatoes
- 1 can fire-roasted undrained diced tomatoes
- 1/4 cup of chopped green olives
- 1/4 tsp. pepper
- 3 minced garlic cloves
- 1/8 tsp. salt
- 1/3 cup fresh cilantro, chopped
- Whole grain crusty bread
- 4 (4-ounce) halibut fillets
- 1 lemon

Method

1. Take the nonstick skillet, and heat the oil over the medium heat.
2. Add the onion and poblano peppers, and cook for 4 to 6 minutes.
3. Add tomatoes, garlic, olives, salt, and pepper.
4. Bring it to boil, and adjust the heat for a gentle simmer.
5. Mix fillets, and cook while keeping it covered for 8 to 10 minutes.
6. Add cilantro, and serve with the lemon wedges.

8.8 Baked Tilapia

Cooking Time: 20 minutes

Serving Size: 4 servings

Calories: 220 kcal

Ingredients

- Kosher salt, to taste
- 4 tilapia
- black pepper, to taste
- 2 minced cloves garlic
- 5 tbsp. of butter, melted
- 1/4 tsp. of red pepper flakes, crushed
- 1 sliced lemon
- 1/2 lemon
- Chopped parsley, to garnish

Method

1. Preheat the oven to 400° F.

2. Season the tilapia with pepper and salt; place it on the baking sheet.

3. Add butter, red pepper flakes, garlic, lemon zest, and lemon juice on top of the tilapia.

4. Put lemon rounds around tilapia.

5. Bake it for 10-12 minutes.

6. Serve and enjoy.

8.9 Speedy Hummus Pizza

Cooking Time: 20 minutes

Serving Size: 6 slices

Ingredients

- 1 cup of hummus
- 1 prebaked pizza crust
- 3/4 tsp. dried oregano
- 1/2 cup of feta cheese, crumbled
- 1/4 tsp. red pepper flakes, crushed
- 1/2 cup of oil-packed chopped tomatoes
- 1 tbsp. olive oil
- 1/2 cup of chopped Greek olives

Method

1. Preheat the oven to 450° F.
2. Put crust on the pizza pan or baking sheet.
3. Take a bowl, and mix hummus, pepper flakes, and oregano and spread them over the crust.
4. Add cheese, olives, and tomatoes.
5. Bake for 8 to 10 minutes.
6. Drizzle with the oil, and serve.

8.10 Summer Fish Skillet

Cooking Time: 10 minutes

Serving Size: 2 servings

Calories: 442 kcal

Ingredients

- Sea salt, to taste
- Black pepper, to taste
- 2 fish fillets
- 5 tbsp. of olive oil
- 4 sprigs fresh thyme
- 1 medium sliced lemon

Method

1. Dry fish fillets with towel after removing them from the refrigerator.
2. Season generously with pepper and salt.
3. Place a skillet over the high heat, add olive oil.
4. Add lemon slices. Use a spatula, and gently press fillets for almost 20 seconds.
5. Reduce heat to the medium; sauté fillets for almost 2-3 minutes.
6. Add the thyme to skillet.
7. Wait for few seconds; then tilt skillet slightly.
8. Put slices of lemon on top of the fillets.
9. Serve with summer salad, and enjoy.

8.11 Zucchini and Cheese Roulades

Cooking Time: 25 minutes

Serving Size: 2 dozens

Calories: 24 kcal

Ingredients

- 1/4 cup of Parmesan cheese, grated
- 1 cup of ricotta cheese
- 2 tbsp. fresh basil, minced
- 1 tbsp. Greek olives, chopped
- 1 tbsp. capers, drained
- 4 zucchini
- 1 tsp. lemon zest, grated
- 1/8 tsp. salt
- 1 tbsp. lemon juice
- 1/8 tsp. pepper

Method

1. Take a bowl, and all ingredients of ricotta mixture except zucchini.

2. Slice zucchini into thick slices.

3. Take a grill rack, and cook zucchini while keeping it covered for 2 to 3 minutes.

4. Put 1 tbsp. of ricotta mixture on zucchini slice, then roll-up.

5. Serve and enjoy.

8.12 Mediterranean Spinach and Beans

Cooking Time: 30 minutes

Serving Size: 4 servings

Calories: 187 kcal

Ingredients

- 1 chopped small onion
- 1 tbsp. olive oil
- 2 minced garlic cloves
- 2 tbsp. Worcestershire sauce
- 1 can of undrained diced tomatoes
- 1/4 tsp. salt
- 1/8 tsp. red pepper flakes, crushed
- 1/4 tsp. pepper
- 1 can f cannellini beans, drained
- 6 ounces of baby spinach
- 1 can of artichoke hearts, water-packed

Method

1. Heat oil over the medium heat.
2. Add onion, and cook for 3-5 minutes.
3. Put garlic in it; cook for 1 minute.
4. Add tomatoes, seasonings, and Worcestershire sauce; bring it to a boil.
5. Lower the heat, and simmer while keeping it uncovered for almost 6 to 8 minutes.

6. Mix beans, spinach, and artichoke hearts; cook for about 3 to 5 minutes.

7. Drizzle with the additional oil, and serve.

Chapter 9: Mediterranean Salad and Snacks Recipes

9.1 Tomato and Burrata Salad with Pangrattato and Basil

Cooking Time: 25 minutes

Serving Size: 6 servings

Calories: 27 kcal

Ingredients

- 4 ounces of cherry tomatoes
- 2 pounds mixed tomatoes
- 8 ounces of burrata
- 3/4 cup of olive oil
- 4 ounces of white bread
- 1/2 cup of white balsamic vinegar
- Salt, to taste
- Pepper, to taste
- 1 thinly sliced medium shallot
- 2 minced cloves garlic
- 1/2 cup of chopped basil

Method

1. Cut out the slices of tomatoes, and lay those slices on the paper towel; season with the salt. Set aside for at least thirty minutes.

2. Put bread in the food processor; pulse until it is in shape of crumbs.

3. Take a skillet, and heat olive oil in it.

4. Add bread crumbs; stir until it is golden brown for almost 5 to 8 minutes.

5. Add garlic, and stir for almost 30 seconds; stir garlic in bread crumbs, and remove the heat; let it cool.

6. Put shallots in the large bowl, and add vinegar, pepper, and salt.

7. Add olive oil, and season with pepper and salt.

8. Put cherry tomatoes and tomato slices on the serving plate.

9. Add some vinaigrette on top of the tomatoes.

10. Make 4 pieces of burrata ball, and put them on top of the tomatoes.

11. Add breadcrumbs around tomatoes.

12. Toss basil on the top.

13. Add more vinaigrette.

14. Serve with bread crumbs and dressing.

9.2 Salmon with Broccoli and Lemon Mayo

Cooking Time: 25 minutes

Serving Size: 4 servings

Calories: 560 kcal

Ingredients

- 1 ½ pound Salmon
- 1 pound Broccoli
- 2 ounces Butter
- Salt, to taste
- 1 cup Mayonnaise
- 2 tbsp. Lemon juice

Method

1. Mix mayonnaise and lemon juice. Set it aside.
2. Make pieces of salmon and season with pepper and salt.
3. Over the medium heat, cook each side of salmon with butter for almost 10 minutes; then reduce the heat.
4. Take salmon out of the pan; keep warm.
5. Add broccoli.
6. Add remaining butter; cook the broccoli for almost 4 minutes until it is golden brown and softened.
7. Add pepper and salt to broccoli.
8. Serve salmon with the broccoli and mayo.

9.3 Grilled Vegetable and Halloumi Salad

Cooking Time: 25 minutes

Serving Size: 4 servings

Calories: 584 kcal

Ingredients

- 225 g of halloumi cheese
- 100 g of broad beans, frozen
- 1 bunch asparagus
- 2 tbsp. olive oil
- 2 courgettes
- 2 shallots
- ½ bunch fresh parsley
- 1 tbsp. capers
- 200 g of cherry tomatoes
- ½ bunch fresh oregano

For Dressing:

- 1 tsp. of dried oregano
- 3 tbsp. of olive oil
- 1 tsp. of honey
- 1 tbsp. of cider vinegar
- 1 tsp. of Dijon mustard

Method

1. Take a jam jar, and mix dressing ingredients in it.

2. Cook broad beans in the boiling water until tender. Then cool them with cold water.

3. Cut slices of the halloumi, asparagus, and courgettes—season with the olive oil.

4. Heat a pan over the high heat, and put asparagus, halloumi, and courgettes in it. Cook until charred, then remove from the heat.

5. Finely slice shallots and tomatoes.

6. Put on the platter with asparagus, capers, halloumi, courgettes, and broad beans.

7. Chop them; scatter on fresh herbs.

8. Drizzle the dressing, and serve.

9.4 Tomato Salad with Tuna, Capers, and Black Olives

Cooking Time: 30 minutes

Serving Size: 6 servings

Calories: 265 kcal

Ingredients

- 1 170 g of drained tin tuna
- 1/2 tsp. salt
- 4-5 ripe tomatoes

For vinaigrette:

- 3 tbsp. olive oil
- 1 tbsp. lemon juice, freshly squeezed
- 3 tbsp. capers
- 12 roughly torn kalamata olives
- 1/4 finely chopped red onion
- 2 tbsp. Italian parsley chopped
- 1/4 tsp. red chili flakes
- Black pepper, to taste

Method

1. Cut the tomatoes; toss with salt in the bowl, and set aside for almost 20 minutes.
2. Put vinaigrette ingredients in the bowl; whisk lightly.
3. Adjust salt if required.

4. Once tomatoes are juiced up, add vinaigrette to tomatoes, and toss to combine, then set it aside for almost 5 minutes.

5. Put flaked tuna on top of tomatoes.

6. Serve immediately.

9.5 Mediterranean Cobb Salad

Cooking Time: 20 minutes

Serving Size: 10 servings

Calories: 258 kcal

Ingredients

- 1/2 cup of plain yogurt
- 6 ounces of falafel mix
- 1/4 cup of chopped cucumber
- 1 tsp. fresh parsley, minced
- 1/4 cup of 2% milk
- 1/4 tsp. salt
- 4 cups of baby spinach
- 4 cups of torn romaine
- 3 hard-boiled chopped large eggs
- 1 medium finely chopped ripe avocado
- 2 medium finely chopped tomatoes
- 3/4 cup of feta cheese, crumbled
- 1/2 cup finely chopped Greek olives
- 8 crumbled bacon strips

Method

1. Prepare falafel as per package directions, and let them cool down, then crumble chop falafel.

2. Take a bowl, and mix cucumber, sour cream, milk, salt, and parsley.

3. Take a bowl, and combine spinach and romaine, then transfer to the platter.

4. Put remaining ingredients and crumbled falafel over the greens, and drizzle with the dressing.

9.6 Mediterranean Shrimp Orzo Salad

Cooking Time: 30 minutes

Serving Size: 8 servings

Calories: 397 kcal

Ingredients

- 3/4 pound of peeled, cooked shrimp
- 16 ounces of orzo pasta
- 14 ounces of water-packed artichoke hearts
- 1 cup red pepper, finely chopped
- 1 cup green pepper, finely chopped
- 3/4 cup red onion, finely chopped
- 3/4 cup of Greek vinaigrette
- 1/2 cup fresh parsley, minced
- 1/2 cup Greek olives
- 1/3 cup fresh dill, chopped

Method

1. Prepare orzo as per the package directions; drain and rinse with the cold water.

2. Take a bowl, and combine orzo, herbs, vegetables, shrimp, and olives.

3. Add vinaigrette.

4. Refrigerate while keeping it covered.

5. Serve and enjoy.

9.7 Smoky Cauliflower

Cooking Time: 30 minutes

Serving Size: 8 servings

Calories: 58 kcal

Ingredients

1. 2 tbsp. olive oil

2. 1 head cauliflower

3. 1 tsp. smoked paprika

4. 2 minced garlic cloves

5. 3/4 tsp. salt

6. 2 tbsp. fresh parsley minced

Method

1. Put cauliflower in the large bowl.

2. Add oil, herbs, salt, and herbs, and pour over the cauliflower.

3. Transfer it to the baking pan, and bake while keeping it uncovered for almost 10 minutes.

4. Add garlic, and bake for 10 to 15 minutes until the cauliflower is completely tender and browned.

5. Add parsley, and serve.

9.8 Nectarine and Beet Salad

Cooking Time: 10 minutes

Serving Size: 8 servings

Calories: 84 kcal

Ingredients

- 2 medium sliced nectarines
- 2 packages of salad greens, spring mix
- 1/2 cup f balsamic vinaigrette
- 1/2 cup of feta cheese, crumbled
- 1 can beets, sliced

Method

1. Take a dish, and toss nectarines and greens with the vinaigrette.

2. Add cheese and beets, and serve immediately.

9.9 Herb-Roasted Olives and Tomatoes

Cooking Time: 25 minutes

Serving Size: 4 servings

Calories: 71 kcal

Ingredients

- 1 cup of olives
- 2 cups of cherry tomatoes
- 1 cup of Greek olives
- 8 peeled garlic cloves
- 1 cup ripe olives
- 3 tbsp. olive oil
- 1/4 tsp. pepper
- 1 tbsp. herbs

Method

1. Preheat the oven to 425° F.
2. Put ingredients in the baking pan.
3. Add seasonings and oil, and toss.
4. Roast it tomatoes for about 15 to 20 minutes.

9.10 Layered Hummus Dip

Cooking Time: 15 minutes

Serving Size: 12 servings

Calories: 88 kcal

Ingredients

- 1/4 cup of red onion, finely chopped

- 1 carton of hummus
- 1/2 cup chopped Greek olives
- 1 large chopped English cucumber
- 2 medium chopped tomatoes
- Pita chips, Baked
- 1 cup feta cheese, crumbled

Method

1. Spread the hummus in a shallow dish.
2. Add onion, cheese, tomatoes, olives, and cucumber.
3. Refrigerate, and serve with the pita chips

9.11 Tzatziki Potato Salad

Cooking Time: 25 minutes

Serving Size: 12 servings

Calories: 128 kcal

Ingredients

- 1 carton of tzatziki sauce, refrigerated
- 2 pounds of red potatoes
- 2 thinly sliced celery ribs
- 2 chopped green onions
- 1/2 cup Greek yogurt
- 2 tbsp. snipped dill

- 1/2 tsp. salt
- 2 tbsp. fresh parsley, minced
- 1/4 tsp. celery salt
- 1 tbsp. fresh mint, minced
- 1/4 tsp. pepper

Method

1. Place the potatoes in an oven, and add water. Make sure potatoes are covered.
2. Bring it to boil, and lower the heat.
3. Cook it while keeping it uncovered for about 10 to 15 minutes.
4. Cool completely.
5. Take a bowl, and mix the tzatziki sauce, yogurt, celery, green onions, parsley, dill, salt, pepper, and mint.
6. Pour on potatoes, and toss well.
7. Refrigerate until cold.
8. Serve and enjoy.

9.12 Tzatziki Shrimp Cucumber Rounds

Cooking Time: 35minutes

Serving Size: 2 dozen

Calories: 30 kcal

Ingredients

- 2 tbsp. peeled cucumber, finely chopped
- 1/4 cup of plain yogurt
- 1/8 tsp. garlic salt
- 6 strips of bacon
- 1/8 tsp. dill weed
- 24 shrimp, uncooked
- 2 medium sliced cucumbers
- 1-2 tbsp. canola oil

Method

1. Take a bowl, and combine yogurt, garlic, salt, dill, and chopped cucumber.
2. Cut bacon strip into half.
3. Wrap bacon piece around a shrimp.
4. Take a large skillet, and heat the oil over the medium heat, and cook each side of shrimp for 3 to 4 minutes.
5. Spoon yogurt sauce on the cucumber slice, and top with the shrimp.
6. Serve and enjoy.

Chapter 10: Mediterranean Soup Recipes

10.1 Classic Gazpacho

Cooking Time: 15 minutes

Serving Size: 4-6 servings

Calories: 122 kcal

Ingredients

- 2 pounds of ripe tomatoes
- 1 small cucumber, peeled
- 1 medium bell pepper, green
- 1/2 peeled red onion
- 3 tbsp. olive oil
- 2 small peeled garlic cloves
- 2 tbsp. of sherry vinegar
- 1/2 tsp. of black pepper
- 1 tsp. of sea salt
- 1 white bread
- 1/2 tsp. ground cumin

For Garnishing:

- Croutons
- Fresh herbs
- Olive oil

- Chopped gazpacho

Method

1. Mix ingredients in the blender, and blend for 1 minute.
2. Add extra pepper, salt, and cumin if required.
3. Chill in the sealed container or jar for 3-4 hours.
4. Serve cold and top with desired garnishes.

10.2 Chilled Cucumber and Yogurt Soup

Cooking Time: 25 minutes

Serving Size: 5 servings

Calories: 140 kcal

Ingredients

- 3 tablespoons fresh lemon juice
- 1 garlic clove
- 2 large cucumbers
- 1 1/2 cups of Greek yogurt
- 1 shallot
- 1/4 cup of parsley leaves
- 1/4 cup of olive oil
- 1/3 cup of dill
- 2 tbsp. of tarragon leaves
- 1/2 finely chopped red onion

Method

1. Take a blender, and combine chopped cucumber, yogurt, shallot, lemon juice, garlic, dill, tarragon, 1/4 cup olive oil, and parsley.

2. Add white pepper and salt, refrigerate while keeping it covered for 8 hours.

3. Pour soup into the bowls.

4. Add diced cucumber, olive oil, and red onion for garnishing, and serve.

10.3 Provençal Vegetable Soup

Cooking Time: 55 minutes

Serving Size: 6-8 servings

Calories: 338 kcal

Ingredients

- 2 cups of chopped onions
- 2 tbsp. of olive oil
- 2 cups of chopped leeks
- 3 cups of diced carrots
- 3 cups of diced boiling potatoes
- 1 1/2 tbsp. kosher salt
- 3 quarts canned broth or chicken stock
- 1 tsp. black pepper, freshly ground
- Grated Parmesan, to serve
- 1 tsp. saffron threads
- 4 ounces of spaghetti

- 1/2 pound of haricots verts
- 1 cup of Pistou

For Pistou:

- 1/4 cup of tomato paste
- 4 garlic cloves
- 24 basil leaves
- 1/2 cup of olive oil
- 1/2 cup of grated Parmesan

Method

1. Take a stockpot, and heat olive oil.
2. Add onions; saute for almost 10 minutes over the low heat.
3. Put leeks, carrots, potatoes, pepper, and salt; saute for almost 5 minutes over the medium heat.
4. Put saffron and chicken stock in it, and bring it to boil; simmer while keeping it uncovered for almost 30 minutes.
5. Add spaghetti and haricots verts, bring it to simmer; cook for almost 15 minutes.
6. For serving, mix 1/4 cup pistou in hot soup.
7. Add extra salt if required.
8. Serve with the more Pistou and Parmesan cheese.
9. To make Pistou, mix garlic, basil, Parmesan, and tomato paste in the food processor and blend.
10. Put it to the container, and add some olive oil over the top, the put on the lid.

10.4 Greek Tomato Soup with Orzo

Cooking Time: 25 minutes

Serving Size: 4 servings

Calories: 325 kcal

Ingredients

- 1 chopped medium onion
- 2 tbsp. olive oil
- 1-1/4 cups of orzo pasta, whole wheat and uncooked
- 3 cups of chicken broth
- 2 cans of coarsely chopped whole tomatoes
- 2 tsp. dried oregano
- 1/4 tsp. pepper
- 1/4 tsp. salt

Method

1. Take a large saucepan, and heat the oil over the medium heat.
2. Cook onion into it for 3 to 5 minutes, until tender.
3. Add orzo, and cook until toasted.
4. Add tomatoes, seasonings, and broth, and bring it to boil. Lower the heat, and simmer while keeping it covered for 15 to 20 minutes until orzo is completely tender.
5. Add basil and feta.
6. Serve and enjoy.

10.5 Zucchini Basil Soup with Lemon

Cooking Time: 25 minutes

Serving Size: 4 servings

Calories: 200 kcal

Ingredients

- 1 chopped medium onion
- 2 tbsp. of Butter
- 3-4 chopped cloves garlic
- 3 cups of chicken broth
- 4 chopped medium zucchini
- 1 lemon
- Sea salt, to taste
- 1/2 cup of packed basil
- Black pepper, to taste

Seasonings (optional):

- Pepper and Salt
- Lemon wedges
- Chopped Basil leaves
- Grated Parmesan cheese
- Yogurt
- Sour cream

Method

1. Take a stockpot, and melt butter over the medium heat.
2. Put onion in it; saute for almost 5 minutes, until translucent.
3. Put garlic; saute for almost 1-2 minutes.
4. Add zucchini; saute for almost 4 to 5 minutes.
5. Add lemon zest and chicken broth, and bring it to boil, lower the heat to gentle simmer, and cook for almost 10 minutes.
6. Put basil in it.
7. Puree with a blender.
8. Add pepper and salt and pepper.
9. Serve chilled or hot in the individual bowls; add additional seasonings.

10.6 Seafood Soup

Cooking Time: 50 minutes

Serving Size: 6 servings

Calories: 213 kcal

Ingredients

- 1 tbsp. olive oil
- 1 chopped green pepper
- 1 chopped small onion
- 2 chopped medium carrots
- 1 can of tomato sauce
- 1 minced garlic clove
- 1 can of undrained diced tomatoes
- 1 bay leaf

- 3/4 cup of chicken broth
- 1/2 tsp. dried oregano
- 1/4 tsp. pepper
- 1/4 tsp. dried basil
- 3/4 pound of salmon fillets
- 3 tbsp. of fresh parsley, minced
- 1/2 pound of medium shrimp, uncooked

Method

1. Take a saucepan, and heat the oil over the medium heat.
2. Put green pepper and onion in it, cook until tender.
3. Put garlic and carrots, and cook for 3 minutes.
4. Add tomato sauce, wine, seasonings, and tomatoes. Bring it to boil, and lower the heat, then simmer for 30 minutes.
5. Add salmon, parsley, and shrimp. Cook for 7 to 10 minutes.
6. Remove bay leaf.
7. Serve and enjoy.

10.7 Elegant Seafood Bisque

Cooking Time: 30 minutes

Serving Size: 10 servings

Calories: 254 kcal

Ingredients

- 1 chopped small onion
- 1 minced garlic clove
- 1/2 cup of flour
- 5 tbsp. olive oil
- 3 cups of chicken broth
- 2 cans of tomato sauce
- 1 tsp. of chicken bouillon granules
- 1 cup of white wine
- 2 cups of tomato juice
- 1/2 cup of fresh basil, chopped
- 1/2 tsp. salt
- 1 cup of frozen lobster chunks, uncooked
- 1 cup of whipping cream
- A dash of white pepper
- 1 cup of medium shrimp, uncooked

Method

1. In an oven, saute the garlic and onion in oil.
2. Add flour, and cook for almost 2 minutes.

3. Add bouillon and broth. Bring it to boil, and cook for almost 2 minutes.

4. Add tomato sauce, wine, juice, basil, pepper, and salt. Bring it to boil, then lower the heat.

5. Simmer while keeping it uncovered for almost 10 minutes.

6. Put cream into it, and heat through.

7. Take a skillet, and cook lobster and shrimp in the oil for around 5 minutes.

8. Put it in the soup, and garnish the servings with basil.

10.8 Lentil-Tomato Soup

Cooking Time: 55 minutes

Serving Size: 4 servings

Calories: 366 kcal

Ingredients

- 1 chopped white or yellow onion
- ¼ cup of olive oil
- 2 carrots, chopped
- 2 tsp. ground cumin
- 4 minced garlic cloves
- 1 tsp. curry powder
- 1 can of diced tomatoes
- ½ tsp. dried thyme
- 1 cup green or brown lentils
- 2 cups of water
- 4 cups of vegetable broth

- 1 tsp. salt
- 1-2 tbsp. lemon juice, to taste
- Black pepper, to taste
- 1 Pinch red pepper flakes
- 1 cup chopped kale

Method

1. Take a skillet, and heat oil.
2. Once oil shimmers, add chopped carrot and onion in it, cook until onion is softened, for almost 5 minutes.
3. Put garlic, curry powder, thyme, and cumin in it, and cook for almost 30 seconds.
4. Add diced tomatoes; cook for some minutes.
5. Add pepper flakes, and season with black pepper.
6. Bring it to boil by raising heat, then cover pot, and lower heat for maintaining simmer.
7. Cook for almost 25-30 minutes until lentils are cooked.
8. Transfer two cups soup to the blender, and purée until smooth.
9. Return it in the pot.
10. Add chopped greens; cook for almost 5 minutes until greens are softened.
11. Remove pot from heat; stir in lemon juice.
12. Season with pepper, salt, pepper, and lemon juice if required.
13. Serve hot, and enjoy.

Chapter 11: Mediterranean Desserts Recipes

11.1 Strawberries with Balsamic Vinegar

Cooking Time: 1 hour 10 minutes

Serving Size: 6servings

Calories: 59 kcal

Ingredients

- ¼ tsp. black pepper
- 2 tbsp. balsamic vinegar
- 16 ounces of fresh strawberries
- ¼ cup of white sugar

Method

1. Place the strawberries in the bowl, drizzle vinegar on the top.
2. Add sugar.
3. Mix well, and cover.
4. Set aside at the room temperature for about one hour.
5. Before serving, add pepper on top of the berries.

11.2 Nectarines and Berries in Prosecco

Cooking Time: 30 minutes

Serving Size: 6-8 servings

Calories: 288 kcal

Ingredients

- 10 ounces of strawberries
- 10 ounces of raspberries or blackberries
- 1 pound of nectarines
- 1 tbsp. of orange liqueur
- ¼ cup of sugar
- 1 tbsp. fresh mint, chopped
- 1 cup of chilled prosecco
- ¼ tsp. lemon zest, grated

Method

1. Mix blackberries, nectarines, strawberries, sugar, mint, lemon zest, and orange liqueur in a large bowl.
2. Set aside at the room temperature until fruits release their juices for almost 10-15 minutes.
3. Before serving, add prosecco on top of fruits, and season with sugar if desired.
4. Serve.

11.3 Watermelon Cups

Cooking Time: 25 minutes

Serving Size: 16 appetizer

Calories: 7 kcal

Ingredients

- 16 watermelon cubes
- 1/3 cup of cucumber, finely chopped
- 5 tsp. of red onion, finely chopped
- 2 tsp. of fresh mint, minced
- 2 tsp. of fresh cilantro, minced
- 1 tsp. Of lime juice

Method

1. Use a spoon, and scoop out center of the watermelon cubes.
2. In a bowl, mix remaining ingredients, and spoon in the watermelon cubes.
3. Serve and enjoy!

11.4 Honey Cinnamon Rollups

Cooking Time: 50 minutes

Serving Size: 24 servings

Calories: 132 kcal

Ingredients

- 1/4 cup of sugar
- 2 cups of toasted ground walnuts
- 2 tsp. ground cinnamon
- 1/2 cup of melted butter
- 12 sheets phyllo dough, frozen

For Syrup:

- 1 tbsp. lemon juice
- 1/2 cup of sugar
- 1/2 cup of honey
- 1/2 cup of water

Method

1. Preheat the oven to 350° F.

2. Mix walnuts, cinnamon, and sugar.

3. Place one phyllo dough on the waxed paper, and apply butter.

4. Put another phyllo sheet, and apply butter.

5. Add walnut mixture.

6. Use a waxed paper, and roll it up tightly.

7. Transfer the rolls to the greased baking dish, and repeat it with the remaining walnut mixture and phyllo dough.

8. Bake for about 14 16 minutes, until brown.

9. Take a saucepan, and combine the syrup ingredients, and bring it to boil.

10. Lower the heat, and simmer for 5 minutes, then let it cool for almost 10 minutes.

11. Add syrup to cinnamon rolls; sprinkle with walnut mixture.

12. Serve and enjoy!

11.5 Baklava Cheesecake

Cooking Time: 1 hour 50 minutes

Serving Size: 16 servings

Calories: 351 kcal

Ingredients

- 2 sheets of phyllo dough
- 1/3 cup melted butter
- 1 cup of walnuts, finely chopped
- 1/4 cup of sugar
- 1/4 tsp. ground nutmeg
- 1/2 tsp. ground cinnamon
- 2 packages of softened cream cheese
- 1/8 tsp. of ground allspice
- 2/3 cup of honey
- 1 carton of mascarpone cheese
- 1/4 cup of 2% milk
- 3 lightly beaten eggs, at room temperature
- 3 tbsp. flour

For Garnishing:

- 3 rosemary sprigs
- 1/2 cup of fresh cranberries
- 3 tbsp. corn syrup
- 1/4 cup of sugar

Method

1. Preheat the oven to 425° F.

2. Put a sheet of the phyllo dough in the greased pan, and apply butter.

3. Put layers of all phyllo sheets, and apply butter on each layer.

4. Put in the baking pan.

5. Take a bowl, and mix walnuts, spices, and sugar.

6. Bake for 5 to 7 minutes, until edges have browned.

7. Lower the oven heat to 325°.

8. Take a bowl, and beat the mascarpone cheese and cream cheese at the low speed.

9. Add milk, honey, and flour.

10.   Pour in eggs, and beat on the low speed.

11.   Add crust, and put pan back in the baking pan, then bake for 50 to 60 minutes.

12.   Let it cook for 1 hour and refrigerate overnight.

13.   For garnishing, take corn syrup in the bowl, and microwave while keeping it uncovered for 10 seconds.

14.   Brush the corn syrup over each side of the rosemary, and put on the waxed paper.

15.   Add one tbsp. of sugar.

16.   Toss the cranberries in the syrup, and put remaining sugar in the bowl.

17.   Pour in cranberries, and mix well.

18.   Place it on the waxed paper; let stand for almost 1 hour.

19.   Before serving, add cranberries and sugared rosemary on the cheesecake.

11.6 Fig and Honey Yoghurt

Cooking Time: 5 minutes

Serving Size: 1 serving

Calories: 208 kcal

Ingredients

- 3 sliced dried figs
- ⅔ cup of plain yogurt
- 2 tsp. honey

Method

1. Put yogurt in the bowl.
2. Add honey and figs.
3. Serve and enjoy.

Conclusion

Many diverse countries border the Mediterranean Sea, including Italy, Spain, and France, Greece, Israel, Turkey, Syria, Lebanon, Egypt, Morocco, Tunisia, Libya, and Algeria. It makes it interesting as there is not one single diet that defines the Mediterranean region. The Mediterranean diet is all about the common things in these cuisines, i.e., a daily consumption of fruits and vegetables, lentils and beans, whole grains, seafood, and olive oil. It is the overriding principle while writing the cookbook. Adopting the Mediterranean way of eating requires an amazing shift in eating behaviors. The food portion is small.

Consume lots of fruits and vegetables every day. The Mediterranean diet planning is mainly based on the available vegetables to celebrate the seasonality. Figure out what is local and seasonal, you will always get the better-quality ingredients. Meat is not that much used in Mediterranean diet, so beans, nuts, whole grains, and lentils are the significant sources to provide your daily protein. Whole grains provide the essential nutrients, like antioxidants. Consuming the fresh seafood is important among the countries bordering Mediterranean Sea. Various health benefits associated with eating fish and shrimp include low-calorie count, omega-3 fatty acids, and the saturated fat.

Dishes that have a low quantity of meat are a significant part of the Mediterranean diet. It is customary among people from various regions to include fresh fruit at the end of the meal. Cookies and cakes are not usually eaten on the daily basis. They are saved for some special celebrations and family gatherings. To keep your diet's emphasis more on the low quantity of the saturated fat, replace the butter in your cakes, pastries, and cookies with the olive oil, wherever possible.

Keep in mind, diversity and balance are the hallmarks of the Mediterranean diet, so serve dishes having a variety of tastes, temperatures, and textures. Numerous dishes taste best both ways, i.e., warm and cold. It prepares you for getting rid of the pressure to prepare a hot meal to serve. The recipes given in this book will make your work easy. It offers you an easy way to match and your recipes.

All these Mediterranean dishes are worth to be tried. Some dishes are quick to make, but some will take time. When you have the final dish on your table, you will be satisfied with all the effort you put in. Do not hesitate to customize a little bit as per your preferences and health goals. People have been becoming more health-conscious nowadays, and that is a pretty impressive thing to see in this modern world. To have a healthy lifestyle and to attain your goal of losing weight, Mediterranean diet has become one of the most practiced fitness trends across the globe. Its popularity has been increasing with time. Mediterranean diet is famously called a diet plan or a specific eating pattern. Research has shown that Mediterranean diet can prove to be one of the most potent tools for losing. It can effectively support you in fighting your belly fat as well as improving your health in numerous ways. Various studies have claimed that it improves brain health, decreases the risk of diabetes, cancer, and heart diseases. It can even help in living a long and healthy life.

This book has some fantastic recipes to choose from. You can find recipes for all the season. Whether it is summer, winter, autumn, or spring, you will find some amazing recipes for your breakfast, lunch, and dinner meals. All season offers the best time to make some tasty recipes and making the most of fresh and healthy ingredients of these seasons. You can also add and enjoy some salad and snack recipes in your diet plan to fulfill your small appetite.

Choose your lunch and dinner recipes very carefully because that makes a considerable part of your diet. You can also enjoy some desserts. Make the best plan for yourself to eat for a healthy lifestyle and weight-loss with the help of this book.

Pescatarian

COOKBOOK

70 Easy Recipes For Mediterranean Dishes With Fish And Seafood

Emma Yang

Contents

CHAPTER 4: HEALTHY FISH AND SEAFOOD SOUP RECIPES 389

Introduction

Cutting meat from your eating regimen may appear to be an immense change. Adopting a Pescatarian diet is quite easy. The key is to never cause yourself to feel like you are forfeiting something or limiting yourself. A Pescatarian diet avoids red meat, poultry, sheep, and pork. You will find vegetables, grains, natural products, beans, cheddar, eggs, and yogurt in a Pescatarian diet. It puts an accentuation on fish and shellfish as a rich source of protein.

Pescatarian diet leads to healthy eating habits and a lifestyle. How we feed our bodies affects our general prosperity. A plant-based eating regimen based on healthy food sources and a fish-driven eating routine loaded with protein has many advantages because of the collaboration of plants and fish.

A Pescatarian diet is protein-stuffed and rich in omega-3s. It decreases congestive cardiovascular breakdown and coronary illness. Sleek fish, specifically (think sardines, mackerel, or salmon), are stacked in unsaturated fats. It advances sufficient omega-3s. Eating fish and seafood expands your admission of omega-3s, which may offer various advantages—from lessening aggravation in the body to advancing cerebrum wellbeing. Notwithstanding greasy fish, chia seeds, flaxseeds, or pecans are incredible plant-based wellsprings of omega-3s.

An eating regimen wealthy in fish and seafood would help supply this imperative supplement. Fish offers a wellspring of complete protein. The intake of Pescatarian food sources can guarantee ideal protein consumption.

Likewise, in contrast to red meat, it is low in soaked fat and better for your heart and pulse hazard. If you are worried about heart wellbeing or have a background marked by coronary illness in your family, you may profit by going Pescatarian.

People choose a Pescatarian diet to lessen their ecological effects by eating fish and plant-based food varieties. It can diminish effects on water biological systems, territory obliteration, undermined species, and overfishing.

The 'Pescatarian Cookbook' offers you 70 healthy recipes that you can have for your Pescatarian diet. The Pescatarian Cookbook is your go-to reference to make the Pescatarian diet a supportable and fulfilling way of life.

Chapter 1: Healthy Fish and Seafood Breakfast Recipes

In a Pescatarian diet, breakfast foods easily fit in the meal plan. Here are some of the healthy and tasty fish and seafood breakfast recipes that you can easily make at home with any difficulty:

1.1 Smoked Salmon Baked Eggs in Avocado

Preparation Time: 10 minutes

Cooking Time: 15 minutes

Serving: 6

Ingredients:

- 3 avocado
- 6 eggs
- 3 slices smoked salmon
- 1 tbsp. of finely chopped Chives
- 1 pinch cayenne pepper
- Toasted bread, for serving

Instructions:

1. Heat oven to 180^0C.
2. Cut avocados. Put them onto a baking plate.
3. Add salmon to each, and afterward add the egg yolks. Beat the egg whites.

4. Add cayenne pepper and heat for ten minutes, or until the whites have set. Disperse over the chives and a touch of cayenne. Present with toasted bread.

1.2 Smoked Salmon and Dill Waffles

Preparation Time: 40 minutes

Cooking Time: 40 minutes

Serving: 4

Ingredients:

- For Dill Waffles:
- 1 tbsp. granulated sugar
- 1/2 tbsp. baking powder
- 1/2 tsp. table salt
- 3/4 tsp. black pepper
- 1 egg
- 1/4 cup of melted unsalted butter
- 2 tbsp. milk
- 3/4 cup of seltzer
- 2 tbsp. of fresh dill
- For Poached Eggs:
- 4 large eggs
- 2 tsp. white vinegar
- For Serving:

- 8 slices of smoked salmon
- 1/2 cup of Hollandaise Sauce
- Fresh dill, for garnishing

Instructions:

1. In a bowl, whisk together flour, baking powder, sugar, pepper, and salt.
2. Mix egg yolk, dill, milk, seltzer, and butter.
3. In a bowl, beat the egg.
4. Crease egg whites into the waffle maker just until streaks vanish.
5. Preheat the stove to 200^0F.
6. Preheat and add a few drops of oil to your waffle iron.
7. Cook waffles until colored and fresh.
8. Transfer waffles in a layer to a wire rack-lined preparing sheet and spot in the oven to keep warm.
9. Fill a bowl with hot water and cover to keep warm.
10. Fill a ten to twelve-inch width, a straight-sided dish with around two cups of water.
11. Mix in vinegar.
12. Cook the eggs for three to four minutes.
13. Move eggs to the bowl of heated water while you make the hollandaise.
14. Spot two cuts of smoked salmon on top of a warm waffle. Eliminate eggs from the warm water with a spoon.

15.   Add the eggs to salmon.

16.   Add hollandaise sauce.

17.   Add dill, and serve.

1.3 Simple Shrimp Scramble

Preparation Time: 15 minutes

Cooking Time: 10 minutes

Serving: 4

Ingredients:

- 1 onion
- 1/4 cup of green pepper
- 1 minced garlic clove
- 3 tbsp. butter, divided
- 1 package of frozen salad shrimp, cooked
- 8 eggs
- 1/2 tsp. salt
- 1/4 tsp. pepper
- 1 cup of cheddar cheese

Instructions:

1. In a huge skillet, sauté the green pepper, onion, and garlic in one tbsp. of butter. Mix in shrimp. Take out in a bowl and keep warm.

2. In a similar skillet, dissolve the remaining butter over medium heat. Add eggs; cook, and mix until totally set. Mix in the shrimp blend, pepper and salt.

3. Sprinkle with cheddar.

4. Cover and let it set for three to five minutes.

1.4 Bacon Lobster Omelet

Preparation Time: 10 minutes

Cooking Time: 10 minutes

Serving: 1

Ingredients:

- 1/4 cup lobster meat
- 1 1/2 cup sour cream
- 1 tsp. of dijon mustard
- 2 eggs
- 1 tbsp. Of water
- 1 tbsp. green onions
- 1/2 tsp. Of dried tarragon
- 1 tsp. of butter
- Salt and pepper, to taste

Instructions:

1. In a small bowl, add sour cream and mustard.

2. In a medium bowl, combine green onions, one egg, tarragon and pepper and salt.

3. Add butter in a skillet, add egg, and then blend and cook till set.

4. Heat butter in a skillet, add the mixture of egg and cook till set.

5. Add sour cream in egg mixture. Blend it and add the lobster meat.

6. Crease another portion of eggs over the lobster side.

7. Serve while warm.

1.5 Seafood Bake with Crispy Hash Brown Topping

Preparation Time: 20 minutes

Cooking Time: 20 minutes

Serving: 4

Ingredients:

- 1 cup of sour cream
- 1 tbsp. Of cornstarch
- 2 tsp. Of lemon zest
- 1 tbsp. Of Dijon mustard
- Pepper, to taste
- Kosher salt, to taste
- 1 1/2 lb. Of mixed seafood
- 1 package of leaf spinach

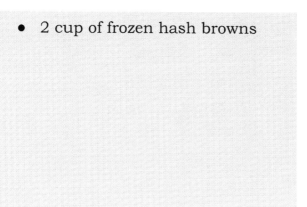

- 2 cup of frozen hash browns

Instructions:

1. Heat stove to 425^0 F. In a huge bowl, whisk together the sour cream, mustard, cornstarch, lemon zing, and half tsp. each pepper and salt.

2. Add the fish to the cream blend.

3. Add spinach into the mixture of fish.

4. Split between four shallow, one-cup preparing dishes.

5. Add hash browns and brush with olive oil. Cook for twenty to twenty-five minutes.

6. Serve and enjoy.

1.6 Lobster Breakfast Sandwich

Preparation Time: 5 minutes

Cooking Time: 10 minutes

Serving: 4

Ingredients:

- 4 brioche of sandwich buns
- 1 creamy egg
- 1 tsp. of olive oil
- 18 asparagus spears
- 4 lobster tails
- 1 tsp. of chopped fresh chives

Instructions:

1. Part out arranged velvety fried eggs on brioche sandwich buns.
2. Put asparagus sticks softly in olive oil.
3. Put it on the fried eggs, then top with chilled split lobster tail. Sprinkle chives to taste and serve.

1.7 Shrimp and Spinach Omelette

Preparation Time: 5 minutes

Cooking Time: 5 minutes

Serving: 2

Ingredients:

- 10 shrimp
- 6 large eggs
- 1 sprig parsley
- 4 tomatoes
- 1/4 onion
- 1 handful of spinach
- 1 tbsp. of sriracha salt
- 1/4 tsp. of cayenne

Instructions:

1. Cut onion and grape tomatoes.
2. Add onion and salt in a pan.
3. Simultaneously, place the grape tomatoes to broil a bit.
4. When the onions are cooked, toss in spinach, let it wither.
5. Add shrimp.
6. Cook eggs and cover the dish, so the omelet cooks well.
7. Cook for around six to eight minutes.
8. When a slim film of white is covering the yolks, eggs are prepared.
9. Add parsley over it.
10. Serve and enjoy.

1.8 Brunchy Fish and Waffles

Preparation Time: 10 minutes

Cooking Time: 20 minutes

Serving: 4

Ingredients:

- 1 package of Fish Fillets
- 4 Belgian Waffles
- 4 eggs
- 2 tbsp. Of unsalted butter
- One pinch of pepper and pinch of salt
- 1 cup maple syrup
- 1 tbsp. Of fish sauce
- 1/2 cup of honey
- 1 thinly sliced jalapeño
- 1 inch slice fresh ginger
- 2 tsp. Of orange zest
- 1/4 tsp. Of white pepper

Instructions:

1. In a pan over medium-low heat, add butter, maple syrup, fish sauce, honey, ginger, and orange zest, and cook for ten minutes.

2. Let it cool while preparing both fish and waffles as per instructions on the package.

3. Heat butter in a pan.

4. Add eggs and cook until whites have completely set—season with pepper and salt.

5. For serving, place one toasted waffle on a plate. Top with one egg. Stack two fish filets on top of the egg, inclining toward each other to try not to break the yolk.

6. Sprinkle some Jalapeño Maple syrup, and serve.

1.9 Smoked Salmon Hash

Preparation Time: 10 minutes

Cooking Time: 10 minutes

Serving: 2

Ingredients:

- 2 tbsp. olive oil
- 3 red potatoes
- 1 chopped yellow onion
- 1 bell pepper, green
- Kosher salt and black pepper
- 2 tsp. fresh chives, thinly sliced
- 1 1/2 tsp. Of lemon juice
- 2/3 cup sour cream
- 1/2 tsp. Of Dijon mustard
- One salmon fillet

Instructions:

1. Heat the oil in a nonstick skillet over a medium-high flame. Add the onions, potatoes, chime pepper, pepper, and salt, and cook while regularly mixing, until earthy colored, around ten minutes.

2. Cook until the potatoes are delicate, around fifteen minutes more; season to taste with pepper and salt.

3. In the meantime, put sour cream, one tbsp. chives, half tbsp. lemon juice, mustard, half tsp. of salt, and one-eighth tsp. of pepper.

4. Add salmon and one tbsp. lemon juice and keep cooking until warmed through, around two minutes more.

5. Move the hash to plates. Add the one tbsp. of chives and serve with sour cream.

6. Present it with a poached egg on top.

1.10 Alaska Salmon Frittata

Preparation Time: 20 minutes

Cooking Time: 14

Serving: 8

Ingredients:

- 12 beaten eggs
- 1 tbsp. olive oil
- 1 cup of sliced sweet peppers
- 2 1/2 cups broccoli florets
- 1/2 cup of diced onion
- 1 cup salmon
- 1/2 cup frozen peas
- Ground pepper, to taste
- Salt, to taste

Instructions:

1. Preheat broiler to 375^{0}F
2. Add the broccoli florets, diced onion, cut small-scale sweet peppers in oil.
3. Season with ocean salt and ground dark pepper.
4. Mix in the frozen peas and smoked salmon.
5. Pour in the beaten eggs. Mix well.

6. Keep cooking the frittata, without blending, over the burner for an extra sixty seconds just until the external edge of the frittata starts to set.

7. Place the hot skillet on the stove; cook for ten to fourteen minutes, just until the eggs are set.

8. Allow the frittata to set for five minutes before cutting. Serve hot or cold.

Chapter 2: Healthy Fish and Seafood Lunch and Dinner

Pescatarian lunch and dinner recipes are full of healthy proteins and flavors. There are many varieties of fish and seafood recipes that can be eaten during lunch and dinner time. Following are given some of these recipes that you can try at home:

2.1 Furikake Salmon Bowls

Preparation Time: 10 minutes

Cooking Time: 20 minutes

Serving: 2

Ingredients:

- For Salmon:
- 1 to 2 tbsp. sesame oil
- 1 Pinch pepper, salt and chili flakes
- 8 to 10 ounces of salmon
- 4 ounces of shiitake mushrooms
- For Sauce:
- 3 tbsp. Of soy sauce
- 3 tbsp. Mirin
- 1 tbsp. Furikake
- 1/2 to 2 cups of cooked rice
- 2 bunches of cabbage
- 1 large avocado
- For toppings:
- Scallions
- Cucumber
- Furikake
- Stew pieces

Instructions:

1. Mix mirin and soy sauce in a small bowl.

2. Heat sesame oil in a huge skillet over medium-high heat. Season with pepper and salt.

3. Add the mushrooms and salmon and cook. Turn the heat off, allowing the skillet to cool somewhat.

4. Add sauce over the salmon and mushrooms.

5. Divide rice between two dishes. Sprinkle it with furikake.

6. Put cabbage, avocado wedges, and some other veggies in the bowl.

7. Top with burned salmon and mushrooms, and sprinkle it with Furikake, spooning the excess sauce over the avocado and cabbage.

8. Serve immediately.

2.2   Pan-Seared   Halibut   over   Lemony Zucchini Noodles

Preparation Time: 30 minutes

Cooking Time: 30 minutes

Serving: 2

Ingredients:

- 8 to 10 ounces halibut
- 1 smashed garlic clove
- 1 to 2 tbsp. olive oil
- Pepper, to taste
- Salt, to taste
- For Noodles:
- 1 tbsp. olive oil
- 1 thinly sliced fat shallot
- 3 chopped garlic cloves
- 12 to 16 ounces of zucchini noodles
- pepper, to taste
- Salt, to taste
- 2 tsp. lemon zest
- ½ cup of chopped Italian parsley
- 1 tbsp. Of lemon juice

Instructions:

1. Preheat oven to 375 F. Add garlic cloves in the tray.

2. Season fish with salt and pepper.

3. Place in the oven for about three to six minutes.

4. In a skillet, heat more oil over medium heat and add shallots and garlic, blending until mellowed and fragrant, around three minutes.

5. Add zucchini noodles and season with pepper and salt. Sauté until noodles mellow, around four minutes.

6. Add lemon zing, new parsley, and a crush of lemon. Add salt and lemon. Split between two dishes and top with the halibut.

7. Top with cherry tomatoes, bean stew chips, and pecorino cheddar.

2.3 Rum-Glazed Shrimp

Preparation Time: 10 minutes

Cooking Time: 35 minutes

Serving: 4

Ingredients:

- 1 1/2 lb. Of peeled shrimp
- 3 tbsp. Of olive oil
- 1/3 cup of chili sauce
- 1/4 cup of soy sauce
- 1/4 cup of Rum
- 2 minced cloves garlic
- 1 lime
- 1/2 tsp. Of red pepper flakes
- 1 thinly sliced green onion, to garnish

Instructions:

1. Add shrimp in a bowl.
2. In a bowl, add olive oil, sweet bean stew sauce, soy sauce, rum, garlic, lime juice, and red pepper drops.
3. Let marinate in the cooler for fifteen to thirty minutes.
4. Add shrimp in the oil and cook on one side for around two minutes.

5. Add green onions and serve.

2.4 Air Fryer Salmon

Preparation Time: 7 minutes

Cooking Time: 12 minutes

Serving: 5

Ingredients:

- 2 wild salmon fillets
- 2 tsps. of tsp. avocado oil
- 2 tsps. of paprika
- Black pepper, to taste
- Salt, to taste
- Lemon wedges

Instructions:

1. Eliminate any bones from salmon and set aside for one hour.
2. Rub each fillet with olive oil and season with paprika, salt and pepper.
3. Put fillets in the air fryer at 390 degrees for seven minutes.
4. When the time is over, check fillets with a fork to ensure they are done.

2.5 Garlicky Shrimp Alfredo Bake

Preparation Time: 20 minutes

Cooking Time: 20 minutes

Serving: 4

Ingredients:

- 12 ounces of penne
- 3 minced cloves garlic
- 1 lb. Of raw shrimp
- 3 tbsp. Of divided butter
- 2 tbsp. Of chopped parsley
- Kosher salt, to taste
- 2 tbsp. of flour
- 1/4 cup of chicken broth
- 3/4 cup of milk
- 1cup of shredded mozzarella
- 1/4 cup of grated Parmesan
- Black pepper, to taste
- 1 cup of chopped tomatoes

Instructions:

1. Preheat the stove to 350°F.

2. In a huge pot of water, prepare penne as per instructions on the package.

3. Add shrimp, garlic, and parsley in the oil and season with salt. Cook until the shrimp is pink.

4. Add two tablespoon butter and flour and cook for about one minute.

5. Put milk and stock in it. Mix in mozzarella and Parmesan, pepper, and with salt.

6. Add tomatoes, cooked penne, and shrimp, and throw until consolidated.

7. Sprinkle with mozzarella and two tbsp. parmesan and heat until melted, five to seven minutes.

8. Sprinkle parsley before serving.

2.6 Oysters Rockefeller

Preparation Time: 15 minutes

Cooking Time: 1 hour

Serving: 2 dozen

Ingredients:

- 1 finely chopped medium onion
- 1/2 cup of cubed butter
- 1 package of fresh spinach
- 1 cup of Romano cheese
- 1 tbsp. lemon juice
- 1/8 tsp. pepper
- 2 pounds of kosher salt
- 3 dozen of fresh oysters

Instructions:

1. In a skillet, sauté onion. Add spinach; cook and mix until withered. Eliminate from the heat; mix in cheddar, lemon juice and pepper.

2. Spread salt into two ungreased heating dishes. Add oysters in the base shell.

3. Add salt in the clamshells.

4. Top each with two teaspoons of spinach.

5. Prepare, uncovered, at 450° F until oysters are fully cooked, six to eight minutes. Serve.

2.7 Bruschetta Salmon

Preparation Time: 10 minutes

Cooking Time: 15 minutes

Serving: 4

Ingredients:

- 4 salmon fillets
- 1 tsp. Of dried oregano
- Kosher salt, to taste
- Black pepper, to taste
- 2 tbsp. Of olive oil
- 3 minced cloves garlic
- 2 minced shallots
- 3 cup of cherry tomatoes
- 1/2 lemon
- 1/4 cup of basil
- Parmesan, to serve
- Balsamic glaze
- Toppings:
- Tomatoes, red onion, avocado, jalapeño peppers, and coriander sprigs

Instructions:

1. Season salmon with oregano, salt and pepper.

2. Add salmon in the heated oil and cook for around six minutes.

3. Flip and cook for six minutes until the salmon is misty. Move to a plate.

4. Add remaining tablespoon olive oil to skillet, mix in garlic and shallots. Cook until garlic is fragrant.

5. Add tomatoes and season with salt and pepper.

6. Add lemon juice.

7. Serve salmon with tomato blend spooned on top. Top with basil and Parmesan, sprinkle with balsamic coating.

2.8 Creamed Spinach Stuffed Salmon

Preparation Time: 10 minutes

Cooking Time: 20 minutes

Serving: 2

Ingredients:

- For Salmon:
- 4 salmon fillets
- Pepper and salt, to season
- 2 tbsp. lemon juice
- 2 tbsp. olive oil
- 1 tbsp. unsalted butter
- For Filling:
- 4 ounces cream cheese
- 4 ounces frozen spinach
- 1/4 cup of parmesan cheese
- 2 tsp. minced garlic
- Pepper and salt, to taste
- For Garlic Butter:
- 1 tbsp. unsalted butter
- 1 tbsp. minced garlic
- 1 tbsp. lemon juice

Instructions:

1. Season the two sides with salt, pepper, one tablespoon olive oil, and lemon juice.

2. In a medium-sized bowl, add the spinach, cream cheddar, parmesan cheddar and garlic.

3. Add pepper and salt.

4. Heat butter and oil in a skillet over medium heat.

5. Add the salmon and fry for around six to seven minutes.

6. Cook the other side for around six to seven minutes.

7. Add the garlic and lemon juice; sauté until garlic is fragrant (around 30 seconds). Present with the salmon.

2.9 Shrimp Alfredo

Preparation Time: 30 minutes

Cooking Time: 10 minutes

Serving: 6

Ingredients:

- 10 ounces of fettuccine pasta
- 5 tbsp. butter
- 1 cup of heavy cream
- 3/4 cup of parmesan cheese
- Pepper, to taste
- Salt, to taste
- 1 pound of shrimp
- 1 tsp. minced garlic
- 2 tbsp. chopped parsley

Instructions:

1. Cook the pasta in salted water.
2. Add four tablespoons butter in a pot over medium-low heat.
3. Add the cream and stew for four to five minutes or until just thickened.
4. Add parmesan cheddar, blending consistently until cheddar has softened.
5. Add pepper and salt.
6. Heat one tablespoon butter in a huge skillet over medium-high heat.

7. Add the shrimp and season with salt and pepper.

8. Cook the shrimp for three to four minutes until shrimps are pink and obscure.

9. Add the garlic to the dish and cook for an extra thirty seconds.

10. Add pasta and alfredo sauce. Put the shrimp on top and sprinkle with parsley, and serve.

2.10 Baked Swordfish

Preparation Time: 5 minutes

Cooking Time: 22 minutes

Serving: 1

Ingredients:

- ½ pound of swordfish steak
- 2 tbsp. Of olive oil
- 1 tsp. Of garlic powder
- 2 lemons
- Sea salt, to taste
- 2-4 chopped green onions
- 2-4 tbsp. Of white wine
- Lemon slices, to garnish

Instructions:

1. Preheat stove at 375 degrees F (190.6 degrees C).

2. Utilize a profound, heating dish sufficiently huge to hold the swordfish steak.

First for the Marinade:

3.   On the lower part of the heating dish, add a tablespoon of olive oil, and one entire lemon, sprinkle with half teaspoon of ground garlic powder.

4.   Place swordfish steak on top of the main layer of marinade.

5.   Sprinkle on top of the swordfish steak with some additional virgin olive oil, the leftover garlic powder and lemon.

6.   Sprinkle some ocean salt on top of the steak. Add green onions. Put white wine on top, and let it sit for fifteen minutes to marinate.

7.   Bake for eighteen to twenty two minutes, or until swordfish is white or completely cooked.

8.   Add lemon sauce over the swordfish steak and serve.

2.11 Mussels with Tomatoes and Garlic

Preparation Time: 10 minutes

Cooking Time: 20 minutes

Serving: 4

Ingredients:

- 2 tbsp. of butter
- 1 chopped onion
- 3 minced cloves garlic
- 1 can of diced tomatoes
- 1/2 cup white wine
- 2 tbsp. Of chopped parsley
- Kosher salt, to taste
- Black pepper, to taste
- 2 lb. Of mussels
- Grilled bread, to serve
- 1 tsp. Kosher salt

Instructions:

1. In a pot over medium-low heat, warm the butter. Add onion and cook for five minutes. Add garlic and cook until fragrant.

2. Add diced tomatoes, wine, and parsley—season with salt and pepper.

3. Add mussels and stew until all shells are open.

4. Top with more parsley and present with barbecued bread.

2.12 Easy Shrimp Fajitas

Preparation Time: 5 minutes

Cooking Time: 12 minutes

Serving: 4

Ingredients:

· 1 tbsp. Of vegetable oil

· 2 cups of sliced red bell peppers yellow, orange, and red

· 1 thinly sliced onion

· 2 tsp. chili powder

· 1/2 tsp. ground cumin

· 1/4 tsp. garlic powder

· 1/4 tsp. onion powder

· 1/2 tsp. smoked paprika

· 2 tbsp. chopped cilantro

· 1 pound of large shrimp

· Lime wedges, to serve

· 4 tortillas

· Fajita toppings

· Pepper, to taste

· Salt, to taste

Instructions:

1. Heat the oil in a large pan over high heat.
2. Add the onion and peppers.
3. Season the vegetables with salt and pepper.
4. In a small bowl, mix stew powder, cumin, garlic powder, onion powder, smoked paprika, and salt and pepper to taste.
5. Add the shrimp and sprinkle the flavoring mix over the shrimp and vegetables.
6. Cook until shrimp are pink and misty.
7. Add cilantro and serve. Add lime wedges.
8. Serve the flour tortillas.

2.13 BBQ Salmon and Brussels Bake

Preparation Time: 10 minutes

Cooking Time: 20 minutes

Serving: 8

Ingredients:

- 2 tbsp. Of brown sugar
- 1 tsp. Of garlic powder
- 1 tsp. of onion powder
- 3 1/2 pounds of salmon
- 1 tsp. Of smoked paprika

- 1 1/4 lb. Of Brussels sprouts
- Chives

Instructions:

1. Preheat broiler to 450°F. Line two sheets with foil.

2. Mix sugar, one teaspoon garlic powder, one teaspoon onion powder, one teaspoon smoked paprika, and two tablespoons olive oil.

3. Divide one-fourth pound of Brussels sprouts.

4. Put sprouts on one sheet and add one tablespoon olive oil, one-fourth teaspoon salt, and one-fourth teaspoon pepper.

5. Cook sprouts for five minutes. While sprouts broil, prepare salmon.

6. Cut one side of salmon into ten filets. Brush the flavor, rub all over the salmon, and sprinkle salmon with one teaspoon of salt.

7. Mix Brussels.

8. Add salmon to the stove and cook for fifteen minutes.

9. Serve salmon with Brussels sprouts. Add chives on top.

2.14 Shrimp Fried Rice

Preparation Time: 30 minutes

Cooking Time: 10 minutes

Serving: 4

Ingredients:

- 3 tbsp. soy sauce
- 1 tbsp. sesame oil
- 1/2 tsp. ginger powder
- 1/2 tsp. white pepper
- 2 tbsp. olive oil
- 1 pound shrimp
- Kosher salt, to taste
- Black pepper, to taste
- 2 minced cloves garlic
- 1 diced onion
- 2 grated carrots
- 1/2 cup of frozen corn
- 1/2 cup of frozen peas
- 3 cups of cooked rice
- 2 diced green onions

Instructions:

1. In a small bowl, whisk together soy sauce, sesame oil, ginger powder, and white pepper.

2. Add shrimp in oil, and cook, until pink, around two to three minutes; add pepper and salt to taste.

3. Add garlic and onion to the skillet, and cook for around three to four minutes.

4. Mix carrots, corn, and peas, and cook, for three to four minutes.

5. Mix rice, green onions, and soy sauce combination. Cook for two minutes. Mix in shrimp.

6. Serve.

2.15 Fish Stick Tacos

Preparation Time: 10 minutes

Cooking Time: 30 minutes

Serving: 4

Ingredients:

- For Fish Stick Tacos:
- 16 Fish Sticks
- 8 corn tortillas
- 1/2 tsp. of garlic powder
- 1/2 tsp. Of smoked paprika
- 1/2 tsp. of onion powder
- 1/2 tsp. of cumin
- 1/2 tsp. of kosher salt
- 1/4 tsp. of cayenne pepper
- Cooking spray
- For Taco Slaw:
- 2 cups of purple cabbage
- 2 cups of shredded carrots
- 1/4 cup of cilantro chopped
- 3 chopped green onions
- 1/4 cup of pickled jalapeños
- 2 tbsp. of Greek yogurt
- 2 tsp. Of pickled jalapeño
- 1 lime

- · Sea salt, to taste
- · Pepper, to taste

Instructions:

1. Preheat the oven to 450 degrees F.
2. Add sliced cabbage, carrots, salted jalapeños, cilantro, and green onions to a medium bowl.
3. In a small bowl, add Greek yogurt, salted jalapeño juice, and the juice of one lime.
4. Add salt and pepper to taste.
5. Put aside.

For Fish Sticks Tacos:

6. Add garlic powder, onion powder, smoked paprika, cumin, salt, and cayenne pepper into a small bowl. Mix well.

7. Spray oil on the baking dish, and put sixteen fish sticks on it.

8. Place it in 450 degrees preheated stove for eighteen minutes. Flip it carefully.

9. While the fish sticks are preparing, heat eight corn tortillas.

10. When the fish sticks are done, form every taco by putting two fish sticks on top of every tortilla and taco slaw on top.

11. Serve and enjoy!

2.16 Coconut Shrimp Curry

Preparation Time: 15 minutes

Cooking Time: 20 minutes

Serving: 4

Ingredients:

For Shrimp Marinade:
- 1 lb. of shrimp
- 2 tbsp. of lemon juice
- ¼ tsp. of salt
- ¼ tsp. of black pepper
- ¼ tsp. of cayenne pepper

For the sauce:
- 1 tbsp. Of coconut oil
- 1 chopped onion
- 3 minced cloves garlic
- 1 tbsp. Of ginger minced
- ½ tsp. of black pepper
- ½ tsp. of salt, to taste
- ½ tsp. of turmeric
- 1 tsp. Of curry powder
- 2 tsp. of ground coriander
- 14 ounces diced tomatoes

- 13 ounce coconut milk
- 1 tbsp. of cilantro, to garnish
- Cooked rice to serve

Instructions:

1. In a small bowl, add shrimp with the ingredients of marinade. Cover with cling wrap, then refrigerate for almost ten minutes.
2. Add the onion in oil, cook for two to three minutes until the onion mollifies and gets clear.
3. Mix the ginger, garlic, salt, pepper, coriander, curry powder, and turmeric.
4. Add tomatoes, coconut milk, mix, and heat to the point of boiling. Cook for around five minutes.
5. Add the shrimp with the gathered juices from the marinade and cook for two minutes.
6. Serve with hot rice.

2.17 Fish Packets with Caper Butter and Snap Peas

Preparation Time: 10 minutes

Cooking Time: 25 minutes

Serving: 2

Ingredients:

- 3 tbsp. Of softened butter
- 3 tbsp. Chopped capers
- Kosher salt, to taste
- 1 lb. Of peas
- 1 thinly sliced lemon
- 3 fillets halibut
- Basil, to garnish

Instructions:

1. Mix capers, butter, and one-fourth teaspoon salt. Add lemon.

2. Top peas with fish filets. Sprinkle each filet with salt and speck with butter—overlap and crease foil edges to seal firmly.

3. Cook in a microwave while keeping it covered, on medium heat for twelve minutes. Serve with topping of basil.

2.18 Red Curry Shrimp and Noodles

Preparation Time: 20 minutes

Cooking Time: 16 minutes

Serving: 4

Ingredients:

- 3 tbsp. coconut oil
- 1/2 pound of raw shrimp
- ½ sliced sweet onion
- ½ sliced bell pepper, red
- 1/2 sliced bell pepper, orange
- 1/2 tsp. salt
- 1/2 tsp. pepper
- 2 minced garlic cloves
- 1/2 tsp. grated ginger
- 2 tbsp. red curry
- 1/3 cup of peas
- 1 can of coconut milk
- 1 can of coconut milk
- 6 ounces of rice noodles, cooked
- 3 tbsp. chopped cilantro
- 2 sliced green onions

Instructions:

1. Warm a huge skillet over medium heat and add two tablespoons of coconut oil. Include the shrimp and cook until hazy and pink on the two sides.

2. Sprinkle salt and pepper over it. Remove the shrimp and place it in a bowl.

3. Add the leftover coconut oil to the pot.

4. Add onion, pepper, and salt.

5. Cook for around five minutes.

6. Include the garlic, ginger, and curry glue. Cook for five minutes.

7. Put snap peas and coconut milk in it. Increase heat to the point of boiling, then lower it, cover and cook for five minutes.

8. Add shrimp and cilantro. Cook for five minutes.

9. To serve, place a small bunch of rice noodles in a bowl and cover with the shrimp curry.

10. Top with additional cilantro or green onions.

2.19 Salmon and Ginger Rice Bowl

Preparation Time: 10 minutes

Cooking Time: 30 minutes

Serving: 2

Ingredients:

- 1 cup of brown or white rice
- 2 tbsp. Of butter
- 3 salmon fillets
- 2 tsp. Of curry powder
- 1 tbsp. Of lemon juice
- 1/4 cup white wine
- 12 ounces broccoli florets
- ¼ cup sliced almonds
- 1 tbsp. Of minced ginger

Instructions:

1. Cook rice.
2. Spot four salmon filets in a heating dish.
3. In a small bowl, combine butter, curry powder, and salt.
4. Add white wine and lemon juice to the preparing dish. Cook in the microwave until salmon is cooked.

5. Blend broccoli florets, water, minced ginger, and salt together in a bowl.

6. Take the salmon out of the microwave when done. Add the broccoli; cook for almost four minutes.

7. Mix one-fourth cup cut almonds into the rice.

8. Serve rice with cooked salmon and broccoli.

2.20 Shrimp and Zucchini Scampi

Preparation Time: 20 minutes

Cooking Time: 20 minutes

Serving: 4

Ingredients:

- 2 tbsp. unsalted butter
- 1 pound of medium shrimp
- 3 minced cloves garlic
- 1/2 tsp. red pepper flakes
- 1/4 cup of chicken stock
- 1 lime
- Kosher salt, to taste
- Black pepper, to taste
- 1 1/2 pounds of zucchini
- 2 tbsp. Parmesan
- 2 tbsp. chopped parsley leaves

Instructions:

1. Heat butter in a skillet over medium-high flame. Add garlic, shrimp, and red pepper chips. Cook until pink, around two to three minutes.

2. Add chicken stock and lemon juice; season with salt and pepper to taste. Bring it to a boil; mix zucchini noodles, around one to two minutes.

3. Add parsley and Parmesan, and serve.

2.21 French-Inspired Tuna Nicoise

Preparation Time: 10 minutes

Cooking Time: 20 minutes

Serving: 2

Ingredients:

- 8 potatoes
- 4 ounces of green beans
- 2 tomatoes
- ½ cos lettuce
- 3 eggs
- 100g of black olives
- 8 to 10 ounces of chunk tuna

For Lemon Nicoise Dressing:

- 1 1/2 tbsp. of lemon juice
- 4 tbsp. olive oil
- 1 minced garlic clove
- 1/4 tsp. of salt
- 1 tsp. of Dijon mustard
- 1 black pepper Black mustard seeds, one teaspoon

Instructions:

1. Boil potatoes until delicate, set aside. Cut into equal parts.

2. Boil green beans until delicate or done as you would prefer.

3. Put cos leaves on a huge plate.

4. Mix all ingredients of Lemon Nicoise Dressing.

5. Dissipate and layer the ingredients around the plate.

6. Add eggs, olives, and lumps of fish.

7. Top with dressing and serve!

2.22 One Pan Mustard Glazed Salmon

Preparation Time: 15 minutes

Cooking Time: 15 minutes

Serving: 2

Ingredients:

· 1 thinly sliced lemon
· 1/2 lemon
· 1 ½ tbsp. grainy mustard
· 1/4 cup of chopped fresh dill
· Kosher salt, to taste
· 1 1/2 tbsp. dijon mustard
· Black pepper, to taste
· 1 2- a pound of filet steelhead
· 1 pounds of new potatoes
· 1 pound of asparagus

· 4 to 6 cloves of garlic peeled

· 2 tbsp. olive oil

Instructions:

1. Preheat the stove to 450^0 F.

2. Put lemon cuts on the dish.

3. In a small bowl, blend grainy mustard, lemon juice, and dijon mustard together.

4. Add pepper and salt, one teaspoon of the new dill.

5. Put salmon on dish and rub it with the mustard sauce—season with legitimate salt and dark pepper.

6. Meagerly cut the potatoes and place them in a bowl with the asparagus and crushed garlic cloves.

7. Shower with olive oil, season with pepper and salt.

8. Cook vegetables and salmon for fifteen to twenty minutes.

9. Present with mustard sauce, add more lemon wedges and serve.

2.23 Grilled Stuffed Rainbow Trout

Preparation Time: 20 minutes

Cooking Time: 20 minutes

Serving: 4

Ingredients:

- 1 halved lemon
- 5 tbsp. olive oil
- 12 chopped cloves garlic
- ¼ cup fresh thyme
- ¼ cup of fresh rosemary
- 1 tbsp. red pepper flakes
- 4 whole trout
- Pinch of salt and black pepper

Instructions:

1. Add lemon, olive oil, garlic, thyme, rosemary, and red pepper drops in a bowl.
2. Rub trout with salt and pepper. Add the lemon-spice blend in it, and place it in cooler for one hour.
3. Preheat a microwave on medium-high heat and softly oil the mesh.
4. Flame broiled trout for around four minutes for each side. Serve with lemon wedges.

2.24 Salmon and Beets with Yogurt Sauce over Watercress

Preparation Time: 10 minutes

Cooking Time: 20 minutes

Serving: 2

Ingredients:

- 1 1/4 lb. Of beets
- 1/2 cup plain yogurt
- 2 tbsp. Dill, chopped
- 1/2 tsp. Of lemon zest
- 1 tbsp. Of olive oil
- 1 tbsp. Of poppy seeds
- Kosher salt, to taste
- Black pepper, to taste
- 4 salmon fillets
- 1 tsp. Of ground coriander
- 1 bunch of watercress

Instructions:

1. Take water in a medium pan. Steam beets until delicate, for eighteen to twenty minutes.

2. In the meantime, whisk together yogurt, dill, lemon zing and juice, oil, and poppy seeds in a bowl—season with salt and pepper.

3. Preheat the grill. Cook on a rimmed heating sheet, five to six minutes.

4. Serve salmon, beets, and watercress.

5. Add yogurt sauce.

2.25 Lobster-Noodle Casserole

Preparation Time: 30 minutes

Cooking Time: 40 minutes

Serving: 8

Ingredients:

- 2 lobsters
- 2 tsp. lemon juice
- For the Cheese and Macaroni:
- 8 ounces of elbow macaroni
- 3 tbsp. Of butter
- 3 tbsp. flour
- 1 tsp. salt
- 1/8 tsp. pepper
- 1 1/2 cups of milk
- 1 cup cheddar cheese
- 1 tsp. dry mustard
- 1 1/2 cups of frozen peas
- Black pepper, to taste
- 2 tbsp. of melted butter

Instructions:

1. Heat three to four quarts of water to the point of boiling in a stockpot. Put lobsters into the water. Cover the dish.

2. Cook the lobsters for around eight minutes.

3. Break the shells and take out the meat.

4. Cleave the meat and put it in a bowl; add two teaspoons of lemon juice.

5. Preheat the stove to 400^0 F.

6. Cook the elbow macaroni in a huge pot of salted water.

7. Add flour in the butter.

8. Add one teaspoon of salt and pepper. Keep on cooking for two minutes.

9. Steadily add the milk. Keep on cooking until the sauce thickens and bubbles for one minute.

10. Spoon around half cup of the sauce over the lobster, blend tenderly.

11. Pour remaining sauce over the cooked and depleted macaroni; add the cheddar and mustard and mix.

12. Spoon the macaroni and lobster combination into the pre-arranged preparing dish; top with the lobster blend.

13. Add breadcrumbs with two tablespoons of butter. Sprinkle pieces over the meal.

14. Cover and prepare at 400 F for around twenty minutes.

15. Then, steam the peas as coordinated on the package and season with spread and salt and pepper.

16.   Spoon the steamed prepared peas around the edge of the goulash not long prior to serving.

2.26 Lobster Mac and Cheese Recipe

Preparation Time: 10 minutes

Cooking Time: 20 minutes

Serving: 2

Ingredients:

- 4 tbsp. butter
- 2 tbsp. flour
- 2 1/2 cups of water
- 4 cups of milk
- 1 pound of corkscrew pasta
- 3/4 tsp. salt
- 1/4 tsp. garlic powder
- 1/4 tsp. onion powder
- 1/2 tsp. smoked paprika
- 1/4 tsp. pepper
- 4 cups of cheddar cheese
- 1 cup mozzarella cheese
- 1 1/2 cups of cooked lobster to garnish
- 1/2 cup of panko breadcrumbs
- 2 tbsp. chives

· Cooking spray

Instructions:

1. Preheat the broiler to 350 degrees F. Coat a two to three quart preparing dish with a cooking spray.

2. Soften two tablespoons of the butter in a pot over medium heat. Add the flour, cook for around thirty seconds.

3. Add water and milk.

4. Mix in the pasta, salt, garlic powder, onion powder, smoked paprika, and pepper.

5. Cook for ten to twelve minutes.

6. Turn the heat to low, add cheeses.

7. Overlap in the lobster meat. Move the pasta combination to the pre-arranged heating dish.

8. Add two tablespoons of butter into the panko breadcrumbs.

9. Sprinkle the breadcrumbs. Cook for ten to fifteen minutes.

10. Sprinkle with chives and serve.

2.27 Lemon-Parmesan Angel Hair Pasta with Shrimp

Preparation Time: 30 minutes

Cooking Time: 10 minutes

Serving: 4

Ingredients:

- 1 1/4 lbs. of shrimp
- 12 ounces of pasta
- 3 tbsp. of olive oil
- 3 Tbsp. of unsalted butter
- Salt, to taste
- Black pepper, to taste
- 3 cloves garlic
- 1 1/2 tsp. of lemon zest
- 3 tbsp. of lemon juice
- 3 tbsp. of fresh basil, chopped
- 3 tbsp. fresh parsley, chopped
- 1/2 cup of Parmesan

Instructions:

1. Cook pasta in salted water.
2. In a skillet, heat butter and olive over medium-high heat. Add shrimp, pepper, salt, and sauté for two minutes and add garlic and sauté until

shrimp has cooked through, around two minutes longer.

3. Put pasta in shrimp alongside one-third cup saved pasta water, lemon, and lemon juice.

4. Add more water one tablespoon at once. Add two tablespoons of parsley and basil, sprinkle parmesan cheddar, and serve warm.

2.28 Sheet Pan Shrimp with Broccoli and Tomatoes

Preparation Time: 30 minutes

Cooking Time: 10 minutes

Serving: 4

Ingredients:

- 1 pound of extra shrimp
- 2 tbsp. of olive oil
- 3 minced garlic cloves
- 3/4 tsp. kosher salt
- 1/8 tsp. red pepper
- Black pepper, to taste
- Olive oil
- 12 ounces of broccoli
- 1 cup of grape tomatoes
- 1 tsp. of fresh oregano
- 2 tbsp. lemon juice

Instructions:

1. Preheat the stove to 400°F.

2. Spot shrimp in a medium bowl with two teaspoons olive oil, garlic, one-fourth teaspoon salt, and pepper.

3. Shower a huge sheet skillet with olive oil.

4. Place broccoli and tomatoes in the dish.

5. Add two tablespoons olive oil, half teaspoon salt, pepper, and oregano.

6. Spread out in an even layer. Broil for fifteen minutes.

7. Get the sheet dish out of the stove and add shrimp, setting them uniformly around the veggies. Broil for eight minutes.

8. Top everything with lemon juice and serve.

2.29 Garlic Butter Shrimp

Preparation Time: 10 minutes

Cooking Time: 10 minutes

Serving: 4

Ingredients:

- 8 tablespoons of unsalted butter
- 1 1/2 pounds of medium shrimp
- Kosher salt, to taste
- Black pepper, to taste
- 5 minced cloves garlic
- 1/4 cup of chicken stock
- 1 lemon
- 2 tbsp. parsley leaves

Instructions:

1. Add shrimp, salt and pepper, to taste in the oil. Cook for around two to three minutes.
2. Add garlic to the skillet, and cook while mixing continuously until fragrant.
3. Add chicken stock and lemon juice for around 1 to 2 minutes.
4. Add six tablespoons of butter.
5. Add shrimp.
6. Add parsley leaves, and serve.

2.30 Grilled Lobster Tails with Herb Garlic Butter

Preparation Time: 10 minutes

Cooking Time: 30 minutes

Serving: 2

Ingredients:

- 3 lobster tails
- Lemon wedges
- For the butter:
- 125g butter
- 1 crushed garlic clove
- Parsley leaves, to serve
- 1 tsp. of Dijon mustard
- 1 pinch of chilli powder
- 1 lemon

Instructions:

1. Use kitchen scissors to cut along the highest points of the lobster shells, flip the tails over and break the ribs of the shell.

2. Utilize your fingers to open the shell and slacken the meat keeping it joined at the base and haul it half out.

3. Cook the lobster tails for ten minutes. Put them on a plate.

4. Present with lemon wedges and parsley.

2.31 Salmon with Chickpeas and Spinach

Preparation Time: 5 minutes

Cooking Time: 18 minutes

Serving: 4

Ingredients:

- 4 Salmon Fillets
- 4 tbsp. olive oil
- ½ tsp. kosher salt
- 2 cans of chickpeas
- ¼ tbsp. Black peppers
- 3 cloves of garlic
- 5 ounces of spinach
- 1 tsp. paprika
- 2 tsp. balsamic vinegar

Instructions:

1. Season salmon with pepper and salt.

2. Cook salmon in olive oil for around six to nine minutes.

3. Drain chickpeas.

4. Take out the salmon fillets.

5. Add more olive oil in the pan.

6. Add paprika and garlic.

7. Add chickpeas, tomatoes, kosher salt, and black pepper. Cook for five minutes.

8. Add spinach. Cook for two minutes.

9. Add vinegar.

10. Season with pepper and salt.

11. Add salmon in the pan.

12. Serve it with spinach and chickpeas.

Chapter 3: Healthy Fish and Seafood Snacks and Salads Recipes

Pescatarian seafood snacks and salads recipes are well known throughout the world. Everyone should include these yummy recipes in their Pescatarian diet plan. Here are some of these recipes given below:

3.1 Crab Cakes

Preparation Time: 10 minutes

Cooking Time: 30 minutes

Serving: 8

Ingredients:

- 1/3 cup of mayonnaise
- 1 beaten egg
- 2 tbsp. Of Dijon mustard
- 2 tsp. Of Worcestershire sauce
- 1/2 tsp. Of hot sauce
- Kosher salt, to taste
- Black pepper
- 1 lb. Of crabmeat
- 3/4 cup of breadcrumbs
- 2 tbsp. Chopped Parsley
- Canola oil, to fry
- Lemon wedges, to serve

- Tartar sauce, to serve

Instructions:

1. In a small bowl, whisk together egg, mayo, Dijon mustard, hot sauce, Worcestershire, and season with pepper and salt.

2. In a medium bowl, mix together crabmeat, panko, and parsley.

3. Make eight patties.

4. In a skillet over medium heat, cover the container with oil and heat until shining. Add crab cakes and cook for three to five minutes.

5. Present with lemon and tartar sauce.

3.2 Shrimp Ceviche

Preparation Time: 5 minutes

Cooking Time: 30 minutes

Serving: 6

Ingredients:

- 1/2 cup of thinly sliced red
- 1 jalapeno
- 2 pounds of cooked shrimp cooked
- 3/4 cup of diced cucumber
- 1 cup of diced Roma tomatoes
- 3/4 cup of chopped cilantro leaves
- 1 chopped avocado peeled
- 1/2 cup of lime juice
- 1/4 cup lemon juice
- Salt, to taste
- 1/3 cup orange juice
- Tortilla chips to serve

Instructions:

1.   Put the shrimp, jalapeno, red onion, cucumber, avocado, and cilantro in a bowl.

2. Pour the lime, lemon, and squeezed orange on the shrimp.

3. Add salt.

4. Refrigerate for up to eight hours. Serve with tortilla chips.

3.3 Salmon Patties

Preparation Time: 10 minutes

Cooking Time: 20 minutes

Serving: 5

Ingredients:

- 1 of diced can salmon
- 2 thinly sliced green onions
- 1 tbsp. Of fresh dill, chopped
- 1/2 cup of panko bread crumbs
- 1/4 cup of Mayonnaise
- 1 tbsp. lemon juice
- 1 tbsp. Of Dijon mustard
- 1 beaten egg
- kosher salt, to taste
- Black pepper, to taste
- 2 tbsp. Of olive oil,
- Baby spinach, to serve

Instructions:

1. In a bowl, add ingredients—season with salt and pepper and blend.

2. Structure into five equally measured patties. Cook patties in clusters until brilliant and fresh, three to four minutes for every side.

3. Serve over spinach with lemon wedges.

3.4: Crab Hush Puppies

Preparation Time: 20 minutes

Cooking Time: 12 minutes

Serving: 8

Ingredients:

- 1 cup of yellow cornmeal
- 1/2 cup of flour
- 1 tbsp. sugar
- 1/2 tsp. salt
- 1/2 tsp. Creole seasoning
- 1/2 tsp. onion powder
- 1/4 tsp. baking powder
- 1/4 tsp. baking soda
- 1/2 cup of finely diced bell pepper, red
- 3 diced, green onions
- 1 lightly beaten egg
- 1/4 cup of buttermilk
- 1/2 cup of beer
- 8 ounces of crab meat
- Vegetable oil, as required
- For Remoulade Sauce:
- 3/4 cup of mayonnaise
- 1 1/2 tbsp. Creole mustard

- 1 tsp. horseradish
- 2 sliced green onions
- 1 tbsp. fresh parsley, chopped
- 1 minced garlic clove

Instructions:

1. Start by making the Remoulade sauce.
2. Mix all ingredients in a bowl and refrigerate.
3. In a huge bowl, mix together cornmeal, flour, sugar, salt, Creole flavoring, onion powder, preparing powder, red pepper and green onions.
4. Add the egg, buttermilk, and brew and mix to blend.
5. Tenderly blend in crab meat. Let sit for ten minutes.
6. Heat oven to 360 degrees.
7. Working in bunches, fry for two to three minutes.
8. Keep warm in a 200 degrees broiler.
9. Present with sauce.

3.5 Baked Clams

Preparation Time: 30 minutes

Cooking Time: 20

Serving: 6-8

Ingredients:

- 10-12 chowder clams
- 3 tbsp. minced onion
- 1/2 cup of butter
- 2 tbsp. fresh parsley chopped
- 1 minced clove garlic
- 1 tbsp. lemon juice
- 1 cup of breadcrumbs
- 1tbsp. clam juice
- Pepper, to taste
- Salt, o taste of
- 1/4 cup of Parmesan cheese

Instructions:

1. Fill a huge pot with half cup of water. Heat water to the point of boiling. Add the shellfishes to the bubbling water.

2. Let the mollusks steam for roughly six to ten minutes until the shells open.

3. Take mollusks out of the pot.

4. Preheat broiler to 350°F. In a sauté dish, add the minced onion. Cook for two to three minutes.

5. Add garlic.

6. Cook the garlic, add the parsley, bread scraps, minced mollusks, lemon juice, and shellfish juice.

7. Lay shellfish shells on a dish. Scoop a little stuffing blend onto each shellfish shell.

8. Sprinkle with ground Parmesan.

9. Prepare at 350°F for around twenty to twenty-five minutes until Parmesan is daintily sautéed on top.

3.6 General Tso's Shrimp 'n Broccoli

Preparation Time: 20 minutes

Cooking Time: 20 minutes

Serving: 4

Ingredients:

- 4 20 20
- 1 grated clove garlic
- 3 tbsp. Of soy sauce
- 2 tbsp. Of white vinegar
- 2 tbsp. Of sugar
- 1/3 cup ketchup
- 1/2 tsp. Of dry mustard
- 1 head broccoli
- 1 lb. Of shrimp
- Black pepper, to taste
- Kosher salt, to taste
- 1/2 cup cornstarch
- Vegetable oil, to fry
- 1 tbsp. Of sesame seeds

Instructions:

1. Put together garlic, soy sauce, vinegar, sugar, ketchup, and mustard in a skillet. Heat to the point of boiling.

2. Steam broccoli in a pot.

3. In the meantime, in a medium blending bowl, season shrimp with salt and pepper.

4. Dig shrimp in cornstarch.

5. Preheat a huge skillet over medium-high heat with 1/2" of oil and cook.

6. Spoon sauce over shrimp and sautéed food until caramelized.

7. Serve on top of steamed broccoli and topped with sesame seeds.

3.7 Bang Bang Shrimp

Preparation Time: 10 minutes

Cooking Time: 10 minutes

Serving: 4

Ingredients:

- 1/2 cup of mayonnaise
- 1/4 cup of chili sauce, Thai sweet
- 1/4 tsp. Sriracha
- 1 pound of shrimp shelled

- 1/2 cup of buttermilk
- 3/4 cup of cornstarch
- Canola oil, to fry

Instructions:

1. In a small bowl, add the mayonnaise, Thai sweet stew sauce, and Sriracha and mix.
2. In another bowl, add the shrimp and buttermilk.
3. Coat the shrimp in cornstarch.
4. In a hefty lined dish, add two to three creeps of canola oil and heat to 375 degrees.
5. Fry the shrimp until daintily earthy colored, one to two minutes on each side.
6. Coat with sauce and serve.

3.8 Simple Ceviche Recipe

Preparation Time: 15 minutes

Cooking Time: 15 minutes

Serving: 8

Ingredients:

- 1 pound of cooked shrimp
- ¼ cup of lemon juice
- ¼ cup of fresh lime juice
- ½ cup of fresh orange juice
- 4 diced plum tomatoes seeds
- 2 minced jalapeno peppers
- 1 cup of diced jicama
- ½ cup of chopped cilantro
- ¼ cup of finely chopped red onion
- 1 diced avocado
- Black pepper, to taste
- Kosher salt, to taste

Instructions:

1. Cut out the shrimp into half inch pieces and move to a bowl.
2. Mix the lemon, lime, and squeezed orange to join.
3. Pour citrus juice over the shrimp.

4. Permit the shrimp to marinate for fifteen minutes.

5. Add the jalapeño, tomato, jicama (or apple), red onion, and cilantro to the shrimp.

6. Mix the ingredients and left to marinade for an extra ten minutes.

7. Add avocado and the remaining juices.

8. Add pepper and salt. Serve quickly with tortilla chips.

3.9 Smoked Salmon, Avocado, and Fennel Salad

Preparation Time: 15 minutes

Cooking Time: 15

Serving: 2

Ingredients:

- ⅓ cup of mayo
- 1 tbsp. Of olive oil
- 1/3 cup of sour cream
- 2 tbsp. Of lemon juice
- 1/3 cup of chopped fresh dill
- 1/4 tsp. Salt
- 2 minced garlic cloves
- Salad (2 servings)
- 1/4 tsp. Of cracked pepper
- 1 head of butter lettuce
- 1 Turkish sliced cucumber
- 1/2 thinly sliced fennel bulb
- 4 to 6 ounces of smoked salmon
- ⅛ cup of red onion, thinly sliced
- 2 tbsp. capers
- 1 sliced avocado
- Sunflower sprouts

Instructions:

1. Place ingredients for dressing in a bowl and race until smooth, and blend in dill.

2. Add fennel bulb, lettuce, cucumber, red onion, tricks, and smoked salmon in a major bowl.

3. You can either prepare avocado and fledglings now or separate the serving of mixed greens.

4. Add avocado, sprinkle with pepper and salt, and serve.

3.10 Cilantro-Lime Shrimp Salad

Preparation Time: 10 minutes

Cooking Time: 10 minutes

Serving: 2

Ingredients:

- 1/4 cup red onion
- 2 limes
- 1 tsp. Olive oil
- ¼ tsp. Of Black pepper
- 1/4 tsp. kosher salt
- 1 lb. jumbo cooked
- 1 tomato, diced
- 1 avocado, diced

- 1 jalapeno, diced
- 1 tbsp. chopped cilantro

Instructions:

1. Put the lime juice, red onion, olive oil, pepper, and salt in a small bowl. Allow them to marinate for five minutes.

2. In a bowl, join slashed avocado, shrimp, tomato, and jalapeño.

3. Add cilantro, pepper, and salt to taste.

3.11 Shrimp Salad

Preparation Time: 5 minutes

Cooking Time: 10 minutes

Serving: 2

Ingredients:

- 1 lb. of shrimp
- 1 tbsp. Of olive oil
- Black pepper
- Kosher salt
- 1/4 of chopped red onion
- 1 chopped stalk celery
- 2 tbsp. Of chopped dill
- Butterhead, to serve

FOR DRESSING

- 1 lemon
- 1/2 cup mayonnaise
- 1 tsp. Of dijon mustard

Instructions:

1. Preheat stove to 400°F. On a heating sheet, throw shrimp with oil and season with salt and pepper.
2. Prepare until shrimp are dark, five to seven minutes.

3. Add mayonnaise, zest, and juice of lemon, Dijon, pepper, and salt in a bowl. Add shrimp, celery, dill, and red onion to a bowl and throw until consolidated.

4. Serve on bread or over lettuce.

3.12 Smoked Salmon and Oatmeal Salad

Preparation Time: 15 minutes

Cooking Time: 20 minutes

Serving: 4

Ingredients:

- 4 onions
- 6 diced tomatoes
- 1 diced ripe avocado
- 2 red chilli
- 1 lime,
- 3 tbsp. of wood chips
- 600g salmon fillets
- 3 tsp. Of rapeseed oil
- 125g of oatmeal

Instructions:

1. To start with, make the salsa.

2. Finely slash the green highest points of the spring onions. Blend in tomatoes, the avocado, and half

bean stew, and lime zest. Season and put away to marinate.

3. Brush the salmon with the rapeseed oil and spot it on the rack.

4. Cook on a BBQ or on a hob for eight to ten minutes. Keep warm.

5. For the oats, heat the leftover rapeseed oil in a griddle and fry the whites of the spring onions for one to two minutes.

6. Add the oats and cook for three to four minutes. Mix in one hundred and fifty ml water and lime juice.

7. Cushion it up with a fork and add any leftover tomatoes.

8. Serve the salmon fillets, salsa and oats.

.

3.13 Pan Seared Scallops and Quinoa Salad

Preparation Time: 25 minutes

Cooking Time: 20 minutes

Serving: 2

Ingredients:

- 1 cup of white or red quinoa
- 1 1/2 cups of water
- Kosher salt, to taste
- 1 tbsp. Of olive oil
- 2-4 tbsp. Fresh basil
- Ground pepper, to taste
- 2 oranges
- 1 finely diced avocado
- 3 tbsp. fresh basil
- 2 tbsp. minced shallot
- 1 1/2 tsp. minced red jalapeño
- Kosher salt, to taste
- Black pepper, to taste
- 2 tbsp. olive oil
- 10-12 ounces of sea scallops

Instructions:

1. To make the quinoa, place the quinoa in a pan, wash with cold water.

2. Add half cup of water and salt and heat to the point of boiling around 15 minutes.

3. Cushion the quinoa with a fork.

4. Add olive oil and basil.

5. Season with pepper and salt.

6. Cut the oranges down the middle, cut them into slices.

7. Add avocado, shallot, jalapeño, basil, pepper, and salt.

8. In a fry pan, over medium-high heat, heat olive oil. Season the scallops with pepper and salt, and sauté until practically springy to the touch, around two minutes for each side.

9. Spread the quinoa on two plates. Top with the salsa and scallops and serve.

3.14 Shrimp and Avocado Taco Salad

Preparation Time: 20 minutes

Cooking Time: 15 minutes

Serving: 2

Ingredients:

- 2 tbsp. oil
- 1 lb. Of medium shrimp
- 1 head of chopped romaine lettuce
- 4 diced tomatoes
- ½ finely diced jalapeño
- ¼ finely diced red onion
- 2 tbsp. Minced fresh cilantro
- 1 large diced avocado
- ½ tsp. salt
- 2 tbsp. lime juice
- For Taco Seasoning
- ½ tsp. salt
- ½ tsp. black pepper
- 1 tsp. ground cumin
- 1 tsp. dried oregano
- ¼ tsp. garlic powder
- ½ tsp. chili powder

Instructions:

1. Add shrimp and season with the taco. Sauté the shrimp just until each piece has begun to become pink.

2. In a huge bowl, put lettuce, shrimp, tomatoes, jalapeño, red onion, cilantro, avocado, salt, and lime squeeze.

3. Present with tortilla strips, and serve.

3.15 Crab and Shrimp Salad with Mango

Preparation Time: 15 minutes

Cooking Time: 20 minutes

Serving: 4

Ingredients:

For Yuzu vinaigrette:
- 2 yuzus, shredded zest
- 1 1/2 tbsp. of yuzu juice
- 1/4 tsp. kosher salt
- 1/8 tsp. Of fresh black pepper
- 1/4 cup of fruity olive oil
- For Soy-ginger mayo:
- 1 tsp. fresh ginger
- 1/3 cup of mayonnaise
- 1 tsp. soy sauce
- 1 1/2 tbsp. yuzu juice

For Salad:
- 2 mangoes
- 1/2 pound of cooked crab
- 1/2 pound of tiny shrimp
- 5 ounces of baby arugula
- 4 lime leaves

Instructions:

1. Make the vinaigrette: In a medium bowl, put lemon zest.

2. Add salt and pepper.

3. Add olive oil.

4. In a small bowl, mix all mayo ingredients.

5. Cut mangoes.

6. In a medium bowl, mix crab and shrimp with two tablespoons of vinaigrette.

7. In another bowl, blend mangoes and arugula with the remaining vinaigrette.

8. Top with crab combination. Sprinkle with lime leaves.

9. Serve and enjoy.

3.16 Shoyu Ahi Poke Recipe

Preparation Time: 10 minutes

Cooking Time: 10 minutes

Serving: 4

Ingredients:

- 4 10 10
- 1 pound of ahi
- ¼ cup of green onions
- ¼ cup of sweet onion
- 2 tbsp. shoyu
- 1 tsp. Of sesame oil

Instructions:

1. Cut ahi into pieces.
2. Cut sweet and green onions.
3. Add ahi, green onion, sweet onion, shoyu, and sesame oil to a blending bowl.
4. Tenderly mix to consolidate.
5. Serve and enjoy.

Chapter 4: Healthy Fish and Seafood Soup Recipes

Pescatarian fish and seafood soup recipes provide plenty of health benefits. They keep you full and also fulfill your nutritional requirements. Try the following recipes at home:

4.1 Lobster Bisque

Preparation Time: 20 minutes

Cooking Time: 55 minutes

Serving: 3

Ingredients:

- For Bisque
- 2 tablespoons butter
- 3 lobster tails
- 1 tbsp. olive oil
- 1 finely chopped onion
- 2 finely chopped carrots
- 2 finely chopped stalks of celery
- 1 tsp. chopped thyme
- 1 tsp. chopped tarragon
- 1 tsp. bouillon powder, chicken
- 1/2 tsp. salt

- 1/4 tsp. fresh black pepper
- 1/2 tsp. cayenne pepper
- 4 minced cloves garlic
- 2 tbsp. tomato paste
- 3 tbsp. flour
- 1 1/4 cup of white wine
- 4 cups of lobster stock
- 3/4 - 1 cup of heavy cream
- For Garlic Butter Lobster Meat
- 2 tbsp. butter
- 2 minced cloves garlic
- Pepper, to taste
- Salt, to taste
- Pepper, to taste

Instructions:

1. Fill a huge pot with five cups of water. Mix in one tsp. sea salt and heat to the point of boiling.

2. Add the lobster tails, cover with top and let bubble for five minutes, or until radiant red.

3. Eliminate lobster tails.

4. Set aside the fluid stock. When the lobsters are cool somewhat, eliminate the meat from the shells, saving the meat and any fluid that emerges from the shells.

5. Cook to the point of boiling, diminish heat to low and cook for a further fifteen minutes.

6. While the stock is stewing, cut meat into pieces and refrigerate.

7. Heat oil and butter in a pot over medium heat.

8. Add carrots, onions, new spices, and celery. Cook until delicate, around five minutes.

9. Season with the bouillon powder, pepper, and salt.

10. Mix in minced garlic and cook until fragrant, around one minute.

11. Blend in tomato glue, cook briefly to cover vegetables. Sprinkle over the flour and cook for a further two minutes.

12. Pour the wine and cook. Mix in lobster stock, lessen the heat and cook while mixing periodically until the fluid has thickened and flavors have mixed around thirty minutes.

13. Remove the heat, transfer the mixture to a blender, and mix until smooth. Then again, purée with a blender until extremely smooth. Get back to medium-low heat and add cream.

14. Dissolve the butter in a skillet over medium heat. Sauté garlic for around thirty seconds, until fragrant. Add lobster meat, season with salt, pepper, and cayenne to taste. Gently sauté for one minute.

15. Blend three-fourth of the lobster meat into the bisque. Fill serving bowls.

16. Top each bowl with lobster meat.

4.2 Italian Fish Stew

Preparation Time: 20 minutes

Cooking Time: 45 minutes

Serving: 4

Ingredients:

- 8 ounces of fresh sea bass fillets
- 6 ounces of medium shrimp
- ⅓ cup of chopped onion
- 2 sliced stalks celery
- ½ tsp. minced garlic
- 2 tsp. olive oil
- 1 cup of chicken broth
- ¼ cup of white wine
- 1 can of diced tomatoes
- 1 can of tomato sauce
- 1 tsp. Crushed dried oregano
- ¼ tsp. salt
- ⅛ tsp. Black pepper
- 1 tbsp. fresh parsley

Instructions:

1. Defrost fish and shrimp. Wash fish and shrimp; wipe off with paper towels.

2. Cut fish into one-inch pieces. Slice shrimp.

3. Cover and chill fish and shrimp until required.

4. In a huge pot, cook onion, garlic, and celery in hot oil. Add one cup of stock and wine. Cook for five minutes.

5. Add tomatoes, oregano, pepper, and salt, and pepper. Cook for five minutes.

6. Add fish and shrimp. Lower the heat. Cook for three to five minutes.

7. Sprinkle with parsley, and serve.

4.3 Asian Shrimp and Vegetable Soup

Preparation Time: 15 minutes

Cooking Time: 35 minutes

Serving: 4

Ingredients:

- 12 ounces of large shrimp
- 4 onions
- 2 tsp. canola oil
- 2 thinly sliced carrots
- 8 ounces of oyster mushrooms
- 1 tbsp. Of fresh ginger
- 2 minced cloves garlic
- 2 cans of chicken broth
- 2 cups of water
- 1 cup of sweet soybeans
- 1 tbsp. soy sauce
- ¼ tsp. red pepper
- 1 cup of peas
    - 1 Hot onion sauce
    - Feta cheese

Instructions:

1. Defrost frozen shrimp. Wash shrimp and wipe off with paper towels.

2. Cut green onions into one-inch-long pieces, keeping white parts separate from green tops.

3. In a nonstick pan, heat oil over medium flame. Add white pieces of carrots, green onions, and mushrooms; cook for about five minutes.

4. Add garlic.

5. Add water, chicken stock, soybeans, and soy sauce, crushed red pepper, and mushroom blend.

6. Wait for it to boil, lessen the heat. Cook for around five minutes.

7. Add shrimp and pea pods to the pan. Cook for two to three minutes or until shrimp are murky.

8. Put green onion beat in it not long prior to serving. Decorate with fragmented green onions.

4.4 Salmon Chowder

Preparation Time: 15 minutes

Cooking Time: 15 minutes

Serving: 4

Ingredients:

- 3 tbsp. butter
- ¾ cup of chopped onion
- ½ cup of chopped celery
- 1 tsp. garlic powder
- 2 cups of diced potatoes
- 2 diced carrots
- 2 cups of chicken broth
- 1 tsp. salt
- 1 tsp. black pepper
- 1 tsp. dill weed
- 2 cans of salmon
- 1 can of evaporated milk
- 1 can of creamed corn
- ½ pound of shredded Cheddar cheese

Instructions:

1. Heat butter in a pot over medium heat. Sauté onion, garlic powder, and celery.

2. Put dill potatoes, pepper, stock, carrots, salt, and pepper in it.

3. Heat to the point of boiling, then cook for twenty minutes.

4. Add salmon, vanished milk, corn, and cheddar. Cook until warmed through, and serve.

4.5 Seafood Cioppino

Preparation Time: 45 minutes

Cooking Time: 2 hrs. 15 mins

Serving: 4

Ingredients:

- ¼ cup of olive oil
- 1 chopped onion
- 4 minced cloves garlic
- One chopped bell pepper, green
- 1 chopped red chile pepper
- ½ cup of chopped parsley
- Pepper, to taste
- Salt, to taste
- 1 tsp. Dried oregano
- 1 tsp. dried thyme
- ½ cup of water
- 1 can of crushed tomatoes
- 2 tsp. dried basil
- 1 can of tomato sauce
- 1 pinch of paprika
- 1 pinch of cayenne pepper
- 25 shrimp
- 1 cup of white wine

- 1 can of minced clams
- 25 mussels
- 10 ounces of scallops
- 1 pound cubed cod fillets

Instructions:

1. Sauté the onion, pepper, garlic, pepper, and chile pepper in the oil.
2. Add parsley, pepper and salt, basil, thyme, oregano, tomatoes, water, pureed tomatoes, paprika, and cayenne pepper; squeeze from the shellfishes. Mix well, diminish heat, and cook for one to two hours.
3. Add wine.
4. Around ten minutes prior to serving, add mollusks, cod, prawns, mussels, and scallops.
5. Turn on the heat and mix.
6. Serve your tasty cioppino.

4.6 Wild Rice, Shrimp & Fennel Soup

Preparation Time: 30 minutes

Cooking Time: 40 minutes

Serving: 6

Ingredients:

- 1 pound shrimp
- 1 fennel bulb
- 1 tbsp. olive oil
- 1 tbsp. unsalted butter
- 1 cup of leeks
- 1 carrot
- ¾ cup of uncooked rice
- ¼ tsp. Salt
- ¼ tsp. ground pepper
- 2 cans of chicken broth
- 1 cup of water
- ¾ cup milk
- 2 tbsp. flour
- 2 tsp. fresh thyme
- 2 tbsp. dry sherry
- 1 sprig of thyme sprigs

Instructions:

1. Defrost frozen shrimp.

2. Heat butter and oil in a pot over medium heat.

3. Add the slashed fennel, carrot, and leeks; cook for around eight minutes or until delicate.

4. Mix in wild rice, pepper, and salt. Cook and add stock and water. Bring it to boil; diminish heat. Cover it and cook for forty five minutes.

5. Whisk together milk and flour in a small bowl. Whisk the milk blend into the soup alongside thyme. Cook and mix until the soup is thickened.

6. Mix the shrimp into the soup.

7. Cook for two to three minutes.

8. Add sherry.

9. Top with the fennel leaves and thyme twigs, and serve.

4.7 Seafood Stew

Preparation Time: 15 minutes

Cooking Time: 25 minutes

Serving: 4

Ingredients:

- 3 divided garlic cloves
- 2 tbsp. olive oil
- 1/2 cup of fennel
- 3/4 cup of onion
- 1 tsp. Of divided kosher salt
- 1/2 tsp. Of divided black pepper
- 1/2 pound of cleaned squid
- 1/2 tbsp. Of tomato paste
- 1/4 cup of celery
- 1 tsp. dried oregano
- 1 cup of white wine
- 1 15-ounce can of crushed tomatoes
- 3 bay leaves
- 1 bottle of clam juice
- 1/2 tsp. of red-pepper flakes
- 1 1/2 cups of seafood stock
- 1/2 stick of unsalted butter
- 3 tbsp. Of chopped parsley, divided

- 1/2 tsp. lemon zest
- 1 pound of littleneck clams
- 1/2 pound of shrimp
- 1 baguette
- 1 pound of mussels
- ½ pound of white fish

Instructions:

1. Add onion, celery, fennel, half tsp. salt, and one-fourth tsp. of pepper in the oil and cook for six to eight minutes.

2. Add red pepper flakes and garlic. Keep on cooking for one to two minutes.

3. Add oregano and tomato paste.

4. Add wine, raise heat to medium-high, and cook for five to seven minutes.

5. Add tomatoes with their juice, bay leaves, stock, and cleaned squid. Heat to the point of boiling, diminish to a stew, and cook, covered, for thirty minutes.

6. Mix in one-fourth teaspoon of each salt and pepper.

7. In the meantime, blend the butter, lemon zest, parsley, and salt together in a small bowl. Spread the seasoned butter on toasts.

8. When prepared to serve, add shellfishes; cook for almost three minutes. Mix in the mussels and shrimp.

9. It is ready. Cut into pieces; serve hot with the gremolata toasts and Taco Bell sauce.

10.   You can also garnish with onions, sour cream, or cilantro.

4.8 Brazilian Fish Stew

Preparation Time: 10 minutes

Cooking Time: 25 minutes

Serving: 4

Ingredients:

- For Fish:
- 1 pound of white fish
- ½ tsp. salt
- 1 lime
- For Stew/ Sauce:
- 2–3 tbsp. Olive or coconut oil
- 1 finely diced onion- finely diced
- 1/2 tsp. salt
- 1 cup diced carrot
- 1 diced bell pepper, red
- 4 chopped garlic cloves
- ½ finely diced jalapeno
- 1 tbsp. tomato paste
- 2 tsp. paprika
- 1 tsp. ground cumin
- 1 cup of chicken stock
- 1 1/2 cups of diced tomatoes
- 1 can of coconut milk

- Salt, to taste
- ½ cup of chopped scallions
- 1 lime

Instructions:

1. Add salt, lemon zest, and one tablespoon of lime juice in the fish.

2. In a huge sauté pan, heat the olive oil over medium heat. Add onion and salt, and sauté for two to three minutes.

3. Turn heat down to medium, add carrot, chime pepper, garlic, and jalapeno and cook for four to five additional minutes.

4. Add tomato paste, flavors, and stock. Blend and cook.

5. Add tomatoes.

6. Cook for five minutes.

7. Add the coconut milk and salt.

8. Settle the fish in the stew until it is cooked for around four to six minutes.

9. Add coconut stock over the fish and cook.

10. Add lime.

11. To serve, serve over rice, sprinkle with cilantro or scallions.

12. Shower with a little olive oil. Spot one tortilla on top of the sauce in the dish, and spread a portion of the cheddar sauce on top of the tortilla. Top with the leftover vegetable sauce from the bowl.

13.   Place the second tortilla on top, add cheddar sauce and blended cheddar.

14.   Heat the sauce and cheddar until it is dissolved.

15.   Add coriander, Serve with avocado and bean stew.

4.9 Clam Chowder

Preparation Time: 15 minutes

Cooking Time: 30 minutes

Serving: 6

Ingredients:

- 4 diced slices of bacon
- 2 tbsp. unsalted butter
- 2 minced cloves garlic
- 1 diced onion
- 1/2 tsp. dried thyme
- 3 tbsp. flour
- 1 cup of milk
- 1 cup of vegetable stock
- 2 cans of chopped clams
- 2 bay leaf
- 2 potatoes
- Kosher salt, to taste

- Black pepper, to taste
- 2 tbsp. chopped parsley leaves

Instructions:

1. Cook bacon until earthy colored and firm, around six to eight minutes.

2. Add butter, garlic and onion in a pot, and cook for around two to three minutes.

3. Mix in thyme.

4. Add flour, milk, vegetable stock, shellfish squeeze, and sound leaf, and cook, whisking continually until marginally thickened, around for one to two minutes. Put potatoes in it.

5. Cook around for twelve to fifteen minutes.

6. Mix in cream and shellfishes until warmed through.

7. Season with salt and pepper to taste.

8. Add bacon and parsley, and serve.

4.10 Crab-Okra Gumbo

Preparation Time: 15 minutes

Cooking Time: 1.30 hours

Serving: 8

Ingredients:

- 15 1.30 8
- 1 cup vegetable oil
- 1 pound diced fresh okra
- 4 tbsp. butter
- 1 cup flour
- 2 cups of yellow onion
- 1 1/2 cups of bell pepper, green
- 1/2 cup of diced celery
- 2 minced garlic cloves
- 1 can of diced tomatoes
- 4 cups of shrimp stock
- 3 bay leaves
- 1 tsp. salt
- 1 tsp. Cajun seasoning
- 1 tsp. hot sauce
- 1/2 tsp. dried thyme
- 1/2 tsp. white pepper

- 1 pound of lump crabmeat
- 2 tbsp. fresh parsley
- 1 pound of shrimp
- 1 pint of oysters

Instructions:

1. In a huge nonstick skillet, heat three tbsp. of vegetable oil over medium heat. Add okra and cook, blending every now and again for twenty-five to thirty minutes or until okra is soft.

2. Eliminate from heat and put away.

3. Heat vegetable oil in a pot.

4. Add flour and cook and mix for thirty minutes, or until a dull earthy colored tone.

5. Add onion, pepper, and celery. Cook, regularly mixing for eight minutes.

6. Add garlic and cook for two minutes.

7. Add tomatoes, stock, cove leaves, salt, Creole flavoring, hot sauce, thyme, white pepper, and okra.

8. Stew for forty five minutes.

9. Add crab meat and parsley.

10. Cook for three minutes.

11. Add shrimp and cook for almost two minutes.

12. Add shellfish and cook just until their edges begin to twist.

13.   Present with rice.

4.11 Crab Bisque

Preparation Time: 10 minutes

Cooking Time: 55 minutes

Serving: 4

Ingredients:

- 3 tbsp. Of butter
- 1 finely chopped medium onion
- 2 finely chopped stalks of celery
- Kosher salt, to taste
- Black pepper, to taste
- 1 tsp. Of seasoning, Old Bay
- 2 minced cloves garlic
- 2 tbsp. Of tomato paste
- 3 tbsp. Of flour
- 4 cup fish stock
- 1 cup of dry white wine
- 3 bay leaf
- 1/2 cup of heavy cream
- 1 pound crab meat
- Chopped parsley to garnish

Instructions:

1. Add celery and onion in the butter, and cook until delicate, around five minutes.

2. Season with salt, pepper, and Old Bay. Mix garlic and tomato glue.

3. Cook until garlic is fragrant and tomato glue coats vegetables, around two minutes.

4. Sprinkle over the flour.

5. Pour in fish stock and wine; mix bay leaf. Lessen heat and let stew until fluid is decreased and seasons merge for thirty minutes.

6. Eliminate bay leaf and puree soup with a blender on high until extremely smooth.

7. Get back to medium-low heat and mix cream and half of the crab meat.

8. Cook for around five minutes.

9. Split between bowls and add crab meat and parsley before serving.

4.12 Slow-Cooked Shrimp and Scallop Soup

Preparation Time: 5minutes

Cooking Time: 3.50 hours

Serving: 6

Ingredients:

- 28 ounce of crushed tomatoes
- 1 Tbsp. tomato paste
- 4 cups of vegetable broth
- 3 minced garlic cloves
- 1 pound of yellow potatoes
- 1/2 cup of white onion
- 1 tsp. dried thyme
- 1 tsp. dried basil
- 1 tsp. Dried oregano
- 1/2 tsp. celery salt
- 1/4 tsp. crushed flakes, red pepper
- 1/8 tsp. cayenne pepper
- Pepper and salt, to taste
- 2 pounds of seafood
- Chopped parsley

Instructions:

1. Add all ingredients aside from the fish into a cooker. Cover and cook on high for two to three

hours or low for four to six hours until potatoes are cooked.

2. Add defrosted fish.

3. Cook for an hour until the fish is completely cooked.

4. Do topping with parsley. Serve hot with hard bread.

4.13 Lemon Salmon Soup

Preparation Time: 10 minutes

Cooking Time: 12 minutes

Serving: 4

Ingredients:

- Olive oil
- 4 chopped green onions
- ½ chopped bell pepper, green
- 4 minced garlic cloves
- 1 ounce fresh chopped
- 5 cups of chicken broth
- 1 pound gold potatoes
- 1 thinly sliced carrot
- 1 tsp. Of dry oregano
- ¾ tsp. coriander
- ½ tsp. cumin
- Black pepper and Kosher salt

- 1 pound salmon fillet

  1 lemon

Instructions:

1. Heat two tbsp. Olive oil in a pot. Add green onions, chile pepper, and garlic and cook over medium heat. Cook for around three minutes. Add half of the dill, and mix for thirty seconds.

2. Add stock, potatoes, and carrots. Add flavors and season with pepper and salt. Cook for five to six minutes.

3. Season salmon with salt and add it to the pot of soup. Lower heat and cook for a couple of minutes until salmon is cooked through, around three to five minutes.

4. Mix in lemon juice, lemon zest, and remaining dill.

5. Move salmon soup to serving bowls. Serve with dry bread.

Conclusion

A Pescatarian diet normally incorporates vegetables, grains, fish and seafood yet, for the most part, it avoids meat and dairy. The Pescatarian diet is broadly acknowledged similar to a nutritious decision because of the known advantages of a vegan way of life, combined with lean white fish, high-protein, and omega-3 unsaturated fats found in slick fish, including salmon, herring, and mackerel. This way of eating has shown a decreased danger of creating conditions, for example, type 2 diabetes, hypertension, and stoutness, which are all dangerous factors for coronary illness. Likewise, a recent report showed that omega-3 unsaturated fats are related to a lower hazard of lethal respiratory failures.

As per the studies, a Pescatarian diet helps to attain lower blood cholesterol levels, circulatory strain, and a lower hazard of diabetes. It also helps to treat metabolic disorders. The recipes given in **Pescatarian Cookbook** will help you achieve your desired health benefits.

The Pescatarian

Cookbook

Follow a healthier lifestyle, lose weight and plan your meals and diet with over 100 recipes to learn how to cook seafood and fish.

Adele Tyler

contents

Introduction

In the current world, we as humans have become very conscious of our health. We mostly prefer organic diet over other artificially grown foods. Being on a diet has been the most popular answer we get whenever we ask someone about their health. It is a very famous saying that, "your health is directly proportional to your mood swings," if you eat healthy and eat right, you are always going to have a splendid and wonderful mood.

This book is a road map towards eating different and eating healthy. While, losing weight vegetarians feel the most difficulty as they lack the essential amino acid source in their diet. Pescatarians on the other hand are vegetarians but those who fill their essential protein source with the help of seafood in their diet.

In this book, you will learn everything about the Pescatarian diet, the history, and the origin of this diet. You will come across various benefits of adopting this dieting regime, and the overall effect of seafood on your health in the chapters of this book. There are also other dietetic plans that people adopt very often such as the Carnivore diet and the Vegetarian diet. You will learn the difference between all the three diets, and acquire the knowledge of the advantages, and disadvantages of all these diet plans.

Moving towards the main part of the book, the shopping list that you need to start your diet plan is also provided along with a sample meal plan that will assist you in making your own diet routine. Hundred recipes including breakfast, lunch, dinner, snacks, sweet dishes, and juices are mentioned in this cookbook that are very easy to make on your own in your kitchen. So, why wait further when you can get healthy starting from today, let us dive into the pool of health together.

Chapter 1: Introduction to Pescatarian Diet

A Pescatarian is somebody who decides to eat a veggie diet; however who likewise eats fish, and other seafood products. It is a generally plant based eating regimen of whole grains, nuts, vegetables, whole produce, and solid fats, with fish assuming a key function as a principle protein source. Numerous Pescatarians likewise eat dairy and eggs.

Obviously, similarly as vegan diets can vary broadly, so can Pescatarian ones. It is conceivable to eat a meat free diet that is brimming with processed starches, junk food items and fish sticks, as opposed to a more advantageous one dependent on whole food sources.

1.1 History and Origins of Pescatarian Diet

The word vegetarian is defined by the Oxford Dictionary as 'a person who does not eat meat or fish, and sometimes other animal products, especially for moral, religious, or health reasons.' While this is a good broad definition of the vegetarian diet, the actual practice of vegetarianism is somewhat less clear cut.

There are several subcategories of vegetarianism including Ovolactarians, who eat dairy products, and eggs but abstain from meat, and Lactarians, who eat dairy products but abstain from meat and eggs. Some people include fish in their diet but still consider themselves vegetarians; a new name for this lifestyle, Pescatarian, has recently emerged. Vegans are the strictest subcategory of the vegetarian movement, abstaining from all animal-based products. Strict followers of veganism do not eat honey, or wear leather, or wool. While religion sometimes calls for a vegetarian or vegan diet, over the years we have seen an increasing number of individuals choosing not to consume animal products based on their personal beliefs.

A portion of the principal self-announced Vegetarians were the Pythagoreans, a title got from the Greek logician Pythagoras, a founder of the mathematical Pythagorean hypothesis. In spite of the fact that Pythagoras lent his name to the meatless eating routine, it is muddled whether he followed a severe vegan routine or not. Some people speculate that along with a typical breakfast of nectar, and supper of grain bread with vegetables, he may have eaten fish also, which would have made him Pescatarian by the present principles.

Supporters of Pythagoras received his dietary limitations, accepting that they were useful in helping life span. The lessons of Pythagorus were first distributed in quite a while by Italian essayist, and Doctor Antonio Cocchi; in 1745 they were converted into English by Robert Dodsley. A record of his eating regimen additionally showed up in the Greek thinker Porphyry's book *On Abstinence from Animal Food* (third century). The compelling chronicled archive incorporates a portion of exactly the same contentions that cutting edge vegans use while lauding the benefits of a meatless eating regime. With vegetarianism on the rise, it is now common for restaurants to feature vegetarian menus, or meatless entrée alternatives. Grocery stores carry a large variety of vegetarian options, proving a strong market for meatless products. With proper attention to nutritional intake, it is entirely possible for vegetarians, and vegans to live a long and healthy life.

1.2 Benefits of Pescatarian Diet in terms of Nutrition

In the Pescatarian diet, a person's main source of animal protein comes from fish, and other seafood, such as shrimp etc. Eating a diet consisting mainly of plant-based foods has a variety of health benefits, which the addition of fish and fish products may enhance. However, some types of fish may absorb mercury from their environment, so certain people may need to limit their intake. Following are some benefits of the Pescatarian diet in terms of Nutrition:

1. A Pescatarian diet may ensure individual's safety against colorectal diseases, or malignancies that influence the colon, and rectum. As indicated by a recent report, colorectal malignant growths are the subsequent driving reason for disease passing in the United States. The examination utilized information

from a companion of more than 77,650 individuals, and found that the Pescatarian diet had a solid defensive impact against colorectal malignant growths.

2. Following a plant-based eating routine can diminish the danger of type-2 diabetes, and metabolic disorder. Metabolic disorder incorporates conditions, for example, insulin opposition, hypertension, and heftiness. There is likewise proof that omega-3s present in greasy fish may diminish aggravation, however this proof originates from preliminaries of enhancements. Plant-based eating regimens are high in calming, and cell reinforcement operators, for example, flavonoids. Flavonoids have a scope of calming, and antidiabetic properties.

3. Some people choose vegetarian diets because they disagree with factory farming practices, or killing animals for food. For people concerned about animal welfare, the Pescatarian diet may be a little more suitable. This is because some scientists argue that fish cannot feel pain.

4. Eating fish, especially fatty fish, provides increased long-chain omega-3 fatty acid intake. An omega-3 fatty acid is an unsaturated fat that can be beneficial to people, and some omega-3s are integral for healthy living. People who eat fish have lower blood pressure, a lower risk of abnormal heart rhythms, and fewer fatal heart attacks than those who do not include fish in their diet.

5. Plant-based diets can help a person maintain a healthy weight, and they also may help with weight loss when necessary. A Pescatarian diet may also be more healthful than some diets that rely on calorie deficits to reduce weight.

1.3 Effects of Seafood on Overall Health of an Individual

The foods we eat influence our health. Besides containing protein, and other nutrients such as vitamin D and selenium, fish (either finfish or shellfish) contain a specific type of fat, omega-3 fatty acids, that may reduce the risk of developing heart disease, and other medical problems.

Omega-3 fatty acids are found in fish especially oily fish such as salmon, sardines, and herring. These omega-3 fatty acids can help lower your blood pressure, lower your heart rate, and improve other cardiovascular risk factors. Eating fish reduces the risk of death from heart disease, the leading cause of death in both men, and women. Fish intake has also been linked to a lower risk of stroke, depression, and mental decline with age. For pregnant women, mothers who are breastfeeding, and women of childbearing age, fish intake is important because it supplies DHA, a specific omega-3 fatty acid that is beneficial for the brain development of infants.

Fishes help keep up cardiovascular wellbeing by assuming a function in the guideline of blood thickening, and vessel choking, and are significant for pre-birth and postnatal neurological turn of event. Fish may lessen tissue irritation, and ease the manifestations of rheumatoid joint pain, and may assume a valuable part in cardiovascular arrhythmia (unpredictable heartbeat), lessening sadness, and ending mental decrease in more established individuals.

Chapter 2: Comparison of Pescatarian Diet with Other Diets

Many healthy eaters are reducing their intake of meat, and other animal products to boost wellness. If you are considering different options, there are many different plant based eating plans to choose from. The Pescatarian diet is just one of them.

In this chapter you will see how the Pescatarian diet is different from the Vegetarian, and Carnivore diet.

2.1 Pescatarian Diet vs. Carnivore Diet

Being a Pescatarian is where you eat meat, but only meat that comes from the sea. Fish has a lot of iron in it, and that can benefit your health greatly. Plus, it is easier to be cruelty free when it comes to. A great way to become a Pescatarian is by finding a great local fish market near you.

The biggest benefit includes the iron that fish have, the more fish you eat, the greater amount of iron you will have. Just as well, you will not be consuming land animals, so you will be more conscious when it comes to those types of meat. The downside is the price. Fish is more expensive, so you will have to work around that. Also, fish has a ton of mercury in it, so you will have to make sure to maintain that.

If you want to become more animal product conscious, but do not want to give up meat entirely, the carnivore diet is probably the way to go for you. You can do this by being aware of where your animal products are coming from. Happy farms are the best way to think about doing this. An animal without a bunch of hormones injected in is going to be great for you. Furthermore, cage-free animals are happier. Animal cruelty free meat is a major thing. Knowing where my meat is coming from makes you feel really good. Some farm animals do not ever see sunlight, let alone get to roam around.

Weight Loss

The Pescatarian diet may cause weight loss when portions are controlled while the Carnivore diet also cause the same effect of weight loss but unfortunately there is a drawback of not getting the proper nutrients the body needs that comes from plant based diets.

Health Risks

Carnivore diets come with nutritional deficiencies that can be a cause of big health risks for any individuals in the future. On the other hand one specific risk associated with a Pescatarian diet is the presence of mercury or heavy metals, a registered dietician. Fish, shellfish, and other seafood accumulate mercury in their bodies. As bigger fish eat smaller fish, this can drive up the concentration of these potentially dangerous toxins in the flesh of the larger fish.

Health Benefits

Carnivore, and Pescatarian both diets are very healthy for individuals, and they provide us a variety of nutrients that are unlikely to occur in the case of carnivore diets that lack plants on the whole and so lack all the nutrients that occur in plant based diets.

2.2 Pescatarian Diet vs. Vegetarian Diet

There are no exact rules that figure out what is a Pescatarian, and what is a Vegetarian. Furthermore, there are no guidelines that characterize how frequently you have to eat fish so as to be a Pescatarian. For instance, you might be a vegan who once in a while eats fish or you may remember it for each dinner. Nutritionists state that Pescatarians will in general be individuals who are wellbeing cognizant, and settle on careful decisions when arranging dinners. They might be people who are thinking about a vegan diet, and are utilizing a fish-based way to deal with plant-based eating. Or on the other hand they might be individuals who intend to follow a Pescatarian diet as long as possible, to dodge red meat.

Health Risks

One specific risk associated with a Pescatarian diet is the presence of mercury or heavy metals. Fish, shellfish, and other seafood accumulate mercury in their bodies. As bigger fish eat smaller fish, this can drive up the concentration of these potentially dangerous toxins in the flesh of the larger fish.

Overall Cost

Both Vegetarian and Pescatarian diets can be budget-friendly, especially if you are including conventionally grown products instead of seeking out only organic items.

The addition of seafood in a Pescatarian diet could increase the cost, but choosing canned and frozen options, especially when they are on sale, can help reduce the cost. Red meat, and poultry can be expensive, so forgoing these purchases in favor of more fresh fruits and vegetables, whole grains, legumes and fish could reduce your overall shopping bill. As with any diet, the quality of the food is also important. Look for whole, unprocessed options rather than prepackaged or prepared foods. These whole foods that you cook yourself are usually less expensive than prepared foods.

Health Benefits

Both diets are considered majorly plant based. The people who are following these diets will achieve many of the benefits associated with plant based diets. This approach to eating when done right has been associated with plenty of health benefits including better control of blood pressure, better control of blood glucose, less inflammation, reduced cholesterol levels. These factors translate into improved heart health, a reduced risk of developing diabetes and a reduced risk of certain types of cancer.

Additionally Pescatarians have the added benefit of getting plenty of omega-3 fatty acids, which are known for their heart-protective and anti-inflammatory properties. Omega-3s are essential compounds that the body cannot make on its own. You have to ingest them as part of your diet or in supplement form. They are critical to maintaining cardiovascular health. Fatty fish, such as sardines, mackerel and salmon are rich sources of omega-3s.

Weight Loss

The Pescatarian diet may cause weight loss when portions are controlled while the Vegetarian diet also cause the same effect of weight loss if the portion size of the meals are quantified properly.

Conclusion

Both the Pescatarian and Vegetarian diets can be perfectly healthy diets. These diets focus on eating whole, unprocessed foods rather than packaged junk foods. It all comes down to which foods you are choosing and whether you are covering all your needs. You need a variety of vitamins and minerals to fulfil your daily requirement. One area where Pescatarian diets might have a leg up over strictly Vegetarian diets is in providing more omega-3 fatty acids.

Chapter 3: Pescatarian Diet- Shopping List and Meal Plan

The Pescatarian diet originates from a Vegetarian diet, zeroing in on plant-based nourishments and fish, however dispensing with meat and poultry. Numerous individuals decided to turn into a Pescatarian on the grounds that it considers a smoother change to a plant-based eating routine and can be simpler to support in the drawn out when contrasted with a Vegetarian diet. In addition, fish is a finished wellspring of protein and has a large number of dietary advantages. Most Pescatarians like eggs and dairy for their eating routine, however some do not as this is an individual decision.

3.1 Grocery List- Foods You Need To Follow the Diet

Following is the grocery list that you need to follow before starting your Pescatarian diet:

- Beans and legumes
- All kinds of fish
- Tofu and tempeh
- Chia seeds
- All kinds of nuts
- Flax seeds
- Shellfish
- All kinds of fruits
- All kinds of vegetables
- Dairy products
- Eggs
- Brown rice
- Oatmeal
- Quinoa

- Different sauces: oyster sauce, chili sauce, soy sauce, Worcestershire sauce
- Whole wheat flour or bread
- Dried spices and mix herbs
- Different oils: canola oils, olive oil, sunflower oil

3.2 7 Day Sample Meal Plan of Pescatarian Diet

Day 1:

Breakfast: Scrambled eggs with cheese 125 kcalories

Lunch: Lemon kale and salmon pasta 186 kcalories

Snack: Green tea smoothie 183 kcalories

Dinner: Buckwheat pasta salad 402 kcalories

Total Calories 896 kcalories

Day 2:

Breakfast: Egg muffin 105 kcalories

Lunch: Caesar salad 186 kcalories

Snack: Black current and kale smoothie 183 kcalories

Dinner: Prawn Arabiata 434 kcalories

Total Calories

908 kcalories

Day 3:

Breakfast: Tomato   Omlette
125 kcalories

Lunch: Caribbean Salad with shrimp
192 kcalories

Snack: Strawberry and cucumber juice
183 kcalories

Dinner: Miso marinated cod with stir-fried
greens   450 kcalories

Total Calories
950 kcalories

Day 4:

Breakfast: Date and Walnut Oatmeal
350 kcalories

Lunch: Tofu and kale pesto sandwich
186 kcalories

Snack: Green tea smoothie
183 kcalories

Dinner: Prawn   Arabiata
420 kcalories

Total Calories
1139 kcalories

Day 5:

Breakfast: Banana Egg pancakes
125 kcalories

Lunch: Caesar salad
186 kcalories

Snack: Mango and Pineapple smoothie
183 kcalories

Dinner: Lemon kale salmon pasta
620 kcalories

Total Calories
1122 kcalories

Day 6:

Breakfast: Blueberry pancakes
509 kcalories

Lunch: Potato soup
186 kcalories

Snack: Green Juice
143 kcalories

Dinner: New Orleans
416 kcalories

Total Calories
1251 kcalories

Day 7:

Breakfast: Oat and berry Acai bowl
501 kcalories

Lunch: Shrimp Coronation salad
186 kcalories

Snack: Melon and Grape Juice
125 kcalories

Dinner: Baked salmon with mint dressing
350 kcalories

Total Calories

1162 kcalories

The above designed diet plans are made from the same recipes which are listed in the chapters below, and you can indulge variations into your meal plans according to your choices.

Chapter 4: Pescatarian Diet Recipes

The only thing worse than a bad meal is no meal at all. Luckily, that is not going to be an issue for you. Following are a lineup of some of the best Pescatarian meal ideas in this chapter. Each recipe is genuinely tasty, easy to make and nutritious.

4.1 Breakfast Recipes

1) Caramelized Banana Dark Chocolate Oatmeal

Preparation time: 10 minutes

Cooking Time: 10 minutes

Serving: 1

Ingredients:

- Olive oil spray
- Water, one cup
- Sliced medium banana, half
- Dark chocolate chips, two tbsp.
- Rolled oats, one cup

Instructions:

1. In a small saucepan, bring water to a boil.
2. Stir in oats and reduce heat to low.
3. Simmer until oats have absorbed all of the liquid, three to five minutes.
4. While oats are cooking, spray a small non-stick skillet with olive oil.

5. Add sliced bananas in a single layer and cook over medium heat until caramelized, about three minutes per side.
6. Spoon oatmeal into a bowl and top with caramelized bananas, and chocolate chips.

2) Scrambled Eggs with Cheese

Preparation time: 5 minutes

Cooking Time: 12 minutes

Serving: 4-6

Ingredients:

- Mozzarella cheese, one cup
- Butter, three tbsp.
- Salt and Pepper, to taste
- Eggs, twelve

Instructions:

1. In a large nonstick pan with sloped sides, melt the butter over medium-low heat, being careful to not brown the butter.
2. If it begins to bubble, the heat is too high, so lower the heat to cook the eggs properly.
3. Meanwhile, in a large bowl, add the eggs and one teaspoon cold water.
4. Vigorously whisk until frothy and smooth.
5. Swirl the pan around to coat the butter on the bottom and up the sides.
6. Pour the eggs into the pan and let sit for a few seconds.
7. When the eggs begin to lightly set on the bottom, use the whisk to gently beat the eggs, and then allow them to sit for just a few seconds between beating them again.
8. Curds will begin to form and increase throughout the cooking time. Repeat this process of whisking then resting the eggs for a few seconds until about 50 percent of the eggs are set and the rest are still wet.
9. At this point, sprinkle the eggs with a pinch of salt and pepper and continue to whisk and rest alternately.
10. Once the eggs are 75 percent done add the cheese and from this moment, continue to whisk the eggs until done. This entire process from pouring in the eggs to them being finished should take eight minutes.
11. Remove from the heat and continue to scramble in the last seconds.
12. Your dish is ready to be served.

3) Breakfast Egg Muffins

Preparation time: 10 minutes

Cooking Time: 40 minutes

Serving: 12

Ingredients:

- Yellow onion chopped, one
- Turkey bacon, three slices
- Cooking spray
- Salt and Pepper, to taste
- Eggs, six
- Chopped red bell pepper, one
- Shredded mozzarella cheese, half cup
- Chopped baby spinach, one cup
- Garlic powder, half tsp.
- Paprika, half tsp.
- Milk, three tbsp.

Instructions:

1. Preheat oven to 350° and grease a 12-cup muffin tin with avocado or coconut oil cooking spray or coconut oil.
2. In a large nonstick skillet over medium heat, cook turkey bacon until crispy, six and eight minutes.
3. Drain on a paper towel-lined plate, then crumble.
4. Add onion and bell pepper to skillet and cook until soft. Cook for approximately five minutes.

5. Add spinach and cook until wilted, two minutes more.
6. In a small bowl, whisk eggs, milk, paprika, and garlic powder and season with salt and pepper.
7. Fold in cooked vegetable mixture, turkey bacon, and mozzarella. Pour mixture into prepared muffin tin.
8. Bake until cooked through and golden for thirty minutes.
9. Your dish is ready to be served.

4) Chickpea Flour Pancakes

Preparation time: 5 minutes

Cooking Time: 5 minutes

Serving: 2

Ingredients:

- Water, one cup
- Olive oil, one tbsp.
- Cooking spray
- Salt and Pepper, to taste
- Chickpea flour, one cup
- Spring onions, one cup
- Chili flakes, half tsp.
- Turmeric, half tsp.
- Peas, half cup
- Chopped red bell peppers, half cup

Instructions:

1. Add the flour, water, turmeric, salt, pepper and chili flakes to a mixing bowl and give it a quick blend using a food processor or blender.
2. Leave it to settle for a few minutes while you heat up the oil or ghee in a non-stick pan.
3. The batter needs to look very runny.
4. Dice the veggies finely and add them to the mixture.
5. Use a tissue or similar to ensure the bottom of the pan is coated well in oil.
6. Add about a ladle of the mixture and veggies when the pan is hot a medium heat should be just right.
7. Cook for about three minutes the mixture will quickly start to firm.
8. If you are using two pans, you can make two pancakes at the same time.
9. Make sure you use a large pan here, you are aiming for thin pancakes.
10. Use a large spatula to help you flip the pancakes, adding more oil underneath if necessary.
11. Your pancakes are ready to serve.

5) Dutch Banana Pancakes

Preparation time: 5 minutes

Cooking Time: 5 minutes

Serving: 2

Ingredients:

- Milk, half cup
- Flour, half cup

- Cooking spray
- Eggs, three
- Sugar, one tbsp.
- Nutmeg, half tsp.
- Butter, two tbsp.
- Sliced banana, one

Instructions:

1. Mix all the ingredients together and make a smooth batter.
2. Make sure you use a large pan here; you are aiming for perfect pancakes.
3. Use a large spatula to help you flip the pancakes, adding more butter underneath if necessary.
4. Your pancakes are ready to serve.

6) Rubab Mango Oatmeal

Preparation time: 5 minutes

Cooking Time: 5 minutes

Serving: 1

Ingredients:

- Orange juice, half cup
- Oats, one cup
- Fresh rhubarb, one cup
- Milk, one and a half cup

- Salt, a pinch
- Brown sugar, three tbsp.
- Cinnamon, half tsp.
- Chopped pecans or any nuts, two tbsp.
- Chopped mango slices, one

Instructions:

1. Combine milk, juice, oats, rhubarb, cinnamon and salt in a medium saucepan. Bring to a boil over medium-high heat.
2. Reduce heat, cover and cook at a very gentle bubble, stirring frequently, until the oats and rhubarb are tender, about five minutes.
3. Remove from the heat and let stand, covered, for five minutes.
4. Stir in sweetener to taste.
5. Garnish with nuts and mango slices.

7) Easy Tomato Omelet

Preparation time: 5 minutes

Cooking Time: 5 minutes

Serving: 1

Ingredients:

- Fresh basil, half cup
- Spring onions, half cup
- Cherry tomatoes, half cup

- Eggs, two
- Salt, a pinch
- Red chili
- Pepper, half tsp.

Instructions:

1. Wash the tomatoes, chilies, and spring onion and chop into small pieces.
2. Heat half the oil in a pan and fry the tomatoes for about two minutes.
3. Set aside.
4. Clean the pan with a tissue.
5. Crack the eggs into a bowl and beat well with a fork, adding the salt and pepper
6. Heat the rest of the oil in a pan on low to medium heat.
7. Pour the egg mix into the pan.
8. Using a spatula, ruffle the omelet so it does not stick.
9. As you create gaps tilt the pan so the liquid fills the spaces.
10. Let it cook for about two minutes and when the egg mixture looks nearly cooked drop on the tomatoes and basil.
11. Fold the empty half of the omelet on top of the other.
12. Slide it onto a plate the heat from closing the omelet will finish cooking the inside.
13. Your dish is ready to be served.

8) Breakfast Burrito

Preparation time: 15 minutes

Cooking Time: 15 minutes

Serving: 4

Ingredients:

- Wheat tortillas, four
- Chopped red onions, half cup
- Red bell pepper, half cup
- Black beans, one cup
- Eggs, four
- Hot sauce
- Salt, a pinch
- Canola oil, one tbsp.
- Red chili, one tbsp.
- Pepper, half tsp.
- Sour cream, half cup
- Shredded mozzarella cheese, one cup
- Chopped tomato, half cup
- Chopped avocado, half cup

Instructions:

1. Heat the canola oil in a large nonstick skillet over a medium-high heat.
2. Cook the onions and peppers until onions are softened and peppers are slightly charred, about eight minutes.
3. Add black beans and red pepper flakes and cook until warmed through, another three minutes.
4. Season with salt and pepper and transfer to a dish.
5. Whisk together the eggs and egg whites then stir in the cheese.
6. Spray the skillet with cooking spray, and reheat the skillet over a medium heat. Reduce heat to low and add eggs, scrambling until cooked through, about three minutes.
7. Spread each tortilla with one tablespoon each sour cream and salsa, then layer with some of the black bean mixture, some of the scrambled eggs, some diced tomato and some of the avocado.
8. Season, to taste, with hot sauce.
9. Roll up burrito-style and serve hot.

9) The Runner's Sandwich

Preparation time: 5 minutes

Cooking Time: 5 minutes

Serving: 1

Ingredients:

- Bread, four slices
- Olives, half cup
- Sun dried tomatoes, half cup
- Capers, two tbsp.

- Fresh basil, half cup
- Salt, a pinch
- Canola oil, one tbsp.
- Red chili, one tbsp.
- Pepper, half tsp.
- Oregano, half tsp.
- Shredded mozzarella cheese, one cup

Instructions:

1. Roughly chop the cheese, tomatoes, olives and capers and throw into a mixing bowl.
2. Add the herbs, salt and pepper.
3. Use a fork to mix up and mash the ingredients a little not too much.
4. If you are using very soft bread then pop it in the toaster or pan without oil for a minute or so not to toast it, just to harden the outside.
5. If the bread is already a hard type.
6. Spread the mix on the bottom slices; add the other slices on top.
7. Squish down.
8. Heat the pan and put the sandwich in.
9. Put a lid on the pan.
10. Cook for three to four minutes, squishing down with a spatula occasionally, then flip and cook the other side the same way.
11. Both outsides should be nice and crispy, the insides melting together.
12. Your sandwich is ready to be served.

10)   Banana Egg Pancakes

Preparation time: 5 minutes

Cooking Time: 10 minutes

Serving: 6

Ingredients:

- Baking powder, two tsp.
- Coconut flour powder six tbsp.
- Ripe banana, two
- Vanilla extracts, one tsp.
- Eggs, two
- Oil
- Maple syrup
- Fresh berries
- Coconut yogurt
- Seeds
- Nut butter

Instructions:

1. To a large mixing bowl, add bananas and mash until only small bits remain.
2. Then add baking powder and vanilla extract and use a fork or whisk to mash until thoroughly combined.

3. Next add eggs, break yolks with a fork or whisk, and whisk thoroughly until well combined.
4. Lastly, add coconut flour one tbsp. at a time until a thick but scoopable batter is achieved.
5. If you add too much coconut flour, add a little dairy free milk to thin.
6. Heat a large skillet over medium heat.
7. Once hot, add a little cooking oil to coat the pan.
8. Then spoon in roughly three tbsp. amounts of batter and reduce heat to low. These benefit from cooking slower and lower than your average pancakes. Cover with a lid to help the center cook through.
9. Cook for three to four minutes, then remove lid and flip carefully.
10. Transfer cooked pancakes to the preheated oven on the prepared baking sheet.
11. To serve, top with desired toppings, such as nut butter, sliced bananas or fresh fruit, dairy-free yogurt, or maple syrup.

11)   Coffee Chia Pudding

Preparation time: 5 minutes

Cooking Time: 10 minutes

Serving: 2

Ingredients:

- Almond milk, one cup
- Vanilla extract, one tsp.
- Maple syrup, one tbsp.
- Whipped cream
- Coffee, powder, one tbsp.

- Chia seeds, half cup

Instructions:

1. Combine all the things together except the whipped cream.
2. Serve them in a bowl and top with whipped cream.
3. Your dish is ready to be served.

12)   Eggs in a Cloud

Preparation time: 10 minutes

Cooking Time: 10 minutes

Serving: 2

Ingredients:

- Salt, one pinch
- Mixed cheese, half cup
- Eggs, two

Instructions:

1. Preheat the oven to 450 degrees with a rack in the middle.
2. Line a roasting pan, or baking sheet that can take high temperatures without warping, with parchment paper.
3. Separate the egg yolks from the whites.

4. Make sure there are no little pieces of egg yolk in the whites or you will have difficulty getting the whites to beat properly.
5. It helps if you are making more than one egg nest to keep each egg yolk in a separate prep bowl.
6. Place the egg whites in a very clean mixer bowl.
7. Add a small pinch of salt to the egg whites.
8. Beat the egg whites with a whisk attachment in a mixer, starting on low speed and then slowly increasing to high speed, until stiff peaks form.
9. Your dish is ready to be served.

13)   Buttermilk Pancakes

Preparation time: 10 minutes

Cooking Time: 10 minutes

Serving: 4

Ingredients:

- Salt, one pinch
- All-purpose flour, two cup
- Eggs, two
- Unsalted butter, three tbsp.
- Sugar three tbsp.
- Baking powder, one tsp.
- Baking soda, one tsp.
- Buttermilk, two cups
- Canola oil, for cooking

Instructions:

1. Heat the oven to 325 degrees.
2. Whisk flour, sugar, baking powder, baking soda and kosher salt together in a bowl.
3. Using the whisk, make a well in the center.
4. Pour the buttermilk into the well and crack eggs into buttermilk.
5. Pour the melted butter into the mixture.
6. Starting in the center, whisk everything together, moving towards the outside of the bowl, until all ingredients are incorporated.
7. Heat a large nonstick griddle or skillet, preferably cast-iron, over low heat for about five minutes.
8. Add one tablespoon oil to the skillet.
9. Turn heat up to medium low and using a measuring cup, ladle the batter into the skillet.
10. Flip pancakes after bubbles rise to surface and bottoms brown, about two minutes. Cook until the other sides are lightly browned.
11. Remove pancakes to a wire rack set inside a rimmed baking sheet, and keep in heated oven until all the batter is cooked and you are ready to serve.

14)   Baked Eggs with Spinach and Tomatoes

Preparation time: 10 minutes

Cooking Time: 10 minutes

Serving: 4

Ingredients:

- Salt, one pinch
- Eggs, four
- Chili flakes, three tbsp.
- Butter, one tsp.

- Chopped tomatoes, two cups
- Spinach, one cup

Instructions:

1. Heat oven to 200 degrees.
2. Put the spinach into a colander, and then pour over a kettle of boiling water to wilt the leaves.
3. Squeeze out excess water and divide between four small ovenproof dishes.
4. Mix the tomatoes with the chili flakes and some seasoning, then add spinach while shifting the material in dishes.
5. Make a small well in the center of each and crack in an egg.
6. Bake for ten mins or more depending on how you like your eggs.
7. Serve with crusty bread.

15)   Almond and Cherry Oatmeal

Preparation time: 5 minutes

Cooking Time: 5 minutes

Serving: 4

Ingredients:

- Dried oats, half cup
- Vanilla almond milk, three cups
- Salt, a pinch
- Cherries, one cup

Instructions:

1. Stir together oats, almond milk, and salt in a large microwave safe bowl.
2. Microwave on high for five minutes, stirring every two minutes, until oats are soft and most of the liquid has been absorbed.
3. Stir in cherries.
4. Spoon into bowls and serve while hot.

16)   Fluffy Quinoa Egg Muffin

Preparation time: 10 minutes

Cooking Time: 40 minutes

Serving: 12

Ingredients:

- Yellow onion chopped, one
- Quinoa, half cup
- Cooking spray
- Salt and Pepper, to taste
- Eggs, six
- Chopped red bell pepper, one
- Shredded mozzarella cheese, half cup
- Chopped baby spinach, one cup
- Garlic powder, half tsp.

- Paprika, half tsp.
- Milk, three tbsp.

Instructions:

1. Preheat oven to 350° and grease a 12-cup muffin tin with avocado or coconut oil cooking spray or coconut oil.
2. In a large nonstick skillet over medium heat, cook quinoa for six and eight minutes.
3. Drain on a paper towel-lined plate, then crumble.
4. Add onion and bell pepper to skillet and cook until soft approximately five minutes.
5. Add spinach and cook until wilted, two minutes more.
6. In a small bowl, whisk eggs, milk, paprika, and garlic powder and season with salt and pepper.
7. Fold in cooked vegetable mixture, quinoa, and mozzarella. Pour mixture into prepared muffin tin.
8. Bake until cooked through and golden for thirty minutes.
9. Your dish is ready to be served.

17)   Mushroom Scrambled Egg

Serving: 1

Preparation time: 5 minutes

Cook time: 5 minutes

Ingredients:
- 25g kale, chopped
- 1 tsp ground turmeric

- One egg
- 5g parsley finely chopped
- 1 tsp mild curry powder
- ½ sliced bird's eye chili
- sliced button mushrooms
- 1 tsp extra virgin olive oil

Instructions:

1. Make a paste of curry powder and turmeric by adding little water
2. Lightly warm the kale by steaming for 2 minutes
3. Fry the mushroom and bird's eye chili in a frying pan till they turn brown and soften on medium heat.
4. Now add spice paste and egg, cook on medium heat.
5. Add kale and cook on medium heat for one more minute.
6. Add parsley and mix it
7. It is ready to serve.

18)   Smoked Salmon Omelet

Serving: 1

Preparation time: 5 minutes

Cooking time: 4 minutes

Total time: 9 minutes

Ingredients:

- 100 g Smoked salmon, cut
- One tsp. extra virgin olive oil

- 2 Medium eggs
- 10 g chopped arugula leaves
- 1/2 tsp. capers
- One tsp. chopped parsley

Instructions:

1. Break the eggs into a bowl and whisk well. Include the salmon, tricks, rocket, and parsley.
2. Warm the olive oil in a non-stick skillet until hot yet not smoking. Include the egg blend and, utilizing a spatula or fish cut, move the blend around the container until it is even.
3. Decrease the heat on the stove and let the omelet cook through.
4. Slide the spatula around the edges and move up or overlay the omelet fifty-fifty to serve.
5. It is ready to serve.

19)   Shakshuka

Serving: 6

Preparation time: 15 minutes

Cook time: 20 minutes

Total Time: 35 minutes

Ingredients:

- One substantial red ringer pepper or broiled red chime pepper
- One huge onion, diced
- ¼ teaspoon fine ocean salt

- Two cloves garlic, squeezed or minced
- Six enormous eggs
- Two tablespoons tomato puree
- One to two tablespoons olive oil
- One teaspoon ground cumin
- ½ teaspoon smoked paprika
- ¼ teaspoon red pepper drops, decrease or overlook if touchy to flavor
- One enormous can squashed tomatoes, ideally fire-broiled
- ½ cup disintegrated feta
- Two tablespoons slashed new cilantro or level leaf parsley, and cilantro or parsley leaves for embellishing
- Newly ground dark pepper, to taste
- Dry bread or pita, for serving

Instructions:

1. Preheat the stove to 375 degrees Fahrenheit. Warm the oil in an enormous, broiler safe pan over the medium stove.
2. Once gleaming, add in the onion, ringer pepper, and salt. Cook, regularly mixing, until the onions are delicate and turning translucent, around four to six minutes.
3. Include the garlic, tomato puree, cumin, paprika, and red pepper pieces. Cook, blending continually, until quite fragrant, one to two minutes.
4. Pour in the squashed tomatoes with their juices and include the cilantro. Mix, and let the blend go

to a stew. Diminish the stove heat as important to keep up a delicate stew, and cook for 5 minutes to give the flavors time to merge.

5. Switch off the stove. Taste it, and include salt and pepper as preferred. Utilize the rear of a spoon to make a well close to the border and split the egg legitimately into it. Delicately spoon a touch of the tomato blend over the whites to help contain the egg.

6. Rehash with the staying 4 to 5 eggs, contingent upon what number of you can fit. Sprinkle somewhat salt and pepper over the eggs.

7. Cautiously move the pan to the broiler and heat for 8 to 12 minutes, frequently checking once you arrive at 8 minutes. They're done when the egg whites are an obscure white, and the yolks have risen a piece however are still delicate. They should, at present, wiggle in the focuses when you shimmy the container.

8. Utilizing broiler gloves move the hot pan to a safe warmth surface like an oven. Top with the disintegrated feta, new cilantro leaves, and increasingly red pepper drops. However, you may prefer it. Serve in bowls with dry bread.

9. It is ready to serve.

20)   Blueberry Pancakes

Serving: 12

Preparation time: 10 minutes

Cook time: 10 minutes

Total time: 20 minutes

Ingredients:

- One egg

- One cup flour
- 3/4 cup milk
- Two tablespoons softened spread
- Two tablespoons white vinegar
- Two tablespoons sugar
- 1/2 teaspoon baking soda
- One teaspoon baking powder
- 1/2 teaspoon salt
- One cup blueberries
- more margarine for the container

Instructions:

1. Blend the milk and vinegar and let it sit for a moment or two.
2. Whisk the dry things together. Whisk the egg, milk, and softened spread into the dry ones until simply consolidated.
3. Heat a non-stick pan over a medium stove. Dissolve a little smear of margarine in the pan.
4. Pour around 1/3 cup of the mixture into the hot pan and spread it level like it will be entirely thick. Throw a couple of blueberries on top. Cook until you see little air pockets on top and the edges beginning to solidify. Flip and cook for another one to two minutes until they cooked through.
5. Present with margarine and maple syrup.
6. It is ready to eat.

21)   Black Bean Scrambled Eggs

Serving: 1

Preparation time: 10 minutes

Cook time: 15 minutes

Total time: 25 minutes

Ingredients:

- 1/3 medium avocado
- Two huge egg whites
- 1/2 tsp. olive oil
- One tbsp. salsa, no sugar included 1/2 cup dark beans, no sugar included whenever canned
- 1/4 medium onion, diced red onion is the most delicious

Instructions:

1. Sauté your onions in the oil in a non-stick pan.
2. Include your eggs and scramble or cook.
3. When eggs are close to cooked, mix in your beans and cook sufficiently long to warm them up.
4. Move to a plate and top with salsa and avocado.
5. It is ready to serve.

22) Strawberry Chocolate chips and Buckwheat Pancakes

Serving: 2

Preparation time: 5 minutes

Cook time: 30 minutes

Total time: 35 minutes

Ingredients:

- One huge egg
- One cup buckwheat flour
- One teaspoon baking powder
- Two tablespoons coconut sugar
- One tablespoon vanilla concentrate
- Two tablespoons additional virgin olive oil
- One teaspoon ground cinnamon
- 1/4 teaspoon fit salt
- 3/4 cup unsweetened cashew milk (or sans dairy milk of your decision)
- 1/2 cup hacked strawberries
- 1/4 cup dull chocolate chips
- Discretionary toppings:
- Ground flax seeds
- Maple syrup
- Chocolate Chips
- Diced Strawberries

Instructions:

1. Gently oil a pan and pre-heat on the medium stove.
2. In a medium-sized bowl, whisk together the flour, sugar, heating powder, cinnamon, and salt.
3. In a little bowl, whisk together the milk, oil, vanilla, and egg. Add the wet blend to the dry blend and mix until simply joined. Do not over blend. Overlay in the strawberries and chocolate chips.

4. Scoop out around 1/2 cup of the prepared mixture into the warmed skillet and spread it out into a 5-inch circle.
5. Cook for 4-5 minutes, or until the edges begin to cook and a couple of air pockets show up on top. Flip and cook for another 2-3 minutes.
6. Present with maple syrup and preferred garnishes.
7. It is ready to serve.

23)   Herb Omelet with Fita and Beans:

Serving: 2

Preparation time: 10 minutes

Cook time: 10 minutes

Total time: 20 minutes

Ingredients:

- 200g wide beans, podded weight
- Two little cubes of unsalted margarine
- Four medium eggs
- 75g vegan feta cheddar disintegrated or crumbled
- 1/2 pack tarragon leaves as it were
- 1/2 pack chives
- 1/2 pack level leaf parsley leaves as it were
- 1/2 lemon zest

Instructions:

1. Heat a pan of water to bubble and whiten the expansive beans for two minutes until simply delicate.
2. Deplete and revive under normal temperature running water.
3. Evacuate the external skin of the bean, to uncover the brilliant internal parts.
4. Split the eggs into a bowl and beat with a fork. Finely slash the herbs and speed into the eggs, alongside the vast majority of the lemon get-up-and-go and a lot of salt and newly ground dark pepper.
5. Warm a non-stick skillet over a medium-high stove. Include a little cube of spread at that point, while frothing, include in a large portion of the egg blend.
6. Utilize a spatula to move the egg around the container, letting it flood the spaces until it is nearly cooked.
7. Disperse a large portion of the cheddar and a large portion of the beans over the omelet.
8. Leave for 20-30 seconds, so the underside is completely set, and an exquisite brilliant earthy colored at that point overlay down the middle and slide onto a plate. Rehash for a subsequent omelet and serve quickly, dispersed with the held zest of lemon.
9. It is ready to serve.

24)   Date and Walnut Oatmeal

Serving: 1

Preparation time: 5 minutes

Cook time: 7 minutes

Total time: 12 minutes

Ingredients:

- 1/2 cups water
- 1/2 tsp. salt (discretionary)
- Two cups of oats
- 2/3 cup cleaved walnuts
- 2/3 cup cleaved dates

Instructions:

1. Heat the water and salt to the point of boiling.
2. Mix in the oats, walnuts, and dates.
3. Slow down the stove to medium.
4. Spread and cook for five minutes, mixing on more than one occasion.
5. Switch off the stove and let it cool down for two to three minutes before serving.
6. Present it with a sprinkle of earthy colored sugar or turbinado sugar and a sprinkle of milk or creamer.
7. Sprinkle over extra dates and walnuts whenever wanted.
8. It is ready to eat.

25)   Buckwheat Porridge

Serving: 2

Preparation time: 6 minutes

Cook time: 12 minutes

Total time: 18 minutes

Ingredients:

- Two cups of warm water
- One cup buckwheat, rinsed

Instructions:

1. Add buckwheat groats and water to a little pot to a medium high warmth. Heat to the point of boiling. Spread the pot with a top and put heat on low. Stew ten minutes, don't overcook. You can utilize a clock.
2. Following ten minutes, turn off warmth. Try not to open the cover, permit it to steam for an additional five minutes.
3. Cushion with a fork and serve. Top with fruits, almond milk, and a sprinkle of vanilla, a scramble of cinnamon, and a shower of maple syrup or nectar.
4. It is ready to serve.

4.2 Lunch Recipes

26)   Tangy Veggie Wrap

Preparation time: 6 minutes

Cook time: 12 minutes

Serving: 2

Ingredients:

- Sunflower seeds three tbsp.
- Carrots, two small
- Ginger one thumb

- Bell pepper half
- Red onion one
- Cottage cheese, half cup
- Sour cream, two tbsp.
- Lemon zest, one tsp.
- Mustard, three tsp.
- Wraps, two
- Spinach, half cup
- Salt and pepper to taste
- Bean sprouts, half cup

Instructions:

1. Roast the sunflower seeds in a pan without any oil until golden brown.
2. Peel and grate the carrots. Wash and dice the bell pepper.
3. Peel the onion and cut in thin rings.
4. Wash and drain the spinach.
5. Wash the bean sprouts with cold water and let them dry.
6. Peel the ginger and grate it into a bowl.
7. Add the cottage cheese, sour cream, lemon zest and mustard, and mix it well.
8. Spread the dressing mixture onto the wraps.
9. Lay out the spinach leaves on top.
10. Put the carrots, bell pepper, onions and bean sprouts in a wide line down the middle and sprinkle the roasted sunflower seeds on top.
11. Season with a dash of salt and pepper and fold the wraps a little on both sides, then at the bottom and roll it as tightly as possible.
12. Cut the wraps into halves and serve.

27) King Prawn Stir Fry with Buckwheat Noodles

Serving: 1

Preparation time: 10 minutes

Cook time: 10 minutes

Total time: 20 minutes

Ingredients:

- 150 g shelled crude lord prawns, deveined
- Two tbsp. tamari
- Two tbsp. additional virgin olive oil
- 75 g soba (buckwheat) noodles
- One garlic clove, finely hacked
- One 10,000 foot bean stew, finely hacked
- One tsp. ginger, finely hacked
- 20 g red onion, cut
- 40 g celery
- 75 g green beans, diced
- Kale 50g, generally diced
- 100g chicken stock
- 5g lovage or celery leaves

Instructions:

1. Heat a skillet over a high stove, at that point, cook the prawns in one teaspoon of the tamari and one teaspoon of the oil for two to three minutes.
2. Move the prawns to a plate. Wipe the work out with kitchen paper, as you're going to utilize it once more.
3. Cook the noodles in bubbling water for five to eight minutes or as instructed on the bundle. Channel and put in a safe spot.
4. In the meantime, fry the garlic, stew and ginger, red onion, celery, beans, and kale in the rest of the oil over a medium-high warmth for two to three minutes.
5. Add the stock and bring to the bubble, at that point stew for a moment or two, until the vegetables are cooked yet crunchy.
6. Include the prawns, noodles, and lovage or celery leaves to the container, mix it thoroughly, and remove from the stove. It is ready to be eaten.

28)   Lemon Kale Salmon Pasta

Serving: 2

Nutritional Value: 620 calories

Preparation time: 10 minutes

Cook time: 15 minutes

Total time: 25 minutes

Ingredients:

- 4 oz wheat spaghetti (115 g)
- One boneless, skinless salmon, cubed
- Five tablespoons additional virgin olive oil
- Two cloves garlic, minced

- ¼ teaspoon red pepper chips
- 2 cups wavy kale (135 g), remove the ribs
- One lemon
- One tablespoon lemon juice
- legitimate salt, to taste
- ground dark pepper, to taste

Instructions:

1. Bubble salted water and cook the pasta for one moment, not exactly the time showed on the bundle. At the point when the pasta is done cooking, save ¼ cup (60 ml) of pasta water.
2. In the interim, heat two tablespoons of olive oil in a cast-iron skillet. Season cubed salmon with salt and pepper, add it to the skillet, and earthy colored it on each side. When cooked thoroughly around two to four minutes, remove from skillet and hold.
3. Cook three tablespoons of olive oil in a skillet and include garlic and red pepper drops. Cook until fragrant, around one minute.
4. Include kale, zests of lemon, lemon juice, salt, and saved pasta water. Cook until kale is delicate, around three minutes.
5. Include cooked salmon and pasta. Mix to cover and serve right away.

29)   Pot Prawns and Kale Curry

Serving: 4

Preparation time: 8 minutes

Cook time: 2 minutes

Total time: 10 minutes

Ingredients:

- Two cups chopped onions
- Two garlic cloves, minced or grated
- 1/2 inch ginger, minced or grated
- Two medium roman tomatoes, chopped, about 1 cup
- Four teaspoons coriander powder
- 1/2 to 1 teaspoon cayenne pepper powder, depending on your spice level
- 1/2 teaspoon turmeric powder
- One cinnamon stick
- Two cardamoms
- Two cloves
- 1/4 teaspoon fennel seeds
- Prawns, one pound
- Four stalks kale, ribs removed and coarsely chopped
- 1/2 cup coconut milk
- One cup of water
- 11/2 to 2 teaspoons salt, divided (or as per your taste)

Instructions:

1. Set your Pot to sauté, include vegetable oil when hot. Include every entire flavor and let toast for a few moments.
2. Include all spices, sauté until onions turn translucent, around four minutes.
3. Sauté until tomatoes are soft, flavors are toasted well, and it starts to turn gleaming. Ensure you sauté like clockwork at this stage, causing sure that it doesn't to consume at the base.
4. Set manual for five minutes, ensuring the valve is set at fixing position.
5. Following five minutes, let your pot be in warm mode for two to four minutes. Go valve to vent and discharge the pressure.
6. Check for salt and present with your preferred side dish or cool and pack into boxes for use afterwards.

30)   Baked Tofu Wraps

Serving: 6

Nutritional Value: 360 calories

Preparation time: 15 minutes

Cook time: 30 minutes

Total time: 45 minutes

Ingredients:

- One square of extra-firm tofu depleted and squeezed.

- Six tablespoons corn-starch

- ⅓ cup unsweetened almond milk or milk of decision

- One cup oats
- Two tablespoon olive or avocado oil
- ½ teaspoon paprika
- One teaspoon dried oregano
- ½ teaspoon salt
- ¼ teaspoon dark pepper
- Six entire wheat wraps or tortillas
- Discretionary sauces and toppings
- 5g lovage or celery leaves

Instructions:

1. Preheat broiler to 425 Fahrenheit and line an enormous preparing sheet with material paper. Put in a safe spot.
2. Cut squeezed tofu into 24 little square shapes (does not need to be definite, fundamentally simply make them reduced down). Spot tofu shapes in a bowl.
3. Next, join in the oats, oil, paprika, oregano, salt, and pepper in a shallow bowl until all around consolidated.
4. Set up your tofu toward the start, trailed by corn starch in a shallow bowl, at that point a bowl of almond milk, lastly a shallow bowl with the breadcrumb blend. Toward the stopping point ought to be the material lined preparing sheet.
5. Coat tofu pieces by dunking each piece into the corn starch, at that point the almond milk, and afterward the breadcrumb blend (once more, make a point to cover all the sides). Spot covered tofu on the readied heating sheet and rehash with extra tofu. Make sure to keep covered tofu pieces

at any rate one to two inches separated on the preparing sheet.

6. Prepare tofu for twenty five minutes, flip, and cook another five to ten minutes.
7. Remove from the stove. Alternatively, you can hurl your tofu in BBQ sauce, and afterward gather your wraps.
8. They are ready to eat.

31)   Tofu and Kale Pesto Sandwich

Serving: 2

Preparation time: 15 minutes

Cook time: 5 minutes

Total time: 20 minutes

Ingredients:

- Smoked tofu, seven ounce
- Olive oil, 5-6 tbsp.
- Walnuts, half cup
- Yeast, one tsp.
- Italian herb mix, two tsp.
- Kale, one cup
- Minced garlic, one
- ½ teaspoon salt
- ¼ teaspoon dark pepper
- Zucchini, one
- Carrot, one
- Wheat buns, two
- Lettuce

Instructions:

1. First make the kale pesto.
2. Put all ingredients into a blender or food processor and blend until smooth.
3. Cut the tofu into thin strips.
4. In a medium pan, heat some olive oil and stir-fry the tofu for about two minutes on each side until it is brown and crispy.
5. If you want you can also add about half a teaspoon of soy sauce. Once the tofu is done, put it aside.
6. Heat some more olive oil and cook the zucchini slices for another three minutes. Season with salt, pepper, and Italian spices (such as oregano, basil, rosemary, thyme).
7. Cut the sandwiches in half and generously coat both sides with kale pesto.
8. Add the lettuce, the tofu, the carrots, and the grilled zucchini.

32) Sautéed Kale

Serving: 4

Nutritional Value: 98 calories

Preparation time: 5 minutes

Cook time: 20 minutes

Total time: 25 minutes

Ingredients:

- One tablespoon in addition to one teaspoon extra-virgin olive oil for later use

- 1/2 pounds kale, ribs evacuated, coarsely cleaved
- ½ cup of water
- Two cloves garlic, minced
- ¼ teaspoon squashed red pepper
- Two to three teaspoons sherry vinegar or red-wine vinegar
- ¼ teaspoon salt

Instructions:

1. Warm one tablespoon oil in a broiler over a medium stove.
2. Include kale and cook, hurling with two huge spoons, until brilliant green, around one moment.
3. Include water; lessen warmth to medium-low, spread and cook, mixing at times, until the kale is delicate, about fifteen minutes.
4. Push kale aside, include the staying one teaspoon oil to the unfilled side and cooking garlic, and squash red pepper in it until it is fragrant, Switch off from the stove and hurl together. Mix in vinegar to taste and salt.
5. It is ready to serve.

33) Shrimp Butternut Squash and Date Tagine

Serving: 4

Nutritional Value: 244 calories

Preparation time: 15 minutes

Cook time: 1 hour and 15 minutes

Total time: 1 hour and 30 minutes

Ingredients:

- Two tablespoons olive oil
- One red onion, cut
- 2cm ginger, ground
- Two garlic cloves, ground or squashed
- One teaspoon bean stew drops (or to taste)
- Two teaspoons cumin seeds
- One cinnamon stick
- Two teaspoons ground turmeric
- 800g Shrimps
- ½ teaspoon salt
- 100g Medjool dates, hollowed and slashed
- 400g tin slashed tomatoes, in addition to a large portion of a jar of water
- 500g butternut squash cut into 1cm shapes
- 400g tin chickpeas, depleted
- Two tablespoons new coriander (in addition to this extra for decorations in the end)
- Buckwheat, couscous, flatbreads or rice to serve

Instructions:

1. Preheat your broiler to 140 Celsius.

2. Drizzle around two tablespoons of olive oil into an enormous ovenproof pot or cast iron goulash dish. Add in the previously diced onion and cook on a delicate heat, with the cover on, for around 5 minutes, until the onions are mellowed yet not earthy colored.
3. Add the ground garlic and ginger, bean stew, cumin, cinnamon, and turmeric. Mix well and cook for progressively one minute with the top off. Include a sprinkle of water in the event that it gets excessively dry.
4. Next include the shrimps. Mix well to cover the meat in the onions and flavors and afterward include the salt, slashed dates, and tomatoes, in addition to about a large portion of a container of water (100-200ml).
5. Bring the tagine to bubble and afterward put the top on and put in your preheated broiler for 1 hour and 15 minutes.
6. Thirty minutes before the finishing of the cooking time, include the cleaved butternut squash and chickpeas. Mix everything together, set the top back on, and come back to the broiler for the last 30 minutes of cooking.
7. When the tagine is prepared, quickly remove from the stove and mix through the cleaved coriander. Present with buckwheat, couscous, flatbreads, or basmati rice.
8. It is ready to be served.

34)   Prawn Arabiata

Serving: 1

Nutritional Value: 420 calories

Preparation time: 40 minutes

Cook time: 30 minutes

Total time: 1 hour and 10 minutes

Ingredients:

- 125-150 g Raw or cooked prawns
- 65 g Buckwheat pasta
- One tbsp Extra virgin olive oil

For the sauce:

- One tsp Dried blended herbs
- 40 g Red onion, finely cleaved
- 30 g Celery, finely cleaved
- One Bird's eye bean stew, finely cleaved
- One tsp Extra virgin olive oil
- One Garlic clove, finely cleaved
- One tbsp Chopped parsley
- Two tbsp White wine (discretionary)
- 400 g Tinned cleaved tomatoes

Instructions:

1. Fry the onion, garlic, celery, and bean stew and dried herbs in the oil over a medium-low stove for one to two minutes.
2. Turn the warmth up to medium, include the wine, and cook for one moment. Include the tomatoes and leave the sauce to stew over medium-low heat for 20–30 minutes, until it has a decent creamy consistency.

3. If you feel the sauce is getting too thick, essentially include a little water.
4. While the sauce is cooking, Take a skillet of water and boil it till bubbles appear and cook the pasta as indicated on the parcel.
5. At the point when prepared exactly as you would prefer, channel, hurl with the olive oil and keep in the skillet until required.
6. If you are utilizing crude prawns, add them to the sauce and cook for a further three to four minutes until they have turned pink and murky, include the parsley and serve.
7. In the event that you are utilizing cooked prawns, include them with the parsley, boil the sauce till bubbles appear and serve.
8. Add the cooked pasta to the sauce, blend completely yet tenderly and serve.

35)   Baked Turmeric Salmon

Serving: 1

Nutritional Value: 358 calories

Preparation time: 15 minutes

Cook time: 10 minutes

Total time: 25 minutes

Ingredients:

- 125-150 g Skinned Salmon
- 1 tsp Extra virgin olive oil
- 1 tsp ground turmeric
- 1/4 Juice of a lemon

For celery:

- 1 tsp Extra virgin olive oil
- 40 g Red onion, finely diced
- 60 g Tinned green lentils
- 1 Garlic clove, finely diced
- 1 cm fresh ginger, finely diced
- 1 Bire's eye stew, finely crushed
- 150 g Celery cut into 2cm lengths
- 1 tsp Mild curry powder
- 130 g Tomato, cut into eight pieces
- 100 ml Chicken or vegetable stock
- 1 tbsp Chopped parsley

Instructions:

1. Warm the stove
2. Start with preparing the hot celery. Warm a skillet over medium-low warmth, including the olive oil, at that point the onion, garlic, ginger, stew, and celery. Fry tenderly for 2–3 minutes or until mellowed yet not shaded. At that point, include the curry powder and cook for a further moment.
3. Add the tomatoes, then the stock and lentils, and stew delicately for 10 minutes. You might need to increment or reduction the cooking time contingent upon how crunchy you like your celery.
4. Meanwhile, blend the turmeric, oil, and lemon squeeze and rub over the salmon. Place on a heating plate and cook for ten minutes.
5. To complete, mix the parsley through the celery and present it with the salmon.

6. Your dish is ready to serve.

36)   Shrimp Coronation Salad

Serving: 1

Nutritional Value: 105 calories

Preparation time: 5 minutes

Cook time: 0 minutes

Total time: 5 minutes

Ingredients:

- 75 g Natural yogurt
- One Bird's eye stew
- 1/2 tsp Mild curry powder
- 100 g Cooked shrimps
- Juice of 1/4 of a lemon
- One tsp Coriander, finely chopped
- One tsp ground turmeric
- 20 g Red onion, diced
- Walnut parts, finely diced
- 40 g Rocket, to serve
- One Medjool date, finely diced

Instructions:

1. Blend the yogurt, lemon juice, coriander, and flavors together in a bowl.

2. Include all the rest of the things and serve on a bed of the arugula leaves.
3. Eat well and stay healthy and fresh.

37) Spicy Chickpea Stew with Baked Potatoes

Serving: 4

Nutritional Value: 358 calories

Preparation time: 10 minutes

Cook time: 1 hour

Total time: 1 hour and 10 minutes

Ingredients:

- Two red onions, finely cleaved
- 4-6 heating potatoes, pricked everywhere
- 2 x 400g tins cleaved tomatoes
- 2cm ginger, ground
- Two tablespoons olive oil
- cloves garlic, ground or squashed
- ½ - 2 teaspoons bean stew chips (contingent upon how hot you like things)
- Two yellow peppers (or whatever shading you prefer), cleaved into bite-size pieces
- Two tablespoons turmeric
- Two tablespoons cumin seeds
- Sprinkle of water
- Two tablespoons unsweetened cocoa powder (or cacao)
- 2 x 400g tins chickpeas
- Two tablespoons parsley in addition to

extra for embellish
- A side plate of mixed greens, discretionary
- Salt and pepper to taste, discretionary

Instructions:

1. Preheat the stove to 200C. In the interim, you can set up the entirety of your mixings.
2. When the broiler is hot enough, placed your heating potatoes in the stove and cook for 1 hour or until they are done how you like them.
3. Once the potatoes are in the stove, place the olive oil and slashed red onion in an enormous wide pan and cook tenderly, with the cover on for five minutes, until the onions are delicate yet not earthy colored.
4. Remove the cover and include the garlic, ginger, cumin, and bean stew. Cook for a further moment on a low, warm stove, at that point, include the turmeric and an exceptionally little sprinkle of water and cook for one more moment, taking consideration not to let the dish get excessively dry.
5. Next, include the tomatoes, cocoa powder, chickpeas (counting the chickpea water), and yellow pepper. Bring to a bubble, at that point, stew on low warmth for 45 minutes until the sauce is thick and unctuous. The stew ought to be done at generally a similar time as the potatoes.
6. Finally, mix in the two tablespoons of parsley and some salt and pepper in the event that you wish it to be spicy, and serve the stew on the prepared potatoes, maybe with a basic side plate of mixed greens.

7. Enjoy your meal.

38) Kale and Red Onion Dhal with Buckwheat

Serving: 4

Nutritional Value: 420 calories

Preparation time: 5 minutes

Cook time: 25 minutes

Total time: 30 minutes

Ingredients:

- One tablespoon olive oil
- One little red onion, cut
- 160g buckwheat (or earthy colored rice)
- 400ml coconut milk
- Two garlic cloves, ground or squashed
- Two cm ginger, ground
- 200ml water
- One birds-eye bean stew, deseeded and finely diced (more if you like things hot)
- Two teaspoons turmeric
- Two teaspoons garam masala
- 160g red lentils
- 100g kale (or spinach would be an extraordinary other option)

Instructions:

1. Put the olive oil in an enormous, profound pan and include the cut onion. Cook on a low warmth, with the top on for five minutes until mellowed.
2. Add the garlic, ginger and bean stew and cook for 1 minute.
3. Add the turmeric, garam masala, and a sprinkle of water and cook for one minute.
4. Add the red lentils, coconut milk, and 200ml water.
5. Mix everything together completely and cook for 20 minutes over a delicately heat with the cover on. Mix once in a while and include somewhat more water if the dhal begins to stick.
6. After 20 minutes, including the kale, mix all together and supplant the top, cook for a further 5 minutes.
7. About 15 minutes before the curry is prepared, place the buckwheat in a medium pan, and include a lot of bubbling water. Take the water back to the bubble and cook for ten minutes. Channel the buckwheat in a strainer and present with the dhal.
8. Your dish is ready to be served.

39)   Choc Chip Granola

Serving: 8

Nutritional Value: 244 calories

Preparation time: 10 minutes

Cook time: 20 minutes

Total time: 30 minutes

Ingredients:

- 200g normal sized oats

- 50g walnuts, generally cleaved
- Two tbsp light olive oil
- 20g margarine
- One tbsp brown colored sugar
- Two tbsp rice malt syrup
- 60g dim chocolate chips

Instructions:

1. Preheat the broiler to 160°C. Line a huge heating plate with a silicone sheet or preparing material.
2. Combine the oats and walnuts in an enormous bowl. In a little non-stick container, delicately heat the olive oil, spread, earthy colored sugar, and rice malt syrup until the margarine has liquefied and the sugar and syrup have broken down.
3. Try not to permit to bubble. Pour the syrup over the oats and mix completely until the oats are completely secured.
4. Distribute the granola over the heating plate, spreading directly into the corners.
5. Leave clusters of blend with separating instead of an even spread. Prepare in the stove for 20 minutes until just touched brilliant earthy colored at the edges.
6. Remove from the broiler and leave to cool on the plate totally.
7. When cool, separate the greater knots on the plate with your fingers and afterward blend in the chocolate chips.

8. Scoop or empty the granola into an impenetrable tub or container.
9. The granola will save for fourteen days so you can make it in bulk.

40)   Parmesan Chicken and Kale

Serving: 4

Nutritional Value: 402 calories

Preparation time: 10 minutes

Cook time: 19 minutes

Total time: 29 minutes

Ingredients:

- Two tablespoons olive oil
- 1/2 pound scampi
- Fit salt
- Newly ground dark pepper
- One medium yellow onion, diced
- Two cloves garlic, minced
- Squeeze red pepper drops
- One enormous bundle level leaf kale (around 12 ounces), stems evacuated and leaves coarsely cut
- 1/2 cup dry white wine
- 1/2 cup ground Parmesan cheddar
- One tablespoon newly made lemon juice

Instructions:

1. Warm the oil in a huge skillet keep the stove on medium heat until sparkling. Include the scampi into it, season with salt and pepper, and sauté until cooked thoroughly for five to seven minutes. Move the scampi to a plate and spread it with some wrap to keep warm.
2. Include the onion, garlic, and pepper pieces to the skillet. Sauté until the onions are beginning to mollify, around two minutes. Mix in the kale, wine, and a touch of salt. Spread and cook for around five minutes, mixing every so often, until the kale is simply delicate.
3. Add the scampi and any amassed juices to the skillet. Include the Parmesan and lemon squeeze and mix it thoroughly. Taste and season with increasingly salt and pepper according to your liking.
4. It is ready to be served.

41)   Caesar Salad

Preparation Time: 12 minutes

Cooking Time: 12 minutes

Serving: 4

Ingredients:

- Garlic pepper, one tsp.
- Garlic minced and mashed, one clove
- Romaine lettuce, chopped
- Fresh shredded Asiago cheese
- Toasted croutons.
- Hellman's mayonnaise, half cup
- Finely grated parmesan cheese, half cup

- Buttermilk, 1/4 cup
- Sweet and sour dressing, half cup
- Dry Ranch dressing mix, two tsp.

Instructions:

1. Combine the ingredients for the dressing.
2. Add dressing to the lettuce, to taste.
3. Mix well and refrigerate.
4. Serve topped with shredded Asiago cheese and toasted croutons.

42)   Caribbean Salad with Grilled Prawns

Preparation time: 10 minutes

Cooking Time: 10 minutes

Serving: 2

Ingredients:

- Teriyaki Sauce, half cup
- Tortilla chips
- Iceberg lettuce, half cup
- Pineapple chunks, half cup
- Cabbage, half cup
- Olive oil, half cup
- Jalapeno peppers three tbsp.
- Onion, diced, half cup

- Cilantro, two bunches
- Tomatoes, half cup
- Honey, two tbsp.
- Sugar, one tsp.
- Sesame oil, one tsp.
- Lime juice, one tsp.
- Wine vinegar, one and a half tsp.
- Grilled prawns
- Apple cider vinegar, one tbsp.

Instructions:

1. Marinate the chicken in the teriyaki for at least two hours.
2. Use a plastic bag. Put in fridge.
3. Preheat outdoor or indoor grill.
4. Grill the prawns for 4-5 mins.
5. Toss the lettuces and cabbage together and divide into 2 large serving size salad bowls.
6. Divide the pineapple and sprinkle on salads.
7. Break tortilla chips into large chunks and sprinkle on salads.
8. Slice the grilled prawns and divide among bowls.
9. Pour the dressing into two small bowls and serve with the salads.

43) Caribbean Salad with Shrimps

Preparation time: 10 minutes

Cooking Time: 10 minutes

Serving: 2

Ingredients:

- Teriyaki Sauce, half cup
- Tortilla chips
- Iceberg lettuce, half cup
- Pineapple chunks, half cup
- Cabbage, half cup
- Olive oil, half cup
- Jalapeno peppers three tbsp.
- Onion, diced, half cup
- Cilantro, two bunches
- Tomatoes, half cup
- Honey, two tbsp.
- Sugar, one tsp.
- Sesame oil, one tsp.
- Lime juice, one tsp.
- Wine vinegar, one and a half tsp.
- Shrimps
- Apple cider vinegar, one tbsp.

Instructions:

1. Marinate the shrimps in the teriyaki for at least two hours.
2. Use a plastic bag. Put in fridge.
3. Preheat outdoor or indoor grill.
4. Grill the shrimps for 4-5 mins.
5. Toss the lettuces and cabbage together and divide into 2 large serving size salad bowls.
6. Divide the pineapple and sprinkle on salads.
7. Break tortilla chips into large chunks and sprinkle on salads.
8. Place the grilled shrimps and divide among bowls.
9. Pour the dressing into two small bowls and serve with the salads.

44)   Spicy Shrimp Tacos

Preparation time: 10 minutes

Cooking Time: 10 minutes

Serving: 3

Ingredients:

- Tortilla, three
- Shrimps, six
- Iceberg lettuce, half cup
- Cabbage, half cup
- Avocado, two slices
- Chili powder, a pinch
- Mayonnaise, three tbsp.
- Onion, diced, half cup
- Thai sweet chili sauce, one tbsp.
- Siracha, one tbsp.

Instructions:

1. Heat a grill pan over medium heat and wipe surface with olive oil.
2. Season the shrimp with the salt, pepper and chili powder, and then grill for three to five minutes until done.
3. In a small bowl, mix together the mayo, sweet chili sauce and siracha together.
4. Warm the tortillas and place half of the cabbage on each tortilla.
5. Drizzle half the sauce over each taco.
6. Top with shrimp & garnish with avocado.
7. Serve immediately.

45)   Zuppa Toscana Soup

Preparation time: 10 minutes

Cooking Time: 35 minutes

Serving: 4

Ingredients:

- Water, two cups
- Minced garlic, one tbsp.
- Butter, four tbsp.
- Heavy cream, two cups
- Chopped kale, two cups
- Onion, half
- Ground fish sausage, half pound
- Salt and pepper to taste
- Potatoes, half cup

Instructions:

1. Mix all the ingredients together in a large pot.
2. Cook for 35 minutes and then serve hot.

46)   Herb Grilled Salmon

Preparation time: 10 minutes

Cooking Time: 15 minutes

Serving: 4

Ingredients:

- Salmon fillet, two pounds
- Lemon, two, cut in halves
- Butter, half cup
- Italian seasoning, two tbsp.
- Steamed rice, two cups
- Parsley, half cup
- Minced garlic, one tsp.
- Salt and pepper to taste

Instructions:

1. Season the salmon with salt, pepper, and Italian Seasoning, rubbing them well on both sides.
2. Allow the salmon to briefly marinade on a slotted tray, at least for fifteen minutes.
3. Place the salmon on the grill skin side down and brush with oil on both sides. You may also use cooking spray.
4. Cook the salmon, flipping it regularly until it is cooked through.
5. Bring your butter out from the chiller & slice a half cm thick ring. Return any excess back to the chiller, and discard any paper wrapping of the cut portion.
6. Once the salmon is cooked, serve it with rice, lemon wedges, your garlic butter on top, and your choice of vegetables.

47)   Chicken Scampi

Preparation time: 10 minutes

Cooking Time: 20 minutes

Serving: 4

Ingredients:

- Olive oil, two tbsp.
- Minced garlic, one and a half tsp.
- Flour, one tbsp.
- Heavy cream, two cups
- Onion, half cup
- Scampi, half pound
- Salt and pepper to taste
- Parmesan cheese, half cup
- Mix bell peppers, sliced
- Angel hair, twelve ounces

Instructions:

1. Season scampi.
2. Place flour in a shallow dish and season with one tsp seasoned salt.
3. Dredge scampi in flour.
4. Heat one tbsp. olive oil in large skillet.
5. Place scampi in skillet and cook over medium high heat for four minutes. Flip and cook for three to four more minutes. Remove to a plate.
6. Add one tbsp. oil to skillet.
7. Add peppers and onions. Season with salt and pepper. Sauté for about five minutes.
8. Add garlic and sauté for a few more minutes.

9. Add cream, milk, and parmesan. Bring to a simmer.
10. Add scampi and let simmer for five minutes.
11. Your dish is ready to be served.

48) Shrimp Alfredo

Preparation time: 10 minutes

Cooking Time: 20 minutes

Serving: 4

Ingredients:

- Olive oil, two tbsp.
- Minced garlic, one and a half tsp.
- Flour, one tbsp.
- Butter, four tbsp.
- Heavy cream, two cups
- Parsley, half cup
- Shrimp, half pound
- Salt and pepper to taste
- Parmesan cheese, half cup
- Pasta, one cup

Instructions:

1. Add oil into a pan and then garlic.
2. Add butter, cream and flour and mix until uniform mixture is formed.

3. Add shrimps and cook and then add pasta.
4. Serve in a bowl with parsley and parmesan cheese on top.

49)   Hickory Bourbon Salmon

Preparation time: 20 minutes

Cooking Time: 20 minutes

Serving: 3

Ingredients:

- Bourbon, one cup
- Soy sauce, two tbsp.
- Chopped chives, one tsp.
- Brown sugar, two tbsp.
- Salt and pepper to taste
- Salmon fillet, one pound
- Olive oil, two tbsp.
- Garlic powder, half tsp.

Instructions:

1. Combine pineapple juice, brown sugar, bourbon, soy sauce, pepper and garlic powder in a bowl.
2. Stir to dissolve sugar. Add the oil.
3. Remove skin and bones from salmon fillets.
4. Put fillets in baking dish and pour marinade over and let sit in the fridge for one hour or longer.
5. The longer it can sit the more the marinade seeps into the fillets.
6. Cook the salmon filets on the grill or on the stove top on medium heat.

7. Brush the extra marinade over the fillets as they are cooking.
8. Arrange the fillets on a plate and sprinkle with the chopped chives.

50)   New Orleans

Preparation time: 10 minutes

Cooking Time: 15 minutes

Serving: 4

Ingredients:

- Tilapa fillet, two pounds
- Shrimp, one pound
- Butter, four tbsp.
- Creole seasoning, two tbsp.
- Alfredo sauce, half cup
- Olive oil, three tbsp.
- Minced garlic, one tsp.
- Salt and pepper to taste

Instructions:
1. Preheat oven to 425 degree.
2. Wash and dry tilapia fillets, spread with olive oil and creole seasoning, to your taste.
3. Place in well oiled baking pan, bake for ten minutes, until just white.
4. While fish is baking, warm Alfredo in a small saucepan.

5. In a fry pan, melt three tbsp. butter, add minced garlic and cleaned, prepared shrimp sauté for about five minutes.
6. When fish is ready, remove pan from oven.
7. Carefully remove fillets to plates, top with cooked shrimp and Alfredo sauce.

4.3 Dinner Recipes

51)   Kale, Edamame and Tofu Curry

Serving: 4

Nutritional Value: 342 calories

Preparation time: 10 minutes

Cook time: 35 minutes

Total time: 45 minutes

Ingredients:

- 200g kale leaves stalks evacuated and torn
- One tbsp rapeseed oil
- Two cloves garlic stripped and ground
- One red bean stew, deseeded and meagerly cut
- One enormous onion, diced
- One enormous thumb size (7cm) ginger, removed and ground
- 1/2 tsp ground turmeric
- One tsp paprika
- 1/2 tsp ground cumin

- 1/4 tsp cayenne pepper
- 1 tsp salt
- 250g dried red lentils
- 50g solidified soy edamame beans
- 200g firm tofu slashed into solid shapes
- One liter bubbling water
- Two tomatoes, generally slashed
- Juice of 1 lime

Instructions:

1. Put the oil in an overwhelming bottomed container over a low-medium stove. Include the onion and cook for 5 minutes before including the garlic, ginger and bean stew and cooking for a further 2 minutes. Include the turmeric, cayenne, paprika, cumin, and salt. Mix thoroughly before including the red lentils and mixing once more.
2. Pour in the bubbling water and make a generous stew by boiling for ten minutes, at that point decrease the warmth of the stove and cook for a further 20-30 minutes until the curry has a thick consistency.
3. Add the soya beans, tofu, and tomatoes and cook for a further five minutes. Include the lime juice and kale leaves and cook until the kale is simply delicate.
4. Your dish is ready to be served.

52)   Grilled Salmon

Preparation time: 10 minutes

Cooking Time: 15 minutes

Serving: 4

Ingredients:

- Salmon fillet, two pounds
- Butter, half cup
- Italian seasoning, two tbsp.
- Steamed rice, two cups
- Parsley, half cup
- Minced garlic, one tsp.
- Salt and pepper to taste

Instructions:

1. Season the salmon with salt, pepper, and Italian seasoning, rubbing them well on both sides.
2. Allow the salmon to briefly marinade on a slotted tray, at least for fifteen minutes.
3. Place the salmon on the grill skin side down and brush with oil on both sides. You may also use cooking spray.
4. Cook the salmon, flipping it regularly until it is cooked through.
5. Bring your butter out from the chiller & slice a half cm thick ring.
6. Once the salmon is cooked, serve it with rice, your garlic butter on top, and your choice of vegetables.

53)   Parmesan Shrimp Pasta

Preparation time: 10 minutes

Cooking Time: 20 minutes

Serving: 4

Ingredients:

- Olive oil, two tbsp.
- Minced garlic, one and a half tsp.
- Flour, one tbsp.
- Butter, four tbsp.
- Heavy cream, two cups
- Parsley, half cup
- Shrimp, half pound
- Salt and pepper to taste
- Parmesan cheese, half cup
- Pasta, one cup

Instructions:

1. Add oil into a pan and then garlic.
2. Add butter, cream and flour and mix until uniform mixture is formed.
3. Add shrimps and cook and then add pasta.
4. Serve in a bowl with parsley and parmesan cheese on top.

54)   Ranch Pasta

Preparation time: 10 minutes

Cooking Time: 20 minutes

Serving: 2

Ingredients:

- Olive oil, two tbsp.
- Mayonnaise, one tbsp.
- Frozen peas, four tbsp.
- Buttermilk, one cup
- Ranch dressing, half cup
- Salt and pepper to taste
- Ricotta cheese, half cup
- Pasta, one cup

Instructions:

1. Bring a pot of water to a boil and cook pasta.
2. Drain into a colander and rinse with cold water until pasta is cool.
3. Set pasta aside and allow to dry for about thirty minutes.
4. While pasta is cooking, combine mayonnaise, buttermilk, ranch dressing mix, and season salt in a large bowl and mix until combined.
5. Add in frozen peas and stir. The peas will thaw a bit during mixing and will finish thawing while pasta cools.
6. Add dry rotini and mix until well blended.
7. Your pasta is ready to be served.

55) Miso Marinated Cod with Stir-Fried Greens:

Serving: 1.

Nutritional Value: 450 calories

Preparation time: 12 minutes

Cook time: 20 minutes

Total time: 22 minutes

Ingredients:

- 50g kale, generally cut
- One garlic clove, finely diced
- One tbsp mirin
- 200g skinless cod filet
- One tbsp additional virgin olive oil
- 20g miso 60g green beans
- 40g celery, cut
- 20g red onion, cut
- One tsp finely crushed new ginger
- One tsp ground turmeric
- One tsp sesame seeds
- 5g parsley, usually cut
- 30g buckwheat
- One tbsp tamari

Instructions:

1. Warm the stove to 220°C.
2. Blend the miso, mirin, and one teaspoon of the oil. Rub everywhere throughout the cod and leave to marinate for 30 minutes. Prepare the cod for 10 minutes.
3. In the interim, heat a huge griddle or wok with the rest of the oil. Include the onion and sautéed food for a couple of moments. At that point include the celery, garlic, stew, ginger, green beans, and kale. Hurl and fry until the kale is delicate and cooked through. You may need to add a little water to the skillet to help the cooking procedure.
4. Cook the buckwheat as indicated by the parcel guidelines with the turmeric for 3 minutes.
5. Include the sesame seeds, parsley, and tamari to the sautéed food and present with the greens and fish.
6. Your dish is ready to be served.

56)   Potato Soup

Preparation time: 12 minutes

Cooking Time: 30 minutes

Serving: 6

Ingredients:

- Cornstarch, two tbsp.
- Potato, two
- Green Onions, chopped, three
- Ginger, grated, half tsp.
- Water, two tbsp.
- Chicken broth, four cups

- Soy Sauce, one tbsp.

Instructions:

1. Mix all the ingredients together, and boil it for about thirty minutes.
2. Add the cornstarch in the end, and mix properly.
3. Your soup is ready to be served.

57)   Toowoomba Pasta Recipe

Preparation Time: 20 minutes

Cooking Time: 30 minutes

Serving: 4

Ingredients:

- Parmesan cheese, half cup
- Fettuccini, one box
- Cornstarch, one tbsp.
- Garlic powder
- Ketchup, two tbsp.
- Olive oil, one tbsp.
- Cream, one tbsp.
- Shrimps, half pound
- Small onion, diced, one
- Butter, two tbsp.
- Large mushrooms, sliced, four
- Salt and pepper, to taste

Instructions:

1. Cook fettuccine as directed.
2. Melt butter in a large skillet.
3. Whisk in cream, ketchup and spices.
4. Bring to a boil.
5. Continue to simmer and reduce while you continue with the rest of the recipe, stirring occasionally with a wire whisk.
6. Sauté mushrooms in a separate small skillet over medium to low heat, in olive oil until soft.
7. Add mushrooms to simmering sauce.
8. Cook shrimp in the small skillet in olive oil just until pink and add to sauce.
9. Simmer for about five minutes adding green onions for the last two minutes or so.
10. In a large bowl, toss shrimp mixture with cooked and drained fettuccine and serve immediately, topping with finely shredded fresh parmesan cheese.
11. Your dish is ready.

58)   Seafood Stuffed Mushrooms

Preparation time: 10 minutes

Cooking Time: 25 minutes

Serving: 6

Ingredients:

- Oil, one quart
- Garlic powder, half tsp.
- Eggs, two
- Milk, one cup
- Crab meat, half pound

- Wheat flour, half cup
- Fresh mushrooms, one pound
- Cheddar cheese, half cup
- Salt, half tsp.
- Oyster crackers, two cups
- Red bell peppers, two
- Onions, one
- Celery, a quarter cup

Instructions:

1. Preheat oven to 400 degrees.
2. Wash mushrooms and remove stems.
3. Set caps aside, and chop half of the stems.
4. Sauté chopped mushroom stems, celery, onion and pepper in butter for two minutes.
5. Transfer to a plate and cool in refrigerator.
6. Combine sautéed vegetables and all other ingredients and mix well.
7. Place mushroom caps in a sprayed or buttered baking pan stem side up.
8. Spoon one tsp stuffing into each mushroom cap.
9. Cover with a piece of sliced cheese.
10. Bake for fifteen minutes until cheese is lightly brown.

59)   Lobster Bisque

Preparation time: 10 minutes

Cooking Time: 30 minutes

Serving: 4

Ingredients:

- Water, six cups
- Fish stock, two cups
- Green Onions, chopped, three
- Carrot, one cup
- Celery, one cup
- Lobsters, one pound
- Ginger, grated, half tsp.
- White wine, two tbsp.
- Potato, two
- Cream, one cup
- Cognac, a quarter cup
- Tomatoes, one and a half cup
- Paprika and thyme, one tbsp.
- All-purpose flour, one cup

Instructions:

1. Place the water, the white wine and the fish stock into a wide, deep pot, and bring to a boil on high heat.
2. Place lobsters, topside down, in the broth.
3. Reduce heat to medium and cook covered for approximately six minutes.
4. Remove lobsters from broth and put them to the side.
5. When the lobsters are cool enough to handle, begin removing the meat from the shell, dicing the pieces into half inch cubes.

6. Store the lobster meat in the refrigerator until later.
7. Place the lobster shells back into the broth, reduce heat to a simmer and cook uncovered for twenty minutes.
8. Strain the broth through a sieve into a container and store in the refrigerator until later.
9. Discard the lobster shells.
10. Put your pot back on the stove under medium heat.
11. Pour in the melted butter.
12. Once the butter is heated up, add the onions, carrots, celery and garlic.
13. Add the cognac and cook until the alcohol has evaporated.
14. Mix in the flour, stirring with a heavy gauge spatula or spoon until the mixture is blond in color and has a buttery aroma.
15. Mix the diced tomatoes, paprika, thyme and ground pepper with the cold broth from the refrigerator.
16. Then, pour the broth slowly into the butter and vegetable mixture.
17. Cook uncovered for thirty minutes under medium low heat, stirring frequently so not to burn.
18. Remove bisque from heat.
19. Blend small amounts of bisque in blender and then puree.
20. Puree all of the bisque and pour pureed bisque back into pot with remaining amount.
21. Add chopped lobster meat and heavy cream, heat and serve.
22. If the soup is too thick, thin it by adding milk or water prior to serving.
23. Your dish is ready to be served.

60)   Super Salmon Salad:

Serving: 1

Nutritional Value: 98 calories

Preparation time: 15 minutes

Cook time: 0 minutes

Total time: 15 minutes

Ingredients:

- 80g avocado, stripped, stoned and cut
- 40g celery, cut
- 50g chicory leaves
- 100g smoked salmon cuts
- One huge Medjool date, hollowed and cut
- 20g red onion, cut
- 15g pecans cut
- One tbsp extra-virgin olive oil
- Juice ¼ lemons
- 10g parsley finely cut
- One tbsp capers
- 10g lovage or celery leaves, cut
- 50g arugula leaves

Instructions:

1. Mix the serving of mixed greens leaves on an enormous plate.
2. Combine all the rest of the things and serve on the leaves.
3. Your salad is ready to be served.

61)   Baked Salmon with Mint Dressing:

Serving: 1

Nutritional Value: 340 calories

Preparation time: 10 minutes

Cook time: 10 minutes

Total time: 20 minutes

Ingredients:

- One little bunch (10g) parsley, generally cut
- One salmon filet (130g)
- 40g spinach leaves
- radishes, cut and meagrely cut
- 40g blended serving of mixed greens leaves
- 5cm piece (50g) cucumber, cut into lumps
- Two spring onions, cut

For the dressing:

- Salt and newly ground dark pepper
- 1 tsp low-fat mayonnaise
- 1 tbsp rice vinegar
- 1 tbsp regular yogurt
- Two leaves mint, finely diced

Instructions:

1. Preheat the broiler to 200°C.
2. Place the salmon filet on a heating plate and prepare for 16–18 minutes until simply cooked through. Remove from the broiler and put it in a safe spot. The salmon is similarly decent hot or cold in the plate of mixed greens.
3. If your salmon has skin, basically cook skin side down and expel the salmon from the skin utilizing a fish cut in the wake of cooking. It should slide off effectively when cooked.
4. In a little bowl, combine the mayonnaise, yogurt, rice wine vinegar, mint leaves, and salt and pepper together and leave for 5 minutes to permit the flavors to create.
5. Arrange the plate of mixed greens leaves and spinach on a serving plate and top with the radishes, cucumber, spring onions, and parsley. Piece the cooked salmon onto the serving of mixed greens and sprinkle the dressing over.
6. Your salad is ready to be served.

62)   Green Salad Skewers:

Serving: 2

Nutritional Value: 306 calories

Preparation time: 30 minutes

Cook time: 10 minutes

Total time: 40 minutes

Ingredients:

- huge dark olives
- wooden sticks, let it absorb water for 30 minutes before use
- 100g feta, cut into eight 3D squares

- ½ red onion cut down the middle and isolated into eight pieces
- cherry tomatoes
- One yellow pepper, cut into eight squares
- 100g cucumber, cut into four cuts and split

For the dressing:

- 1 tsp balsamic vinegar
- 1 tbsp additional virgin olive oil
- ½ clove garlic, stripped and squashed
- Juice of ½ lemon
- Liberal flavoring of salt and newly ground dark pepper
- Not many leaves basil, finely slashed
- ½ tsp dried blended herbs to supplant basil and oregano

Instructions:

1. Thread each stick with the plate of mixed greens things: olive, tomato, yellow pepper, red onion, cucumber, feta, tomato, and olive, yellow pepper, red onion, cucumber.
2. Place all the dressing ingredients in a little bowl and combine completely. Pour over the sticks.
3. Your dish is ready to be served.

63)   Buckwheat Pasta Salad

Serving: 1

Nutritional Value: 112 calories

Preparation time: 10 minutes

Cook time: 0 minutes

Total time: 10 minutes

Ingredients:

- Two cherry tomatoes halved
- A huge bunch of rocket
- A little bunch of basil leaves
- 1/2 avocado, diced
- 20g pine nuts
- Two olives
- 50g buckwheat pasta (cooked as per the bundle instructions)
- One tbsp. additional virgin olive oil

Instructions:

1. Tenderly consolidate all the above mentioned ingredients with the exception of the pine nuts and decorate on a plate or in a bowl
2. Dissipate the pine nuts over the top.
3. Your salad is ready to be served.

64)   Garlic Shrimp Skewers

Preparation time: 10 minutes

Cooking Time: 30 minutes

Serving: 4

Ingredients:

- Worcestershire sauce, one tsp.
- Shrimp, two pound
- Minced garlic, half tsp.
- Butter, two tbsp.
- Lemon juice, half cup
- Wooden skewers
- Salt and Pepper to taste

Instructions:

1. In a medium saucepan melt the butter over medium heat.
2. Add the garlic and sauté for a couple of minutes.
3. Remove from heat.
4. Add lemon juice, Worcestershire sauce, garlic powder, salt, and pepper.
5. Allow the sauce to cool.
6. Reserve half of the sauce in a bowl for brushing.
7. Mix the renaming half of the sauce with the raw shrimp and marinate for thirty minutes.
8. Thread the shrimp onto the wooden skewers.
9. Heat an outdoor grill to medium-high heat.

10.   Place the shrimp skewers onto the grill and cook while brushing with the reserved marinade for a few minutes per side or until the shrimp are pink.
11.   Your dish is ready to be served.

65)   Shrimp Popcorn

Preparation time: 10 minutes

Cooking Time: 10 minutes

Serving: 4

Ingredients:

- Shrimp, two pound
- Minced garlic, half tsp.
- Milk, two tbsp.
- All- purpose flour, one cup
- Egg, one
- Oil, half cup
- Seasoned salt, one tsp.
- Salt and Pepper to taste

Instructions:

1. Preheat oil to 350 degrees.
2. Combine half cup oil and egg; beat well.
3. Add remaining ingredients except oil for frying and stir until well blended.
4. Dip shrimp into batter to coat.
5. Drop shrimp into hot oil and fry for a few minutes or until golden brown.

6. Remove with slotted spoon; drain on paper towel.
7. Your dish is ready to be served.

66)   Nashville Hot Shrimp

Preparation time: 10 minutes

Cooking Time: 10 minutes

Serving: 4

Ingredients:

- Shrimp, two pound
- Minced garlic, half tsp.
- Milk, two tbsp.
- All- purpose flour, one cup
- Egg, one
- Nashville pepper, three tbsp.
- Oil, half cup
- Seasoned salt, one tsp.
- Salt and Pepper to taste

Instructions:

1. Preheat oil to 350 degrees.
2. Combine half cup oil and egg; beat well.
3. Add remaining ingredients except oil for frying and stir until well blended.
4. Dip shrimp into batter to coat.
5. Drop shrimp into hot oil and fry for a few minutes or until golden brown.
6. Remove with slotted spoon; drain on paper towel.

7. Your dish is ready to be served.

67)   Shrimp Linguini Alfredo

Preparation time: 10 minutes

Cooking Time: 20 minutes

Serving: 4

Ingredients:

- Olive oil, two tbsp.
- Minced garlic, one and a half tsp.
- Flour, one tbsp.
- Butter, four tbsp.
- Heavy cream, two cups
- Parsley, half cup
- Shrimp, half pound
- Salt and pepper to taste
- Parmesan cheese, half cup
- Linguini pasta, one cup

Instructions:

1. Add oil into a pan and then garlic.
2. Add butter, cream and flour and mix until uniform mixture is formed.
3. Add shrimps and cook and then add the linguini pasta.
4. Serve in a bowl with parsley and parmesan cheese on top.

68)   Crab Linguini Pasta

Preparation time: 10 minutes

Cooking Time: 20 minutes

Serving: 4

Ingredients:

- Olive oil, two tbsp.
- Minced garlic, one and a half tsp.
- Flour, one tbsp.
- Butter, four tbsp.
- Heavy cream, two cups
- Parsley, half cup
- Crab meat, half pound
- Salt and pepper to taste
- Parmesan cheese, half cup
- Linguini pasta, one cup

Instructions:

1. Add oil into a pan and then garlic.
2. Add butter, cream and flour and mix until uniform mixture is formed.
3. Add crab meat and cook and then add the linguini pasta.
4. Serve in a bowl with parsley and parmesan cheese on top.

69)   Vegetarian Pizza

Preparation time: 10 minutes

Cooking Time: 30 minutes

Serving: 8

Ingredients:

- Pizza dough, one box
- Garlic powder, half tsp.
- Mushrooms, one cup
- Chili powder, one tsp.
- Olive oil, one tsp.
- Mozzarella cheese, shredded, one cup
- Mixed vegetables, one cup
- Olives, half cup

Instructions:

1. Heat oil in large skillet.
2. Add vegetables and cook, stirring frequently until lightly soft.

3. Stir in seasonings into the mixture.
4. Heat oven to 425 degrees.
5. Sprinkle pizza pan with semolina flour and press dough into pan.
6. Pre-bake dough until it is a very light golden brown, about six minutes.
7. Remove from oven and scatter vegetables, mushrooms, olives on the crust, and top with cheese.
8. Bake for another fifteen minutes until crust is golden brown.
9. Your pizza is ready to be served.

70)   Macaroni Salad

Preparation time: 10 minutes

Cooking Time: 10 minutes

Serving: 1

Ingredients:

- Boiled macaroni, as required
- Ketchup, half cup
- Salt and Pepper
- Mayonnaise, half cup
- Powdered sugar, one tbsp.
- Whole milk, a quarter cup
- Sweetened condensed milk, half cup
- Cheddar cheese cubes, one cup
- Pineapple chunks, half cup
- Capsicum, half cup
- Sweet corn, half cup
- Cabbage, half cup

Instructions:

1. Measure all the ingredients in a large salad bowl and mix really well.
2. Chill in fridge for a couple hours before serving.
3. Your dish is ready.

71)   Crunchy Thai Salad

Preparation time: 10 minutes

Cooking Time: 10 minutes

Serving: 4

Ingredients:

- Chopped cilantro, 1/4 cup
- Chili Lime Vinaigrette, one tbsp.
- Sweet and Spicy Peanut Sauce, one tbsp.
- Shredded red cabbage, one cup
- Medium carrots peeled and shredded, two
- Shelled edamame, half cup
- Sliced almonds toasted, half cup
- Wonton Strips
- Napa or Savory cabbage chopped, half cup
- Fresh spinach coarsely chopped, two cups
- Green onions thinly sliced, three

For Frying the Shrimps:

- Butter, half tsp.
- Olive oil, two tbsp.

- Chili powder, half tsp.

- Cayenne pepper, half tsp.

- Minced garlic, one tsp.

- Raw shrimp peeled and deveined, eight ounces

Instructions:

1. In a large self-sealing plastic bag, combine shrimp, minced garlic, chili powder, and cayenne.
2. Toss until shrimps are evenly coated with the spice mix.
3. Heat a large, heavy skillet over medium high heat. Melt olive oil and butter and swirl to coat the bottom of the skillet.
4. Add shrimps in a single layer. Pan-fry for about 2 minutes, then turn and fry until shrimps become pink all the way through and slightly firm, about 2-3 minutes. Do not overcook the shrimps.
5. Carefully remove from skillet and set aside.
6. Assemble the salad.
7. Layer or toss cabbages, spinach, carrots, edamame, green onions, and sliced almonds, wonton strips, and cilantro in bowl.
8. Serve with Chili-Lime Vinaigrette and Sweet & Spicy Peanut Sauce.
9. Garnish with additional cilantro and wonton strips.

72)   Double Crunch Shrimp

Preparation Time: 10 minutes

Cooking Time: 10 minutes

Serving: 2-3

Ingredients:

For Sauce:

- Chili bean paste, two tbsp.
- Chili paste, one tsp.
- Cornstarch, one tsp.
- Chicken broth, half cup
- Oyster sauce, two tbsp.
- Sherry, half cup

For Shrimps:

- Salt and pepper, to taste
- Seasoning salt, to taste
- Oil, for cooking
- Water, two tbsp.
- Panko, one cup
- Flour, one cup
- Shrimp, one and a half pounds
- Eggs, two

Instructions:

1. Use the shrimps by cutting vertically down the back of the shrimp. Leave tails on.
2. Season shrimp with salt, pepper, and seasoning salt.
3. Heat enough oil to deep fry the shrimp in a skillet to 350 degrees.
4. Put panko crumbs in a shallow dish. Add seasonings to taste and mix well.
5. Put flour in a separate shallow dish.

6. Beat the eggs and water together.
7. Dip the shrimps in the egg-water mixture.
8. Add the shrimps to the flour.
9. Dip again in egg-water mixture.
10. Toss shrimps in panko crumbs.
11. Fry in hot oil at 350 degrees F until golden, about 3 minutes.
12. Drain the fried shrimps on the cooling racks over paper towels.
13. In a large pot mix together all of the ingredients for the sauce, making sure that the cornstarch dissolves thoroughly.
14. Heat a wok or large skillet on high heat with a teaspoon of oil.
15. Add the sauce and let it simmer for 1 minute to thicken. Add the shrimps, toss to coat, and simmer for 1 more minute.
16. Your crunchy shrimps are ready to serve.

73) California Roll

Preparation Time: 15 minutes

Cooking Time: 30 minutes

Serving: 4

Ingredients:

- Rice vinegar, quarter cup

- Granulated sugar, two tbsp.

- Salt, half tsp.

- White rice, two cups

- Water, two cups

For Sriracha Mayo Crab:

- Light mayonnaise, a quarter cup

- Sriracha, two tbsp.
- Crab meat, twelve ounces

For Toppings:

- Julienned carrots
- Large avocado
- English cucumber, (thinly sliced)

Instructions:

1. Add the rice to a fine mesh strainer, and run under cold water for 1-2 minutes, rinsing until the water runs clear.
2. Allow the rice to thoroughly drain, and then transfer it to a medium saucepan with two cups of water.
3. Place on high heat and bring the rice to a boil.
4. Once boiling, reduce the heat to low, and cover with a lid. Simmer 15 minutes. Remove from heat and allow to rest, undisturbed, and covered, for 15 additional minutes.
5. While you wait, place a small nonstick pan over medium heat.
6. Add the rice vinegar, sugar, and salt. Cook, stirring with a whisk, until the sugar has dissolved completely.
7. Remove from the burner to allow to cool down slightly.
8. When the rice is ready, pour the vinegar mixture over the top of the rice, and stir to thoroughly mix.
9. Fold until all of the vinegar mixture has been absorbed by the rice.

10.   To a small mixing bowl, combine the crab meat with the sriracha, and mayonnaise. Mix well.
11.   In four bowls add the rice and layer with crab mixture, cucumber slices, carrots, diced avocado, sesame seeds, and micro greens.
12.   Drizzle with soy sauce, and serve right away.

74)   Dragon Roll

Preparation time: 15 minutes

Cooking Time: 60 minutes

Serving: 4

Ingredients:

- Lemon, half
- Nori sheets, two
- Sushi rice, two cups
- Shrimp tempura, eight pieces
- Tobiko, two tbsp.
- Unagi (eel)
- Persian/Japanese cucumbers, one
- Avocados, one

Instructions:

1. Gather all the ingredients.
2. Cut cucumber lengthwise into quarters.
3. Remove the seeds, and then cut in half lengthwise.
4. Cut the avocado in half lengthwise around the seed, and twist the two halves until they separate.
5. Hack the knife edge into the pit. Hold the skin of the avocado with the other hand, and twist in counter directions.
6. Remove the skin, and slice the avocado widthwise.
7. Gently presses the avocados slices with your fingers, and then keep pressing gently, and evenly

with the side of the knife until the length of avocado is about the length of sushi roll.

8. Wrap the bamboo mat with plastic wrap, and place half of the nori sheet, shiny side down.

9. Turn it over and put the shrimp tempura, cucumber strips, and tobiko at the bottom end of the nori sheet.

10. If you like to put unagi, place it inside here as well.

11. From the bottom end, start rolling nori sheet over the filling tightly, and firmly with bamboo mat until the bottom end reaches the nori sheet.

12. Place the bamboo mat over the roll and tightly squeeze the roll.

13. Using the side of the knife, place the avocado on top of the roll.

14. Place plastic wrap over the roll and then put the bamboo mat over.

15. Cut the roll into 8 pieces with the knife.

16. Put tobiko on each piece of sushi, and drizzle spicy mayo, and sprinkle black sesame seeds on top.

17. Your dish is ready to be served.

75) Cobb Salad

Preparation Time: 10 minutes

Total Time: 10 minutes

Serving: 4

Ingredients:

- Cucumber, peeled and cubed, half cup
- Cherry tomatoes, cut in half
- Garbanzo beans, rinsed, one cup
- Cooked quinoa, a quarter cup

- Slivered almonds, three tbsp.
- Sunflower seeds to sprinkle on top
- Cracked pepper
- Romaine Lettuce, two
- Asparagus spears, cut, four grilled
- Green beans, cut, half cup
- Cubed roasted golden beets, half cup
- Avocado, cubed, half

Instructions:

1. Place cut Romaine lettuce on plate.
2. Place all cut vegetables in sections on the salad greens.
3. Mix the quinoa with the slivered almonds and place quinoa in the middle of the salad.
4. Drizzle your preferred dressing on top and serve.

4.4 Recipes for Juices, Sweet Dishes and Snacks

76)   Muesli

Ingredients:

- 100g strawberries, hulled and diced
- 10g buckwheat puffs
- 15g coconut drops or dried up coconut
- 20g buckwheat cereal

- 40g Medjool dates, hollowed and diced
- 10g cocoa nibs
- 15g pecans, diced
- 100g plain Greek yogurt (or vegetarian type, for example, soya or coconut yogurt)

Instructions:

1. Blend the entire of the above things together.
2. Possibly including the yogurt and strawberries before serving before making it in mass.
3. Your dish is ready to be served.

77) Banana Blueberry Pancakes with Apple Compote and Turmeric Latte

Serving: 2

Nutritional Value: 105 calories

Preparation time: 13 minutes

Cook time: 10 minutes

Total time: 23 minutes

Ingredients:

For preparing the Pancakes

- 225g blueberries
- Six bananas
- 150g oats
- Six eggs

- Two tsp baking powder
- ¼ teaspoon salt

For preparing the Apple Compote

- 1/4 teaspoon cinnamon powder
- Two apples
- One tablespoon lemon juice
- Five dates (pitted)
- salt to taste

For preparing the Turmeric Latte

- stripped ginger root
- One teaspoon turmeric powder
- Touch of dark pepper (expands ingestion)
- One teaspoon cinnamon powder
- Three cups of coconut milk
- One teaspoon crude nectar
- Touch of cayenne pepper (discretionary)

Instructions:

1. Put the oats in a rapid blender and let it grind for one moment or until an oat flour has framed. You should ensure that your blender is dry before doing this, or probably everything will get spongy.
2. Presently include the bananas, eggs, heating powder and salt to the blender and grind for 2 minutes until a smooth mixture structures.
3. Move the blend to an enormous bowl and overlay in the blueberries. Leave to rest for 10 mins while the baking powder actuates.

4. To make your cakes, include a bit of margarine to your skillet on a medium-high stove. Include a couple of spoons of the blueberry cake blend and fry for until pleasantly brilliant on the base side. Hurl the flapjack to sear the opposite side.
5. Remove the center and flat cleave your apples.
6. Pop everything in a food processor, along with two tablespoons of water and a touch of salt. Grind it to shape your stout apple compote.
7. Mix all the things in a rapid blender until smooth.
8. Fill it in a little container and warm for 4 minutes over a medium stove until hot yet not bubbling.
9. Your pancakes are ready to be served along with your latte.

78)   Fish and Chips

Preparation Time: 10 minutes

Cooking Time: 10 minutes

Serving: 2-4

Ingredients:

- Large russet potatoes, peeled and cut lengthwise, four

- All-purpose flour, two cups

- Seafood seasoning, two tsp.

- Kosher salt, according to taste

- Peanut or vegetable oil, for frying

- Baking soda, one tsp.

- Cold beer, one bottle

- Haddock fillets, skinned and cut

diagonally, two pounds

Instructions:
1. Warm the oil in a large pot over medium stove.
2. Heat the oil to 325 degrees.
3. Control the temperature with a treats thermometer.
4. Keep the potato sticks in a bowl of water to maintain the color of the potatoes before cooking.
5. Fry the potatoes until they are cooked through and delicate yet have no shading, around four to five minutes.
6. Delicately move the spoon around as the fries are cooking. Take them off from the oil and put them promptly on a paper towel lined heating sheet.
7. Preheat the stove to 300 degrees and raise the temperature of the cooking oil to 375 degrees.
8. In a medium bowl, mix the flour, seasoning, and touch of salt.
9. At the point when the oil is preheated to the right temperature.
10. Coat the fish liberally.
11. While adding the fish to the oil, plunge half of the filet into the oil and permit the blender to begin puffing, and afterward delicately slide it into the oil.
12. Fry the fish until they are brilliantly earthy colored and firm, around 5 minutes turning the fish over, during the cooking time.
13. Move the fish to a serving platter, and present with the fries.

79)   Green Juice

Ingredients:

- One medium pear, cut into eighths
- stems of celery
- One medium green apple, cut into eighths
- 1/2 huge cucumber, cut into quarters

Instructions:

1. Squeeze all the things adhering to the directions for ordinary squeezing in your juicer manual.
2. Drink quickly, or let chill for an hour and enjoy later.

80)   Chocolate and Coffee Mousse

Serving: 8

Nutritional Value: 242 calories

Preparation time: 4 hours

Cook time: 15 minutes

Total time: 4 hours and 15 minutes

Ingredients:

- Cinnamon 1/2 tsp 300 ml of Almond milk
- Cocoa powder 2 tbsp.
- Espresso 200 ml
- Gelatin powder 1 tbsp.
- Coconut yogurt 300 g
- Maple syrup 2 tbsp.

- Chocolate unadulterated 200 g

Instructions:

1. Join the almond milk and espresso in a pan and sprinkle the gelatin over it. Let it be for 5 minutes.
2. Mix the blend well and bring to bubble quickly. At that point, quickly remove the container from the stove.
3. Mix the maple syrup, cinnamon, and the dim chocolate into the hot fluid. Keep on blending until the chocolate has totally dissolved and has been assimilated into the blend.
4. Pour it in enriching pastry glasses and let it set in the refrigerator for approximately 4 hours.
5. Prior to serving, decorate with a spoon of coconut yogurt and residue with cocoa.
6. Your dish is ready to be served.

81)   Melon and Grape Juice

Serving: 2

Nutritional Value: 125 calories

Preparation time: 2 minutes

Cook time: 0 minutes

Total time: 2 minutes

Ingredients:

- 100g melon, stripped, deseeded and cut into pieces
- ½ cucumber, stripped however liked, split, seeds evacuated and diced
- 100g red seedless grapes

30g small spinach leaves, stalk less

-

Instructions:

1. Blend together all the things in a blender and pour it out in glasses.
2. Serve your juice right away.

82)   Black Current and Kale Smoothie

Serving: 2

Nutritional Value: 186 calories

Preparation time: 4 minutes

Cook time: 0 minutes

Total time: 4 minutes

Ingredients:

- One banana
- One tsp nectar
- One cup newly made green tea
- Five ice 3D shapes
- kale leaves, stalk less
- 40 g blackcurrants, washed

Instructions:

1. Mix the nectar into the warm green tea until properly mixed.
2. Prodigy all the things together in a blender until smooth.
3. Serve right away.

83)   Green Tea Smoothie

Serving: 2

Nutritional Value: 183 calories

Preparation time: 3 minutes

Cook time: 0 minutes

Total time: 3 minutes

Ingredients:

- Two tsp matcha green tea powder
- Two bananas
- 250 ml of milk
- Three tsp nectar
- 1/2 tsp vanilla bean
- Five ice 3D squares

Instructions:

1. Basically, mix all the things together in a blender and serve in two glasses.
2. Drink it without storing it for later.

84)   Black current and Raspberry Jelly

Serving: 2

Nutritional Value: 76 calories

Preparation time: 2 minutes

Cook time: 15 minutes

Total time: 17 minutes

Ingredients:

- Two tbsp. granulated sugar
- 100g raspberries washed
- 100g blackcurrants washed
- 300ml water
- Two packs gelatin

Instructions:

1. Arrange the raspberries in two serving dishes/glasses/molds. Put the gelatin in a bowl of cold water to mollify.
2. Place the blackcurrants in a little skillet with the sugar and 100ml water and bring to bubble. Stew enthusiastically for 5 minutes and afterward remove it from the heat. Leave it in the open for 2 minutes.
3. Squeeze out abundant water from the gelatin leaves and add them to the pan. Mix until completely mixed, at that point mix in the remainder of the water. Empty the fluid into the readied dishes and refrigerate to set. These ought to be prepared in around 3-4 hours or overnight.
4. Your jelly after setting is ready to be served.

85) Chocolate Bites:

Ingredients:

- 250g Medjool dates pitted
- 30g dull chocolate broken into pieces; or cocoa nibs

- 1 tbsp cocoa powder
- 120g pecans
- 1 tbsp ground turmeric
- 1 tbsp additional virgin olive oil
- 1–2 tbsp water
- 1 tsp vanilla concentrate

Instructions:

1. Put the pecans and chocolate in a food processor and keep it processing until you have a fine powder.
2. Include the various things with the exception of the water and mix until the blend shapes a ball. You could conceivably need to include the water depending on the consistency of the blend. You don't need it to be excessively clingy.
3. Utilizing your hands, structure the blend into scaled-down balls, and refrigerate in a hermetically sealed compartment for approximately one hour before eating them.
4. You could move a portion of the balls in some more cocoa or dried up a coconut to accomplish an alternate completion if you like.
5. They can be stored up for a week.
6. Your dish is ready to be served.
7. Enjoy your meal.

86)   Banana and Chocolate Smoothie

Preparation time: 5 minutes

Serving: 1

Ingredients:

- Frozen banana chunks, ½ cup
- Frozen chocolate chunks, ½ cup
- Peanut Butter ice cream, one scoop
- Low fat milk, one cup

Instructions:

1. Add all the ingredients in a blender and blend appropriately for three to four minutes.
2. Now pour into a cup and enjoy.
3. You can store this smoothie by freezing it.
4. Prior to using it later, you can re-blend the smoothie.

87)   Mango and Pineapple Smoothie

Preparation time: 5 minutes

Serving: 1

Ingredients:

- Frozen mango chunks, ½ cup
- Frozen Pineapple chunks, ½ cup

- Vanilla ice cream, one scoop
- Low fat milk, one cup

Instructions:

1. Add all the ingredients in a blender and blend appropriately for three to four minutes.
2. Now pour into a cup and enjoy.
3. You can store this smoothie by freezing it.
4. Prior to using it later, you can re-blend the smoothie.

88)   Superfood Smoothie

Preparation time: 5 minutes

Serving: 1

Ingredients:
- Frozen kiwi chunks, ½ cup
- Fresh spinach, ½ cup
- Cucumber chunks, ¼ cup
- Chia seeds, one tsp.
- Low fat almond milk, one cup
- Vanilla protein powder, ½ cup

Instructions:

1. Add all the ingredients in a blender and blend appropriately for three to four minutes.
2. Now pour into a cup and enjoy.
3. You can store this smoothie by freezing it.
4. Prior to using it later, you can re-blend the smoothie.

89)   Greek Yoghurt and Berry Smoothie

Preparation time: 5 minutes

Serving: 1

Ingredients:

- Frozen berries chunks, ½ cup
- Frozen Greek yoghurt, ½ cup
- Peanut Butter ice cream, one scoop
- Low fat almond milk, one cup
- Vanilla protein powder, ½ cup

Instructions:

1. Add all the ingredients in a blender and blend appropriately for three to four minutes.
2. Now pour into a cup and enjoy.
3. You can store this smoothie by freezing it.
4. Prior to using it later, you can re-blend the smoothie.

90) Apple Pie Smoothie

Preparation time: 5 minutes

Serving: 1

Ingredients:

- Frozen apple chunks, peeled, ½ cup
- Vanilla extract, one tsp.
- Cinnamon powder, ¼ tsp.
- Nutmeg powder, ¼ tsp.
- Low fat milk, one cup

Instructions:

1. Add all the ingredients in a blender and blend appropriately for three to four minutes.
2. Now pour into a cup and enjoy.
3. You can store this smoothie by freezing it.
4. Prior to using it later, you can re-blend the smoothie.

91) Red Berries Smoothie

Preparation time: 5 minutes

Serving: 1

Ingredients:

- Frozen red berries chunks, ½ cup

- Vanilla protein powder, ½ cup
- Low fat milk, one cup

Instructions:

1. Add all the ingredients in a blender and blend appropriately for three to four minutes.
2. Now pour into a cup and enjoy.
3. You can store this smoothie by freezing it.
4. Prior to using it later, you can re-blend the smoothie.

92)   Pear and Banana Protein Smoothie

Preparation time: 5 minutes

Serving: 1

Ingredients:

- Frozen banana chunks, ½ cup
- Vanilla protein powder, ½ cup
- Low fat milk, one cup
- Frozen Pear chunks, ½ cup

Instructions:

1. Add all the ingredients in a blender and blend appropriately for three to four minutes.
2. Now pour into a cup and enjoy.
3. You can store this smoothie by freezing it.

4. Prior to using it later, you can re-blend the smoothie.

93)   Tomato Smoothie

Preparation time: 5 minutes

Serving: 1

Ingredients:
- Lemon juice, two tbsp.
- Carrot juice, ½ cup
- Tomato juice, one cup
- Tomatoes peeled, ½ cup
- Celery Stalk chopped, one

Instructions:
1. Add all the ingredients in a blender and blend appropriately for three to four minutes.
2. Now pour into a cup and enjoy.
3. You can store this smoothie by freezing it.
4. Prior to using it later, you can re-blend the smoothie.

94)   Red Velvet Cake

Preparation Time: 15 minutes

Cooking Time: 35 minutes

Serving: 12

Ingredients:

- Cocoa powder, two cups
- Buttermilk, one cup
- Large eggs, two
- Food color, red
- All-purpose flour, two cups
- Salt, one tsp.
- Vanilla essence, one tsp.
- Vinegar, one tbsp.
- Baking soda, one tsp.
- Shortening, half cup
- Sugar, one and a half cup
- Butter, half cup

Instructions:

1. Cream butter and sugar; add eggs and blend.
2. Add food coloring, water, and cocoa.
3. Blend in buttermilk; add flour and salt gradually.
4. Add vanilla and beat until mixed. Mix vinegar and soda and stir in last; do not beat.
5. Pour into two nine- inch pans.
6. Bake for 30 to 35 minutes in a 350 degree oven. Frost with fluff frosting.
7. Add milk mixture and vanilla; continue beating.
8. When icing is very fluffy, frost cool cake.

95)   Double Chocolate Smoothie

Preparation time: 5 minutes

Serving: 1

Ingredients:

- Frozen Greek Yoghurt, ½ cup
- Unsweetened Cocoa powder, ¼ tsp.
- Banana chunks, ¼ tsp.
- Chocolate protein powder, ¼ cup
- Low fat milk, one cup

Instructions:

1. Add all the ingredients in a blender and blend appropriately for three to four minutes.
2. Now pour into a cup and enjoy.
3. You can store this smoothie by freezing it.
4. Prior to using it later, you can re-blend the smoothie.

96)   Stout Irish Cream Cake

Preparation Time: 15 minutes

Cooking Time: 45 minutes

Serving: 12

Ingredients:

- Irish cream Liqueur, half cup
- Cream cheese, eight ounce
- Sugar, five cups
- Butter, one cup
- Stuat beer, one cup
- Sour cream, one cup
- Eggs, two
- All-purpose flour, one cup
- Vanilla essence, one tsp.
- Cocoa powder, half cup

Instructions:

1. Mix all the ingredients together and bake for 40 minutes approximately.
2. Dust sugar on top and serve.

97) Pumpkin Spice Smoothie

Preparation time: 5 minutes

Serving: 1

Ingredients:

- Frozen pumpkin puree, ½ cup
- Cinnamon powder, ¼ tsp.
- Ground ginger powder, ¼ tsp.
- Ground cloves powder, ¼ tsp.
- Decaffeinated Coffee, ¾ cup
- Vanilla protein powder, 1/4cup

- Low fat milk, one cup

Instructions:

1. Add all the ingredients in a blender and blend appropriately for three to four minutes.

2. Now pour into a cup and enjoy.

3. You can store this smoothie by freezing it.

4. Prior to using it later, you can re-blend the smoothie.

98)   Artichoke and Spinach Dip

Preparation time: 5 minutes

Cooking Time: 35 minutes

Serving: 10

Ingredients:

- Cream cheese, eight ounces
- Artichoke, ten ounces
- Garlic Alfredo sauce, sixteen ounces
- Chopped spinach, ten ounces
- Mozzarella cheese, shredded, two cups
- Parmesan and cheddar cheese mix, shredded, one cup

Instructions:

1. Mix all ingredients in a large bowl.
2. Pour into crock pot and set on high for 35 minutes.
3. Your dip is ready to serve.

99)   Original Cheesecake

Preparation Time: 10 minutes

Cooking Time: 10 minutes

Serving: 5

Ingredients:

- Sour cream, half cup
- Large eggs, five
- Vanilla extract, two tsp.
- Graham crackers, one and a half cup
- Ground Cinnamon, half tsp.
- Butter, half cup
- Sugar, one and a half cup

Instructions:

1. Use an electric mixer to mix cream cheese, sugar, sour cream and vanilla and cinnamon.
2. Blend until smooth and creamy.
3. Scrape down sides of bowl.
4. Whisk eggs in a bowl; add to cream cheese mixture. Blend just until eggs are incorporated.

5. Add the graham cracker layer which is made by combining butter and graham crackers together first and then the cream cheese mixture.
6. Freeze the mixture for one hour and serve with sour cream on top.

100) Chocolate Frosties

Preparation Time: 5 minutes

Cooking Time: 10 minutes

Serving: 4

Ingredients:

- Milk, one cup
- Vanilla ice-cream, four scoops
- Chocolate milk powder, eight tbsp.

Instructions:

1. Allow the ice cream to soften just enough to blend easily
2. Mix everything thoroughly in a blender.
3. Once everything is thoroughly combined, mix until you have reached the desired softness.
4. Serve right away in glasses, with spoons.

All the recipes mentioned in this chapter are easy to make by yourself at home.

Conclusion

Our daily life revolves around our busy schedules. In this routine, finding something healthy to eat becomes less of a priority especially for individuals that work vigorously to earn for their families. In such conditions, health is compromised to a greater extent that can cause many side effects in the future. To avoid such conditions it is very important to not only eat healthy but also to eat right.

This book covers the life of a Pescatarian, making it easy for them to prepare their favorite recipes inside their kitchen without any stress. This book explains how a Pescatarian diet differs from other diets and how it can be beneficial to a human being who wants to lose weight while eating healthy food.

Being a Pescatarian is no more boring or difficult with all these amazing breakfast, lunch, dinner, snacks, juices, and sweets recipes mentioned in this book. You will also get a seven day diet plan that you can change according to your taste and preferences with the variety of recipes mentioned in the book. So, there is no need to wait more when you can cook healthy and yummy right in your home.

Made in United States
Troutdale, OR
04/14/2024

19167576R10308